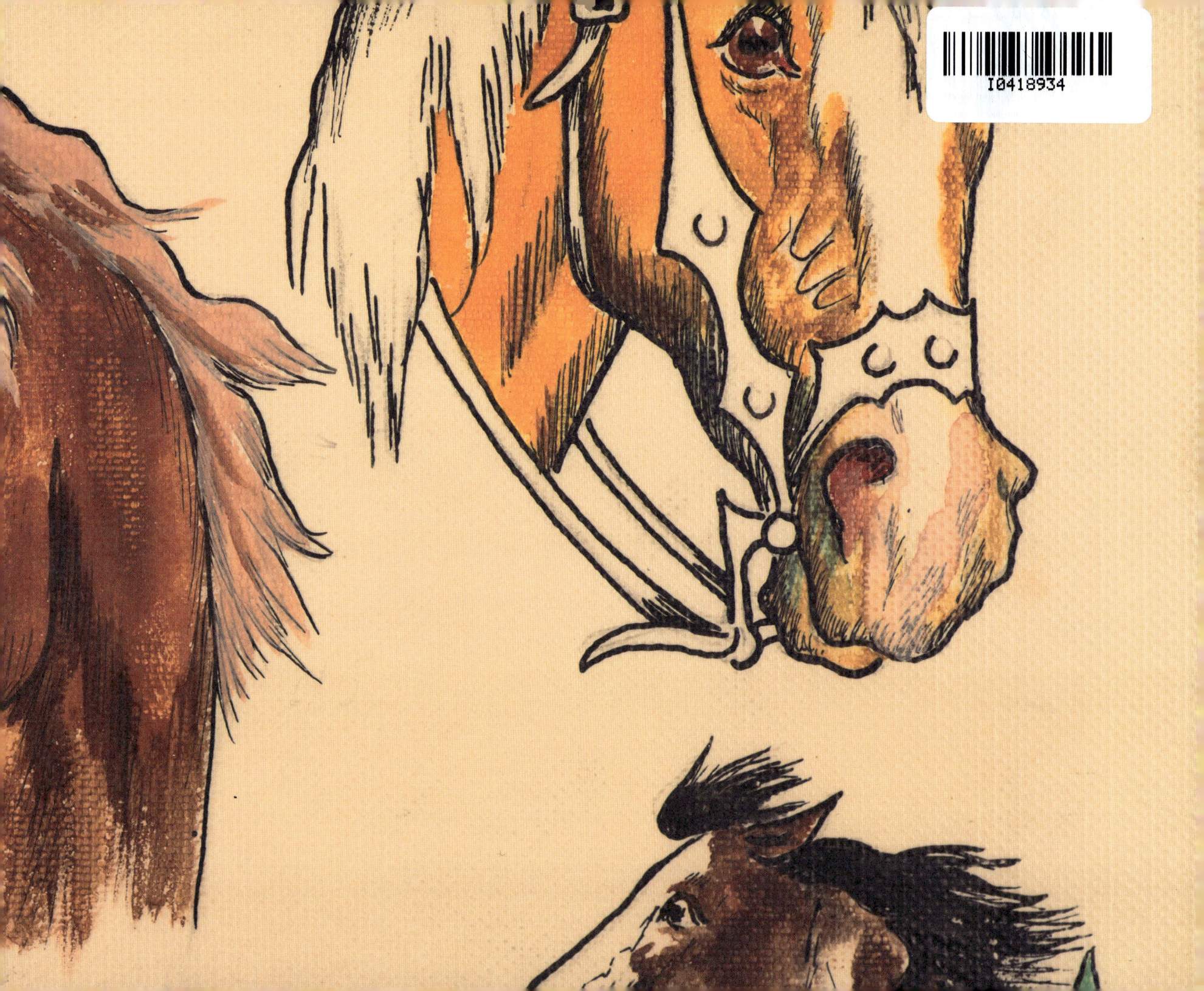

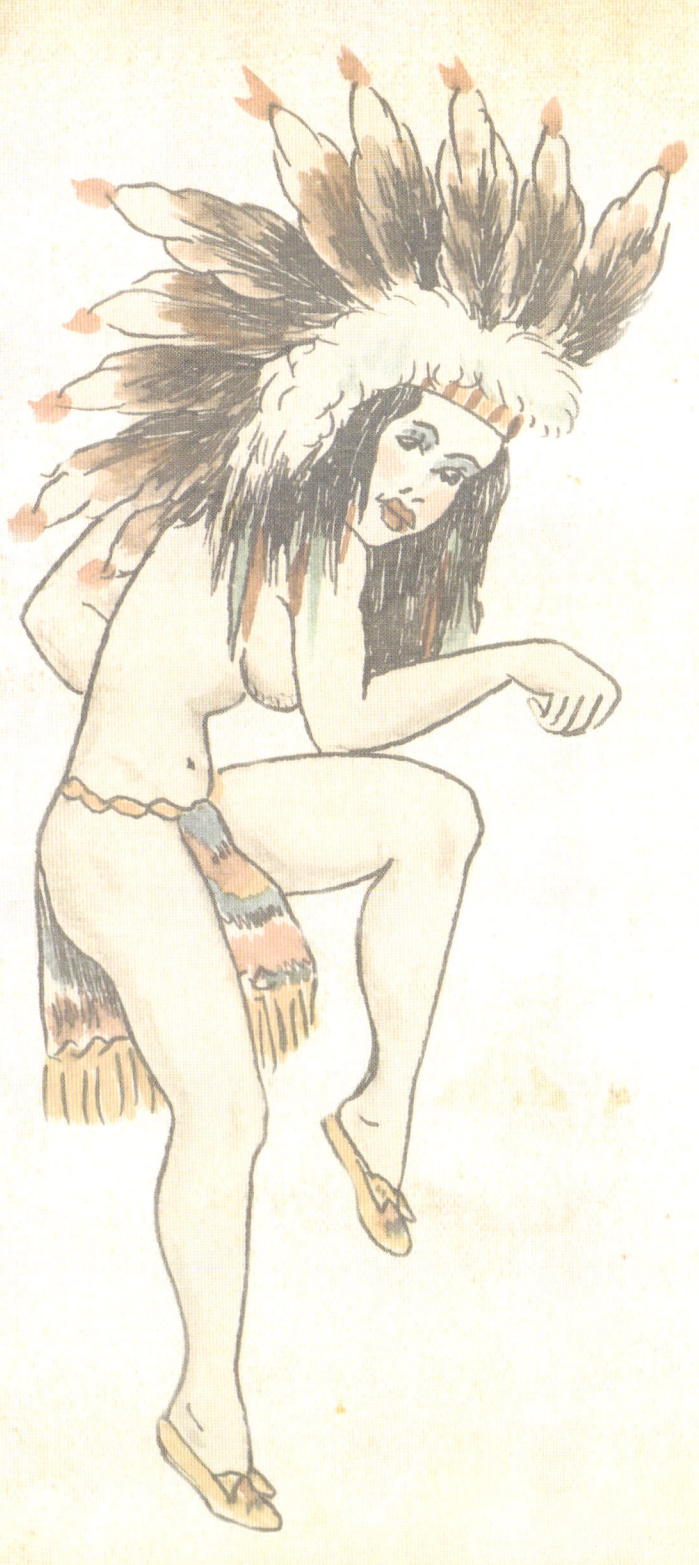

LOTTEVA WAGNER DAVIS

HAND TATTOOIST ⁊AND⁊ ARTIST OF THE AMERICAN WEST

ALAN GOVENAR

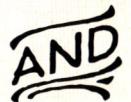

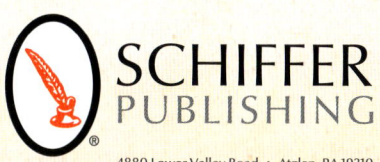
SCHIFFER PUBLISHING

4880 Lower Valley Road • Atglen, PA 19310

Other Schiffer Books by the Author:
Gus Wagner: Globe Trotter and Hand Tattoo Artist, ISBN 978-0-7643-6728-1
Maud Stevens Wagner: Mona Lisa of American Tattoo, ISBN 978-0-7643-6930-8
Stoney Knows How: Life as a Sideshow Tattoo Artist, 3rd Edition, ISBN 978-0-7643-6400-6

Designed by Beth Oberholtzer
Cover design by Molly Shields
Photographs, flash, ephemera, artifacts, and scrapbook pages on pages 11, 15-19, 21-22, 27-30, 32, 33, 46-49, 61-63, 66, 67, 74-76, 98 (left), 102 (right), 104 (right), ca. 1897-1941, courtesy of The Alan Govenar and Kaleta Doolin Tattoo Collection at the South Street Seaport Museum, New York. Photographs on front and back covers and pages 1, 3-10, 12-14, 20, 24, 25, 31, 34-40, 42-45, 54-56, 64, 65, 68-73, 77-97, 98 (right), 99-101, 102 (left), 103, 104 (left), 105-126, private collection.

Photographs on pages 50-53, courtesy Clay Hutchison, The Carousel of Smiles, Sandpoint, Idaho, thecarouselofsmiles.org, inbox@thecarouselofsmiles.org.
Photograph on page 57, courtesy of Patricia "Pat" Waynette Hook.
Photographs on page 59, courtesy of Ron Dolecek.
Photographs on pages 41 and 60, courtesy of Library of Congress.

Type set in Citrus Gothic/Cambria

ISBN: 978-0-7643-6983-4
Epub: 978-1-5073-0604-8
Printed in China

Published by Schiffer Publishing, Ltd.
4880 Lower Valley Road
Atglen, PA 19310
Phone: (610) 593-1777; Fax: (610) 593-2002
Email: info@schifferbooks.com
Web: www.schifferbooks.com

For our complete selection of fine books on this and related subjects, please visit our website at www.schifferbooks.com. You may also write for a free catalog.

Schiffer Publishing's titles are available at special discounts for bulk purchases for sales promotions or premiums. Special editions, including personalized covers, corporate imprints, and excerpts, can be created in large quantities for special needs. For more information, contact the publisher.

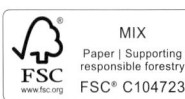

MIX
Paper | Supporting
responsible forestry
FSC® C104723

Opposite: Painting by Lotteva Wagner Davis

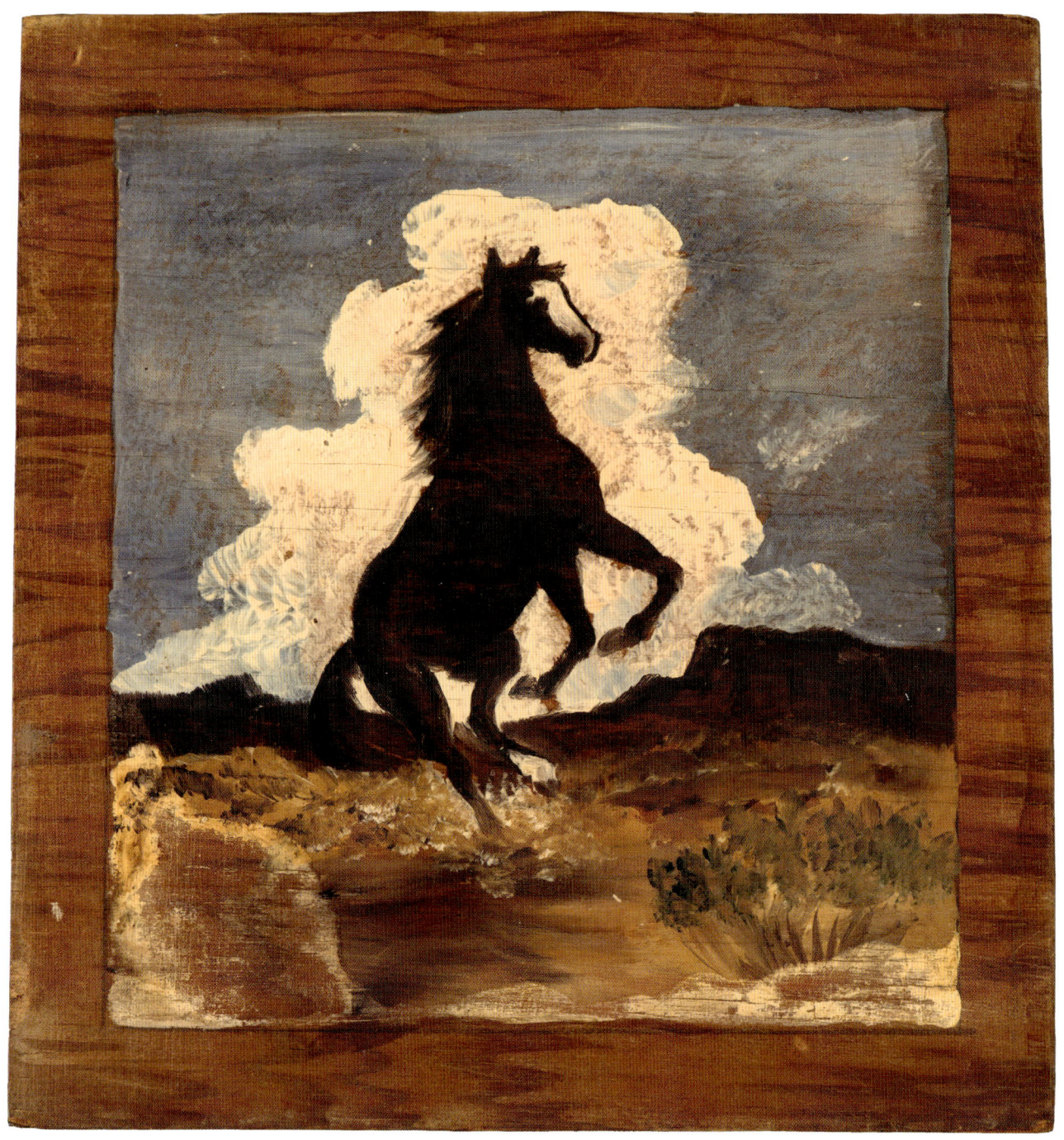

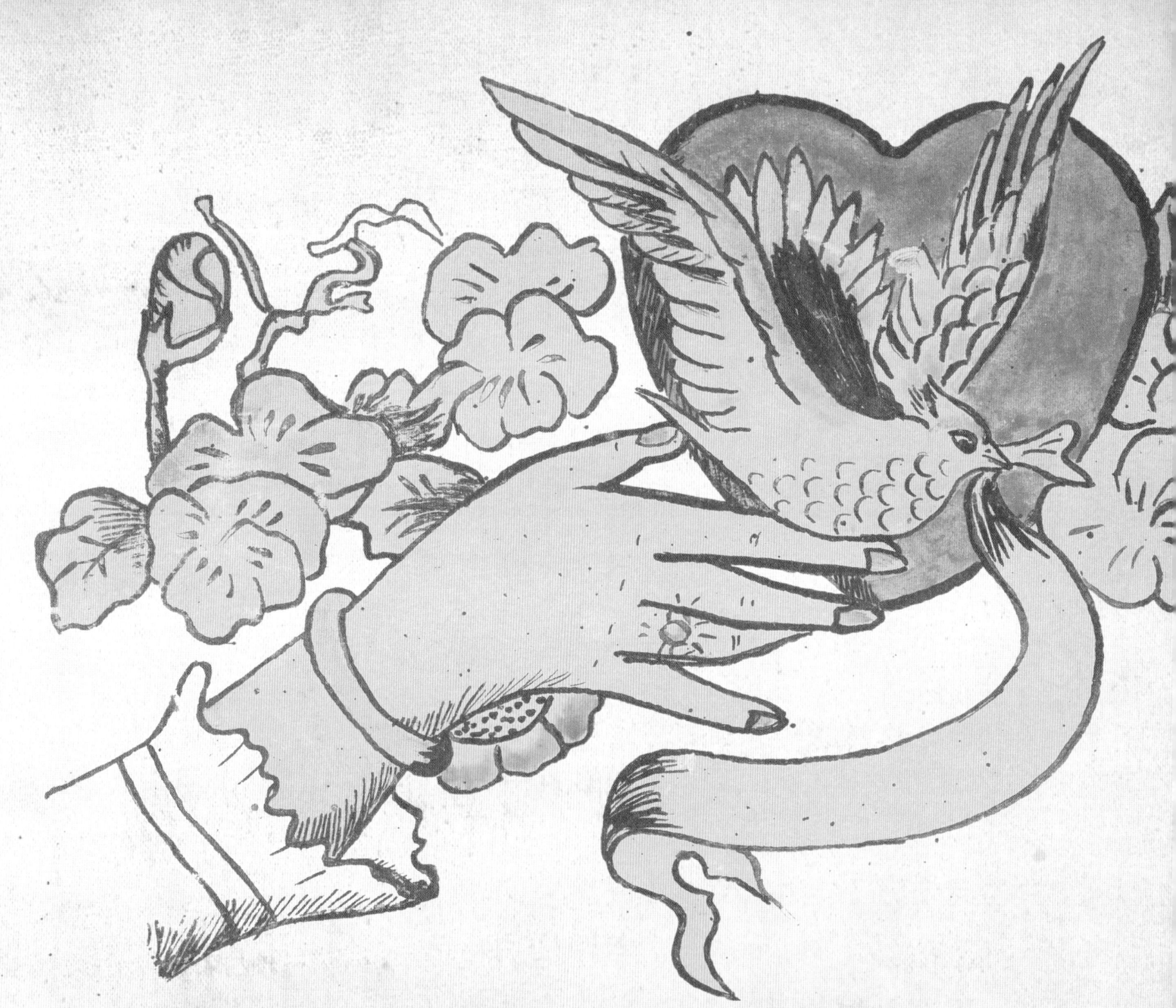

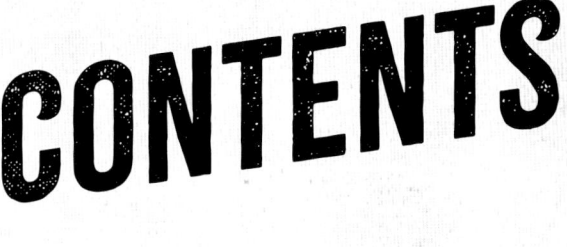

CONTENTS

ACKNOWLEDGMENTS

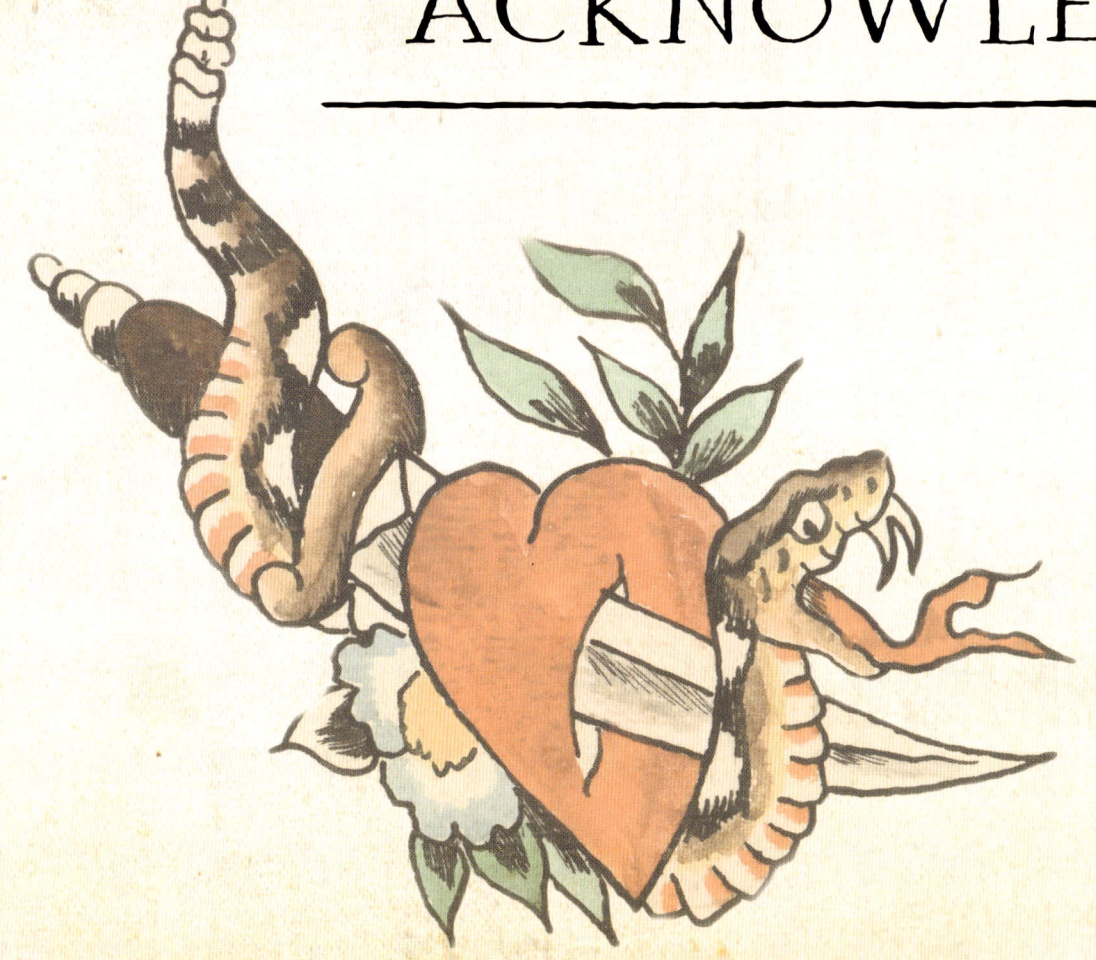

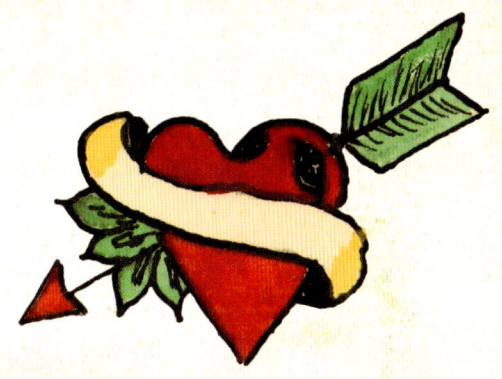

First and foremost, I am grateful to Rockey Reisner for entrusting me with his family treasures, and to my family for believing in my work. Martina Caruso, director of collections and exhibitions at the South Street Seaport Museum, provided scans and documentation and has guided the preservation and conservation of the Alan Govenar and Kaleta Doolin Tattoo Collection. Ed Hardy and Chuck Eldridge offered good counsel as my work advanced. Ron Dolecek contributed his photographs of Gus's and Maud's graves in Kansas and introduced me to Lisa Soller at the Lion County Museum, who offered insights into the history of Maud's family. Patricia "Pat" Waynette Hook, in Manhattan, Kansas, provided her handwritten notes and snapshots from her meeting with her distant cousin Lotteva Wagner Davis. Clay and Reno Hutchison shared photographs of carousel panels painted by Lotteva. Jason Johnson-Spinos assisted with copyediting and the preparation of photographs and images for publication.

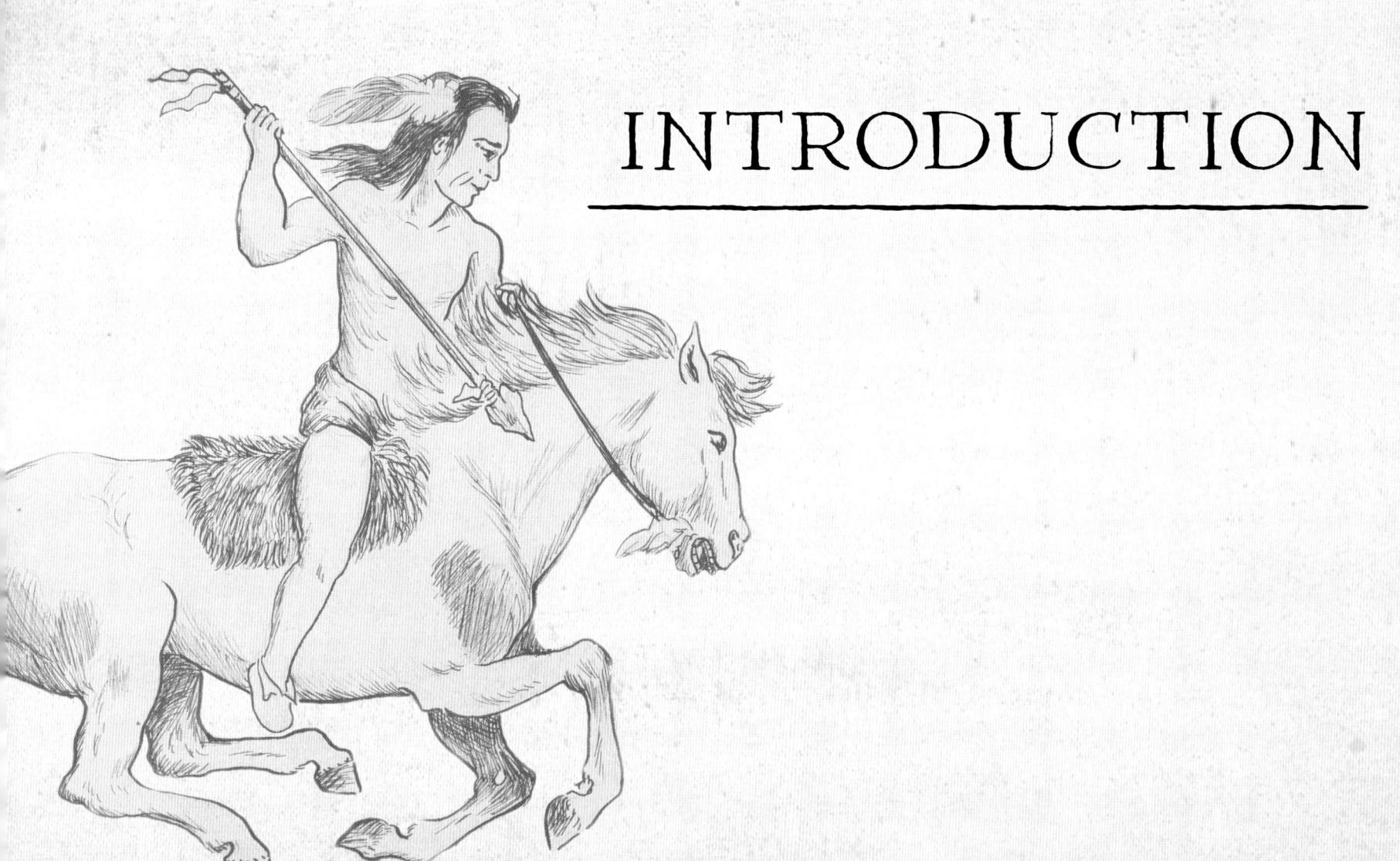

INTRODUCTION

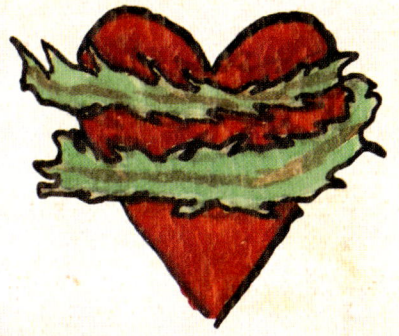

At the 1989 National Tattoo Association convention in Arlington, Texas, Lotteva Wagner Davis was a diva. With reddish-orange poofed-up hair, she regaled passersby, flashing her fancy rings and turquoise bracelets and making tattoos with ancient-looking handmade tools.

Chuck Eldridge, founder of the Tattoo Archive, recalls that he and renowned tattoo artist Ed Hardy were "blown away by her presence, her charisma, her being. She had a classic Texas drawl and talked with her hands. She had a sly sense of humor, making catty asides and endearing gestures to curiosity seekers who wanted to know more. She remembered the past vividly. The stories didn't seem rehearsed, but she jumped from subject to subject, as if she had done this bally many times before."

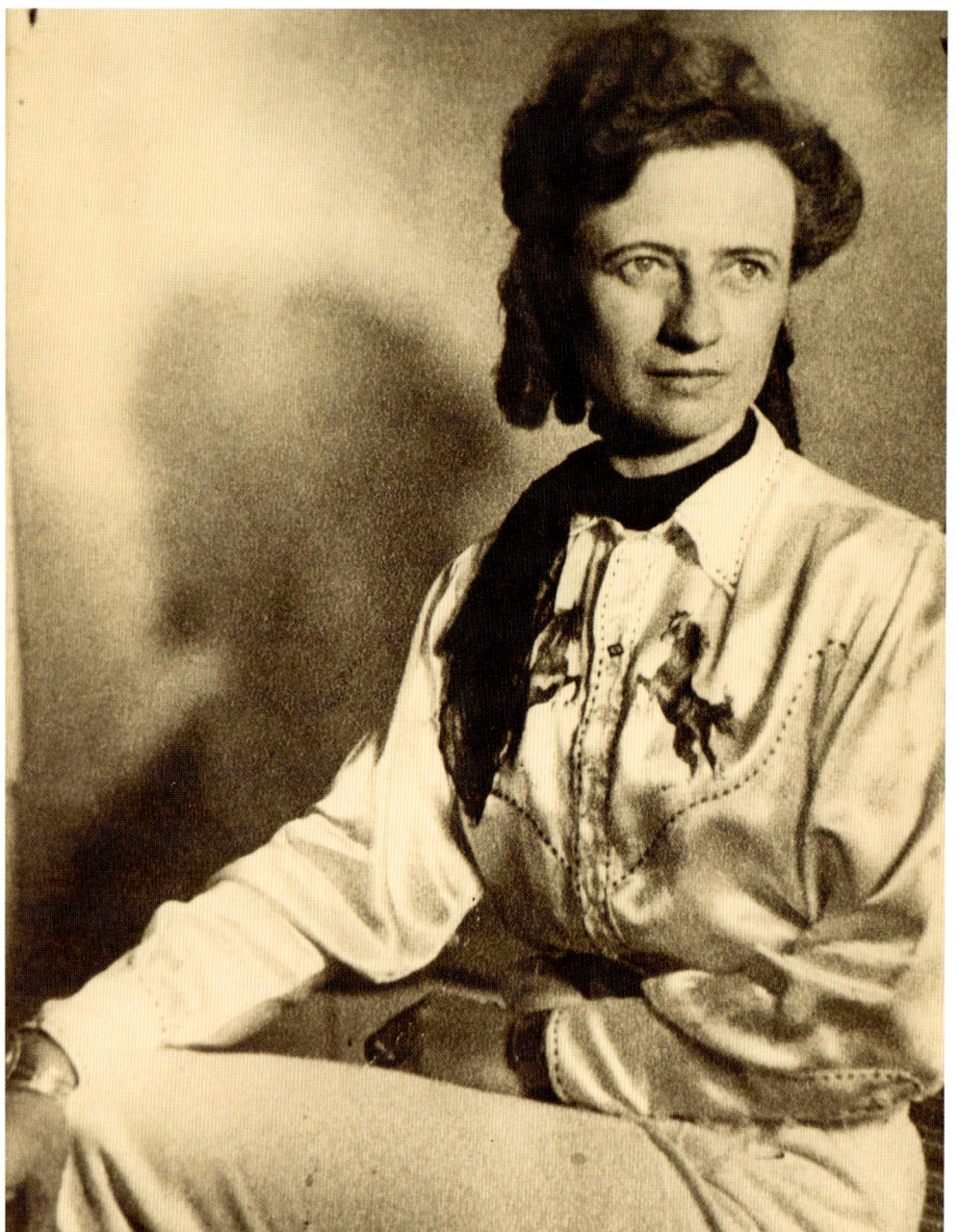

Lotteva Wagner Davis, Elk City,
Oklahoma, 1946

In her hotel room, after a long day of working the convention floor, Lotteva was joined by an entourage of old friends. Like her parents, Augustus "Gus" Wagner and Maud Stevens Wagner, Lotteva relished being the center of attention. Lotteva had agreed to an interview with Chuck, and while he asked her questions, others chimed in.

One man, who Chuck thought may have been Lotteva's husband, said he had met Lotteva in 1943, when he was eighteen and in the Army and Lotteva was thirty-three. The man clearly knew Lotteva well, commenting on the quality of her tattoos and the cleanliness of her shop. He also remembered Lotteva's mother, Maud, whom he described as having "more bullshit than they had in the Kansas City stockyard . . . I'll tell you. Her mother was about her height and maybe 10 pounds heavier. Wore cowboy boots and a skirt about here, with her knees showing."

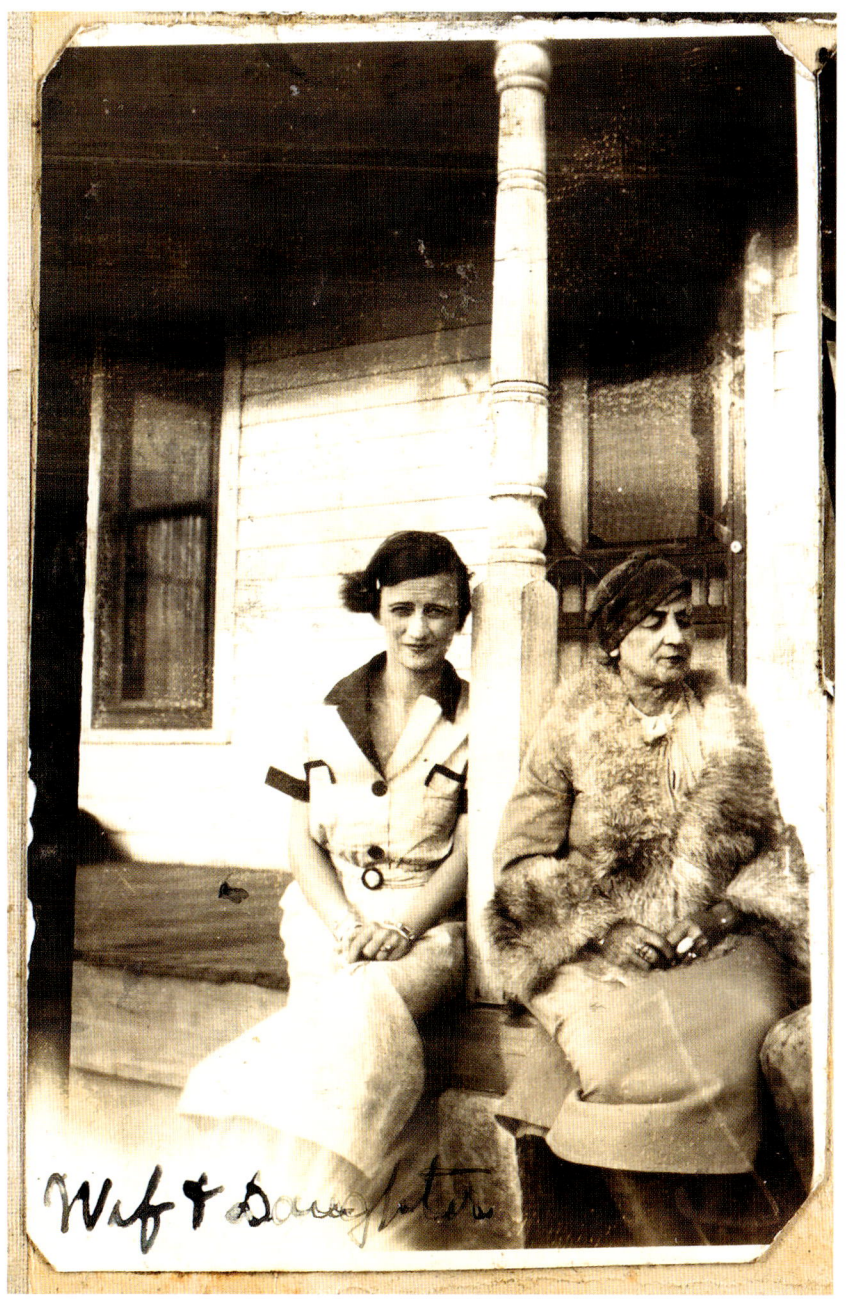

Lotteva and Maud. *Detail from Gus Wagner's scrapbook*

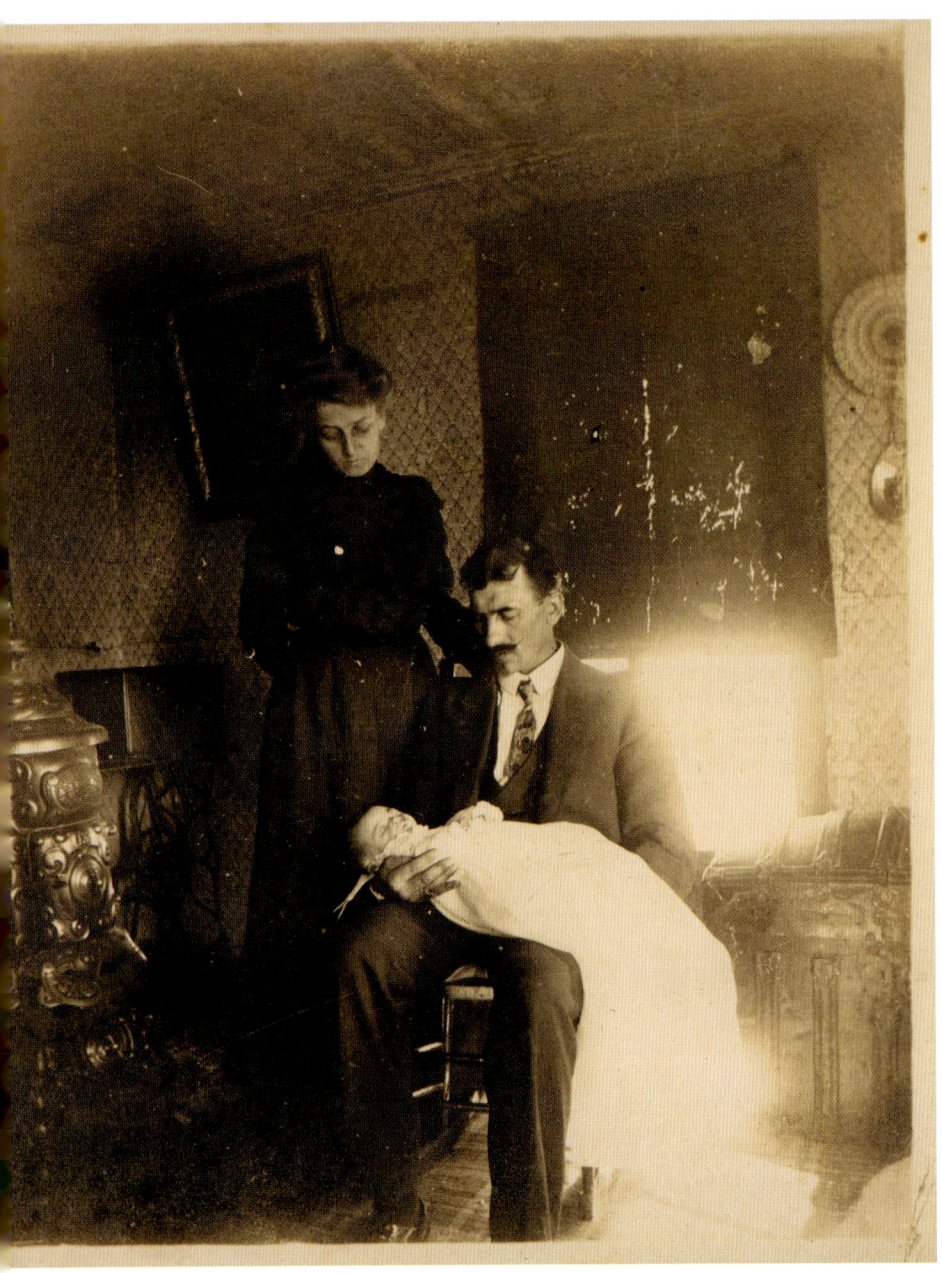

Maud, Gus, and Lotteva, ca. 1910

"Remember what she had on her knees?" Lotteva grinned. "Alice and Jumbo. And she used to sing, 'I got Alice and Jumbo on my knees.' And she'd move them like that [bringing her knees together and spreading them apart]. She had sunflowers on each elbow, here, and the stem would run down here. It's brown in the center and had yellow leaves, and she said, 'They answer two purposes: they show my patriotism to my native state, Kansas, and I don't have to wash my elbows.'"

Lotteva remembered her mother fondly. Born on March 12, 1910, Lotteva grew up on the road with her parents. In conversations with her distant cousin, Patricia "Pat" Waynette Hook, Lotteva talked at length about her childhood years and life with Gus and Maud. Lotteva said she "only got spanked once, and that was for running out in front of a team of horses. After that happened, a woman suggested that Maud 'put the baby in a harness.' Maud was shocked, but the woman said, 'You would harness a dog or cat that you loved to protect it. Don't you love your child as much as a dog?' So, Maud got Lotteva a little red harness, and Lotteva said she loved her harness because it meant Maud loved her."

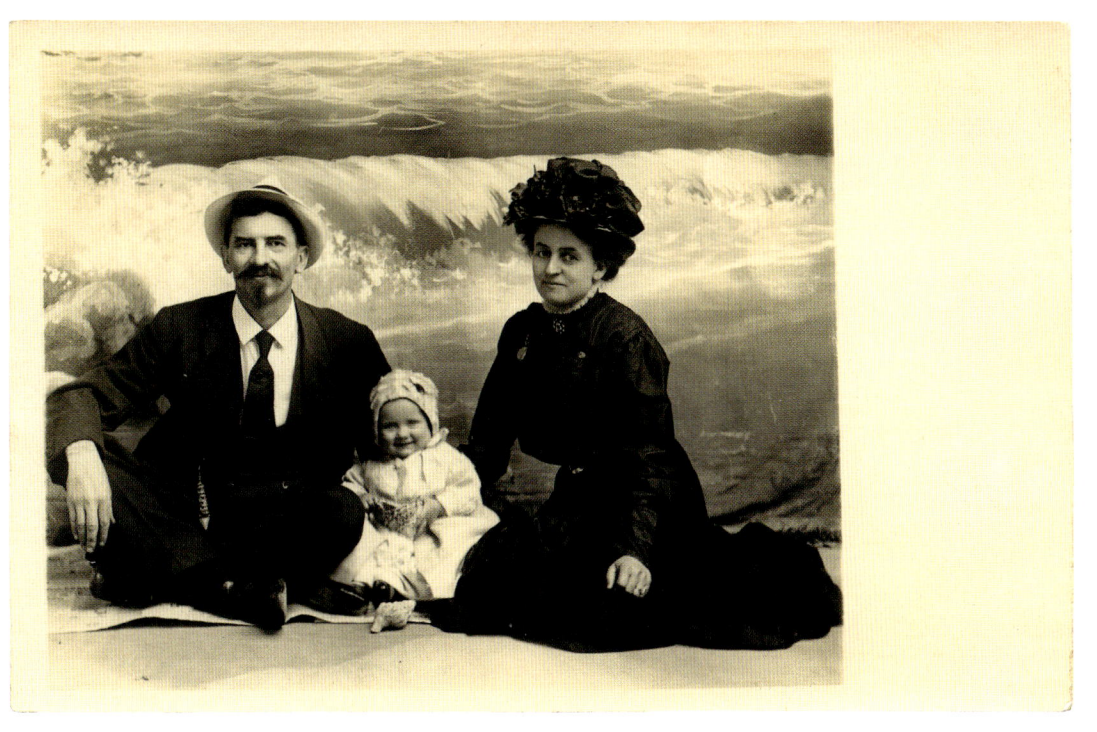

Gus, Lotteva, and Maud in Venice, California. Real photo postcard, 1911.

"Dear parents + sister: Here we are looking in the southern sun while we sit in the sand where the cool sea breezes blow the spray of the Pacific on us. As ever, Maud, Gus + Lotteva." Back of postcard, May 9, 1911.

"Lotteva could spell and write words when she was only two. She could write little notes to her grandma. When they traveled back to Kansas, she learned to spell the name of each state as they traveled through it. She learned the capitals too."[1]

Lotteva told Pat Hook that as a girl growing up, she worked hard and loved helping her family. "Lotteva's grandma, Sarah Jane Stevens, had to be 'led' because of an injury to her neck. Lotteva wanted to lead grandma, but she was too young and too tiny. Aunt Dora [Maud's sister] sectioned an orange and let Lotteva take it to grandma. She was very proud to get to do that. She always wanted to help. She was also allowed to get Grandma a glass of water.

"Lotteva was named for her father's mother, Charlotte Wagner. This was combined with Eva from Little Eva in *Uncle Tom's Cabin*. Actually, Lotteva sounds a lot like Little Eva. Lotteva has never used a nickname, but she has used the name 'Beatrice Hill' when she didn't want to use her own name.

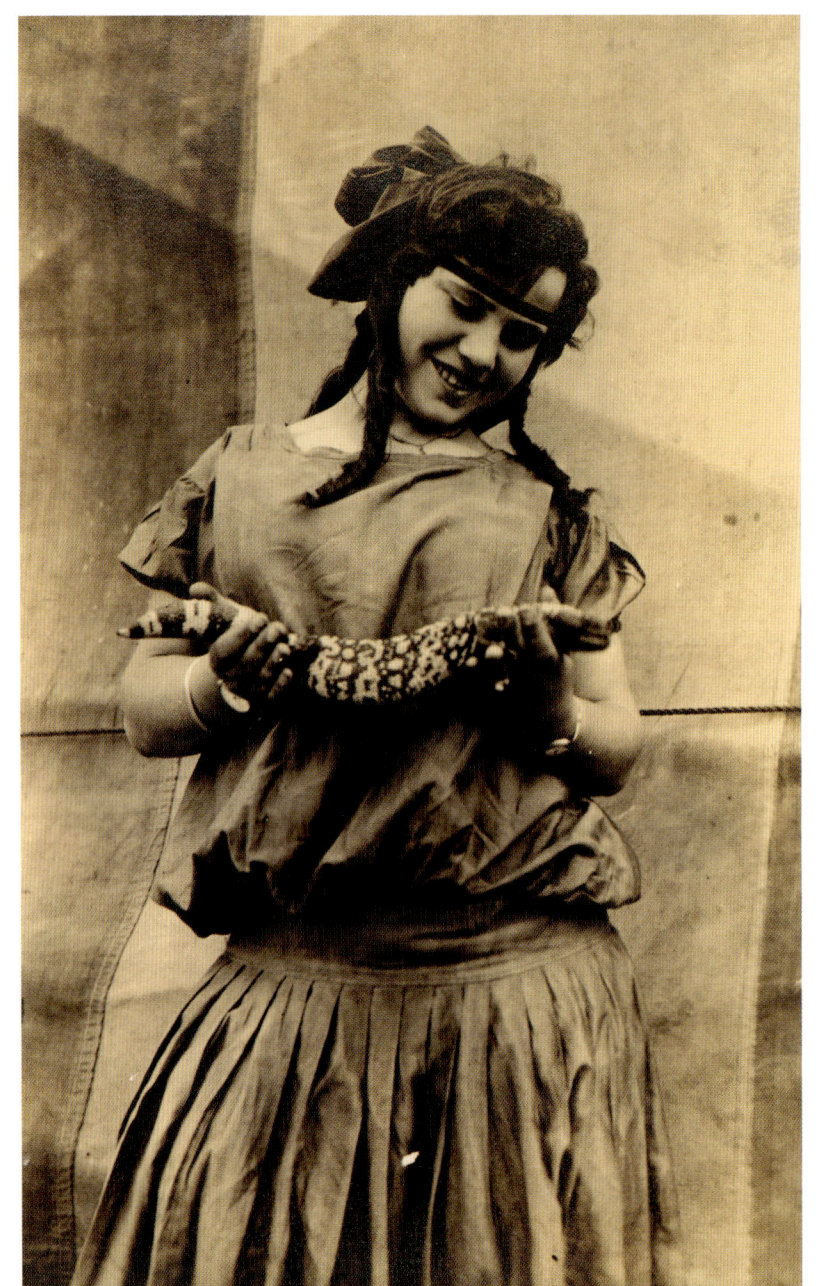

Lotteva, ca. early 1920s

"Lotteva had lots of dolls. But she didn't play with them. She liked to play with a stuffed iguana that she had. Mounted lizards and squirrels were her favorites. Lotteva never did go to school at all. She was taught at home. Maud got her the same books as the school children used. She had a desk for doing lessons. Sometimes people would complain about her not being in school. Then the superintendent would come out to check on matters. Lotteva had a jigsaw puzzle map of the forty-eight states. Maud challenged the superintendent to put it together with her. She started Lotteva on the 'easy' side with California, just to be sure. The superintendent admitted defeat, and Lotteva finished the map. Then he had her read out loud, and he wrote out a paper saying she was ahead of her grade and didn't have to go to school. She could add figures without having to put them in a column. Lotteva would say, 'But I got the right answers, didn't I?' She would be reading the herpetology book, and her mother would come in and tell her to get to her regular lessons. By the age of ten, she had completed a study of the herpetology of North America and had begun on entomology. Her dad helped her make Riker mounts, using old ranch house windows for the glass tops. They were held together with black tape. She had 16,000 specimens; 8,000 were under glass. Some were microspecimens.

"Lotteva's first pet was a guinea pig. She had a white rat too. It had an affair with one or more wild rats, and for a while there were some mottled rats around the place.

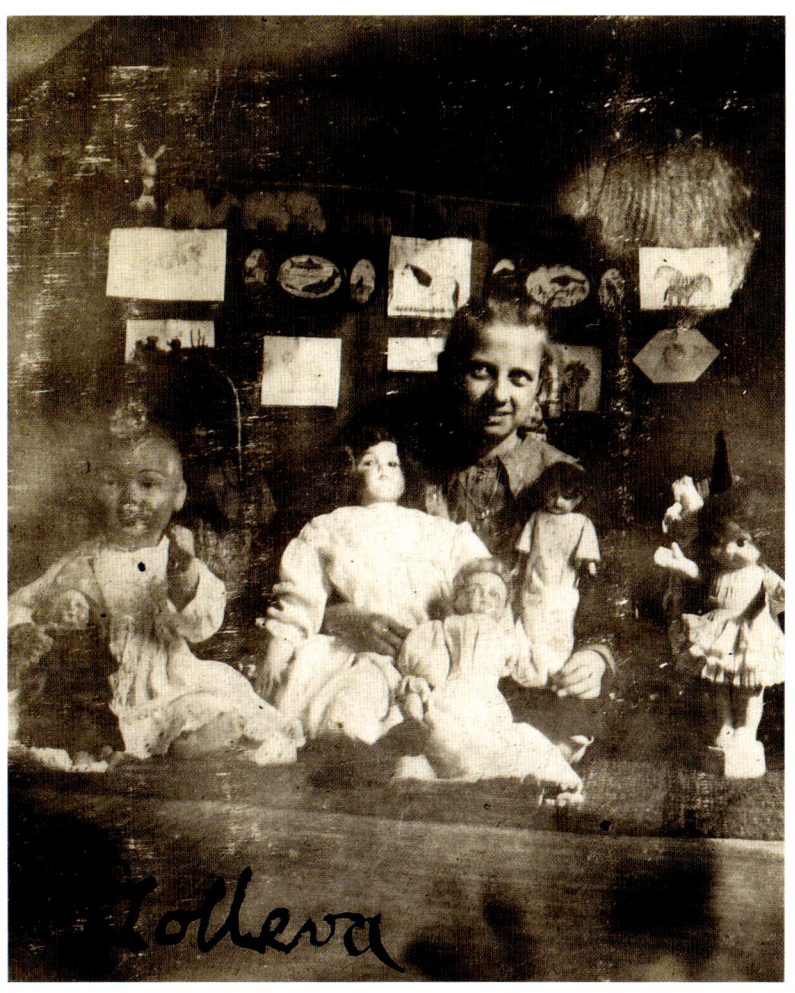

Lotteva with dolls, ca. early 1920s.
Detail from Gus Wagner's scrapbook

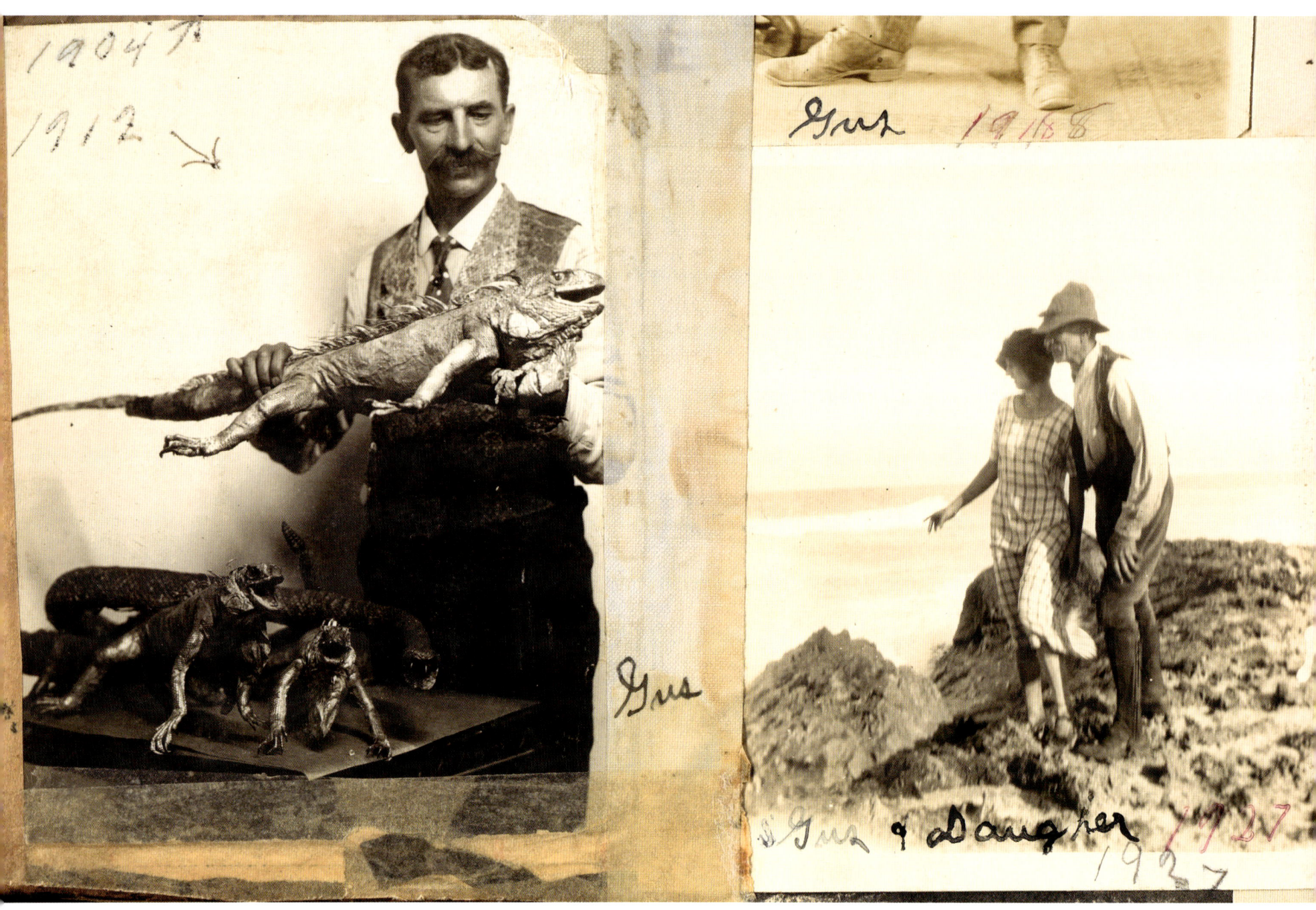

Detail from Gus Wagner's scrapbook

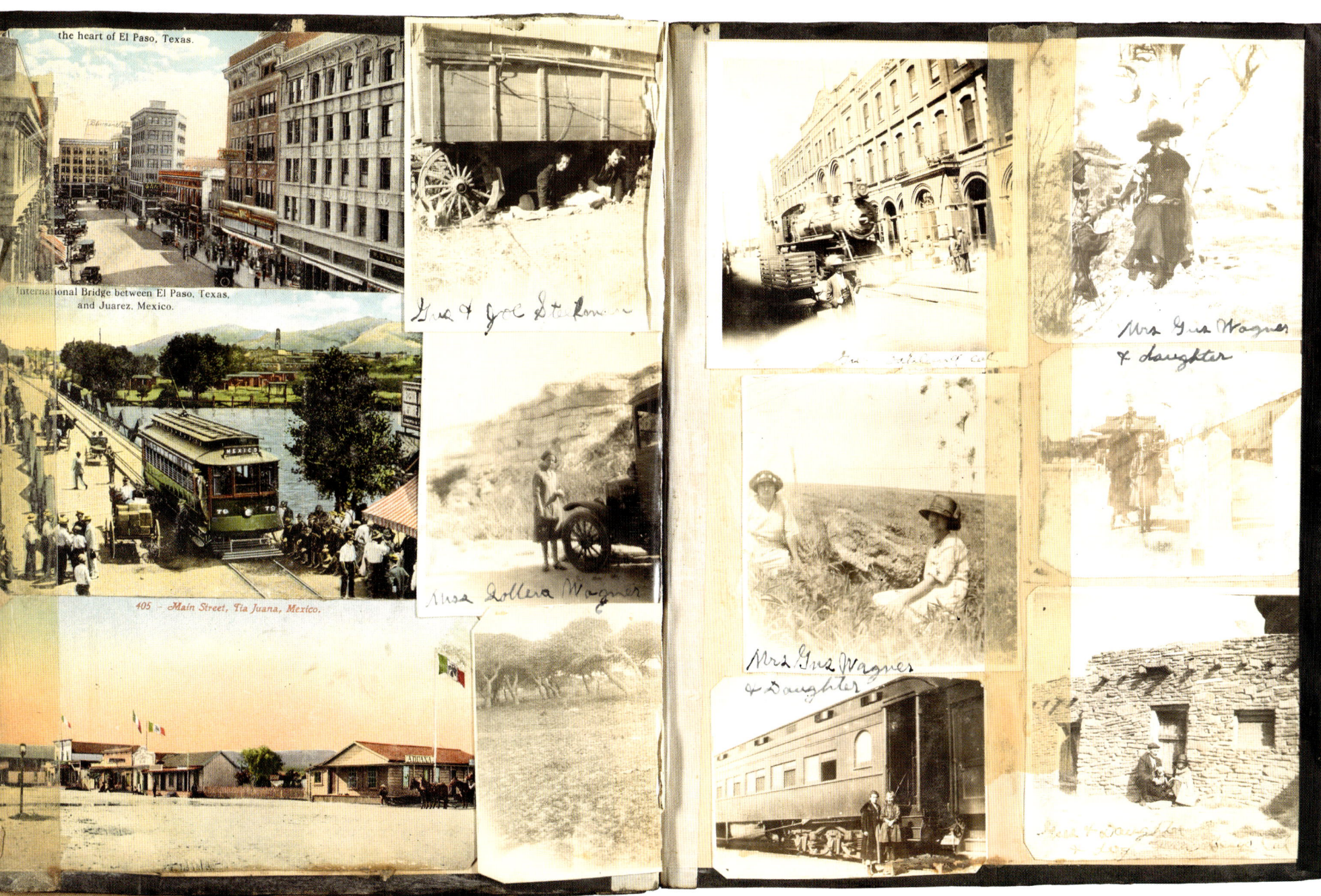

Pages from Gus Wagner's scrapbook

"One day when they were driving along, Lotteva saw a good-sized turtle. 'You don't have anything to put it in,' Gus said. There was no question about whether it was okay for her to have the turtle. Of course, she could have it. She found a paper grocery bag and put the turtle in it. When they got into town, they went to a restaurant. She took the bag with the turtle in with her. As they were eating, people began to stare. She realized the turtle was upside down in the sack and had managed to stick its head out through a hole near the bottom of the bag. She turned it right side up and went on eating. The turtle's name was Pete. It needed to be watched because it liked to go down stairs.

"One time they had a possum in the yard. It could not be intimidated, which seemed unusual. They took it into the house to show to Grandpa David V. Stevens—this was after his stroke. In a few minutes they heard him laugh. Baby possums had come out of her pouch—six babies, three black and three silver. Their dogs had torn the pouch, and that was why the possum was behaving strangely.

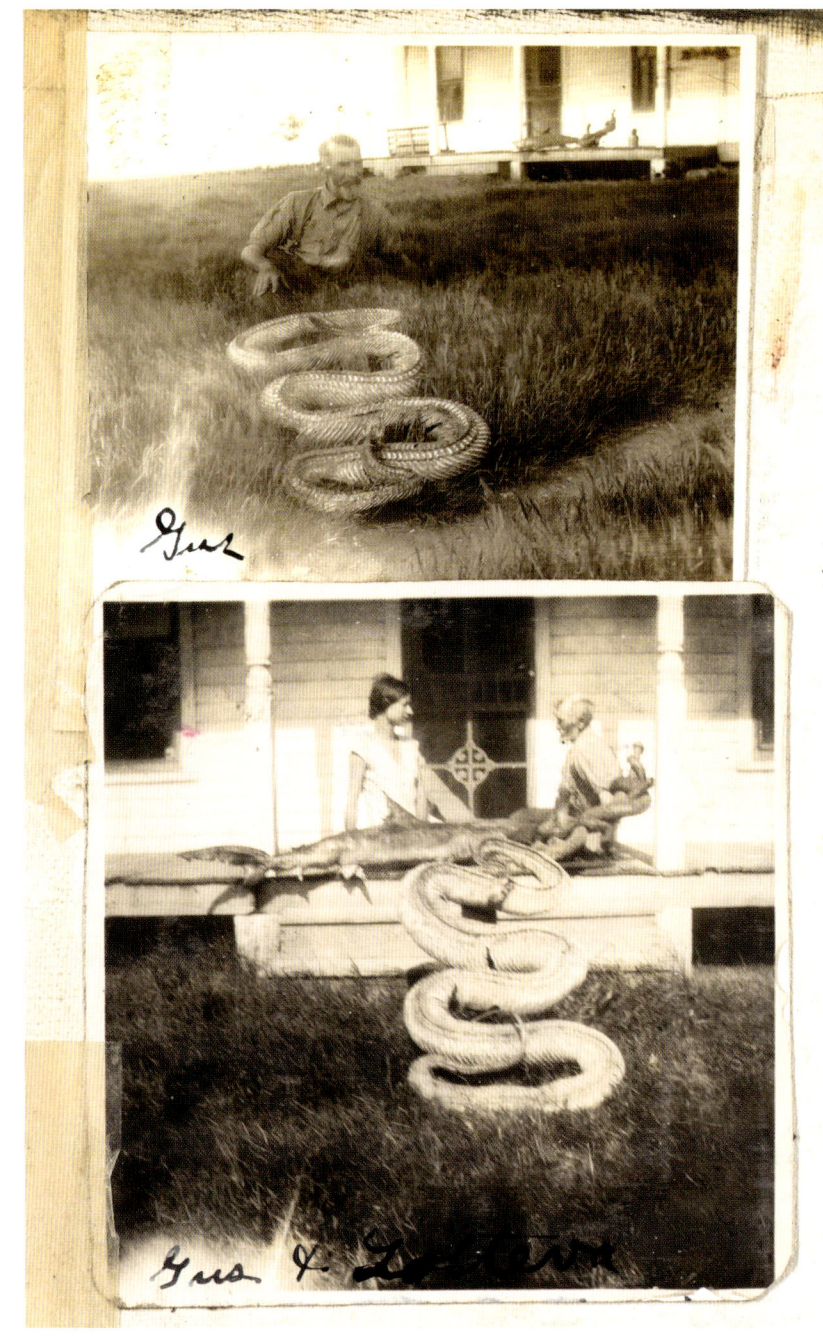

Detail from Gus Wagner's scrapbook

"Santos was their great big python. One day when Lotteva was quite small, Santos decided to eat her. She said she knew what he was up to because she had seen him give prey 'that look.' She couldn't move. She just squealed, 'Mama! Mama! Mama!' Maud came in and said, 'What?' 'Santos,' whispered Lotteva. Then Maud rescued her.

"Santos had to be kept warm. Maud and Gus would put him in his case and take him to bed with them under the covers on cold nights to keep him warm. One night he chilled to death anyway. The next day, Gus skinned him and coiled the body into a cooking pot with herbs and spices. After he [Santos] was boiled, Gus poured him onto a screen to drain the water away. Then the show people gathered around and ate the meat off the bones. Gus wanted the skeleton. Some people only tasted the snake. Others really gorged on the snake meat. Lotteva didn't try it.

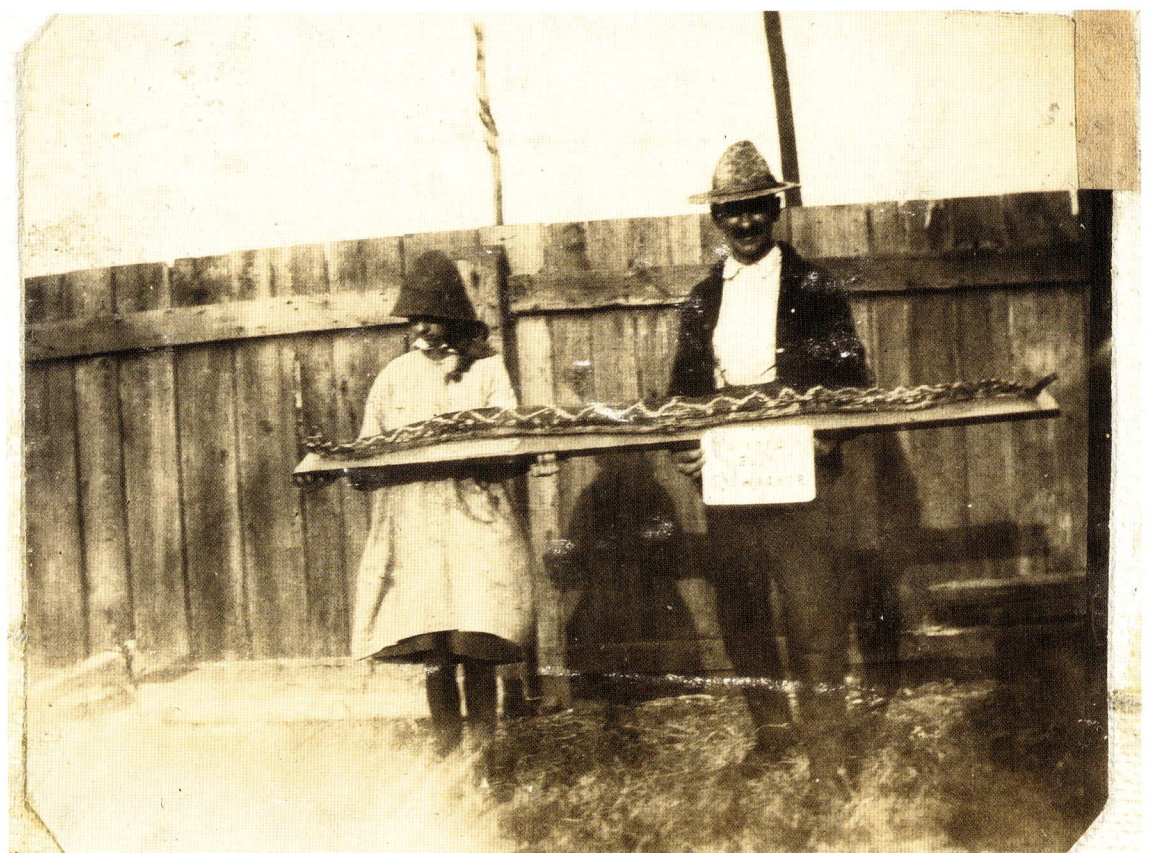

Detail from Gus Wagner's scrapbook

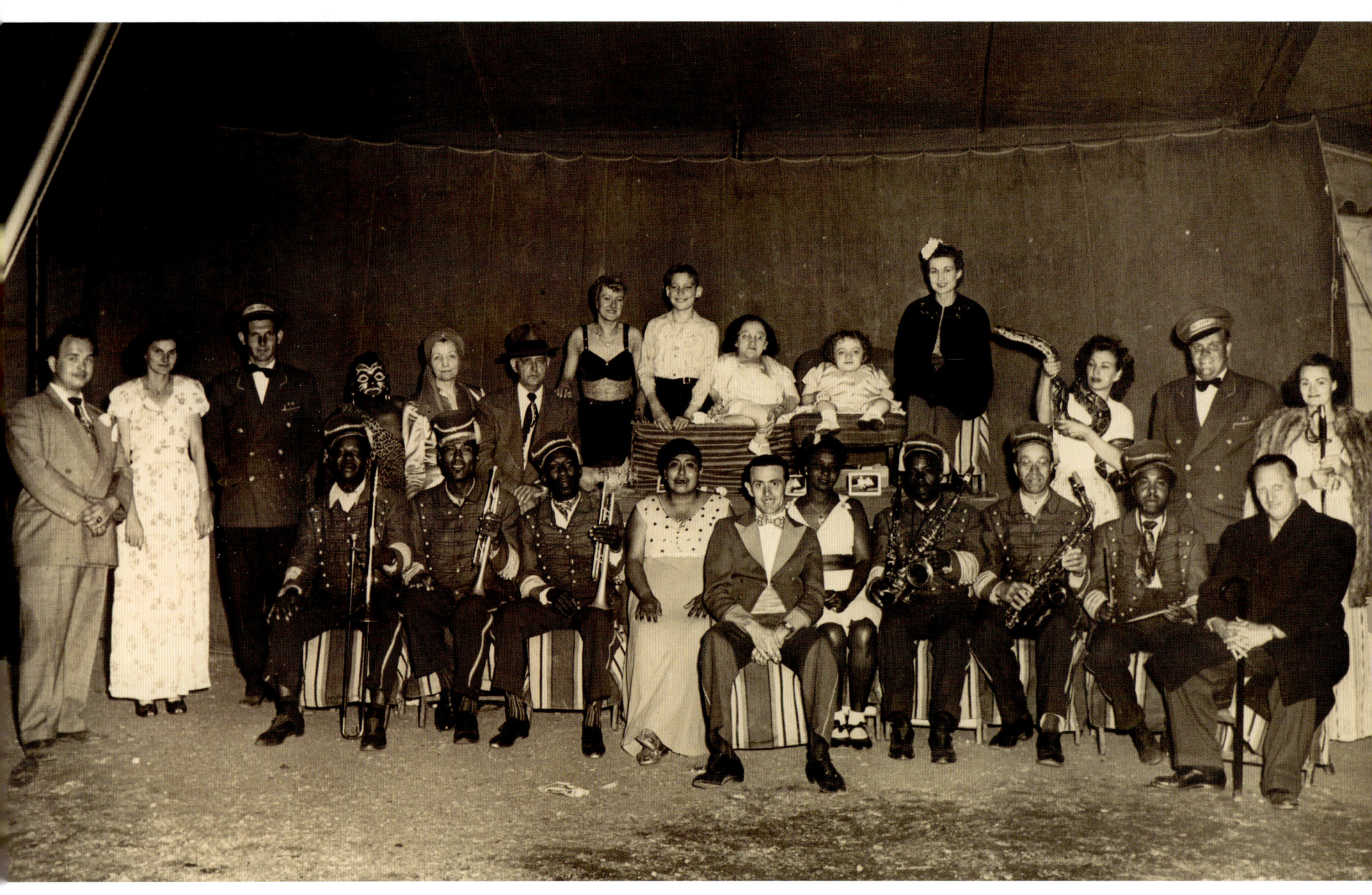

Lotteva with snake, with circus sideshow,
ca. early 1930s

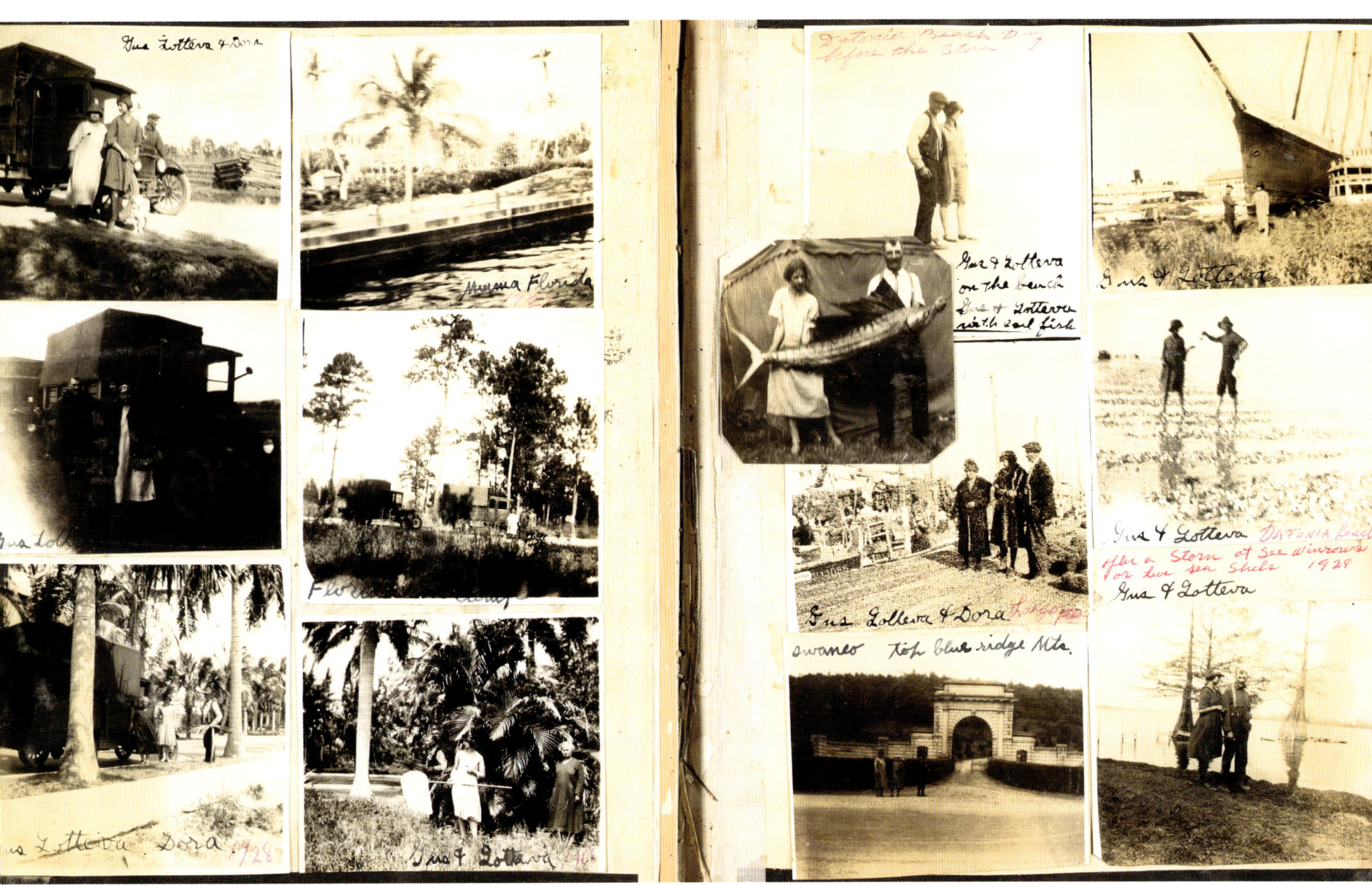

Pages from Gus Wagner's scrapbook

"Lotteva had a business of her own by age twelve. She sold pet stock and wild animals. Their address was RR#1 Box 31— Clements, Kansas. She used the name L. Davis. Nobody knew she was female, much less still a girl. When she was thirteen, she shipped out a badger. It was about half grown and golden red and white. Someone gave it to her. She put it in a barrel with iron mesh over the top, held by a wheel and some rocks. The badger was mean, so she had to lower a water bucket into the barrel. To ship it, she built a wooden cage lined with tin. The opening was covered with hail screen. Harry Dickerson was the buyer. He and Harry Mason were good customers. Dickerson thanked Gus Wagner for the badger and said the cage was the best he had seen. Gus had a hard time convincing him that L. Wagner was his daughter and that she had built the cage."

At an early age, Gus and Maud imbued Lotteva with an entrepreneurial outlook—how to make the most with whatever she had or found. One time, according to Pat Hook, "Gus made a model of a human, using papier mâché and some real human bones. It even had some real human hair on it. When it was all fixed up, it was pretty strange. They would put it under the stage in a box of sorts when they performed. They never mentioned it, but it attracted interest. If anybody asked about it,

Detail from Gus Wagner's scrapbook

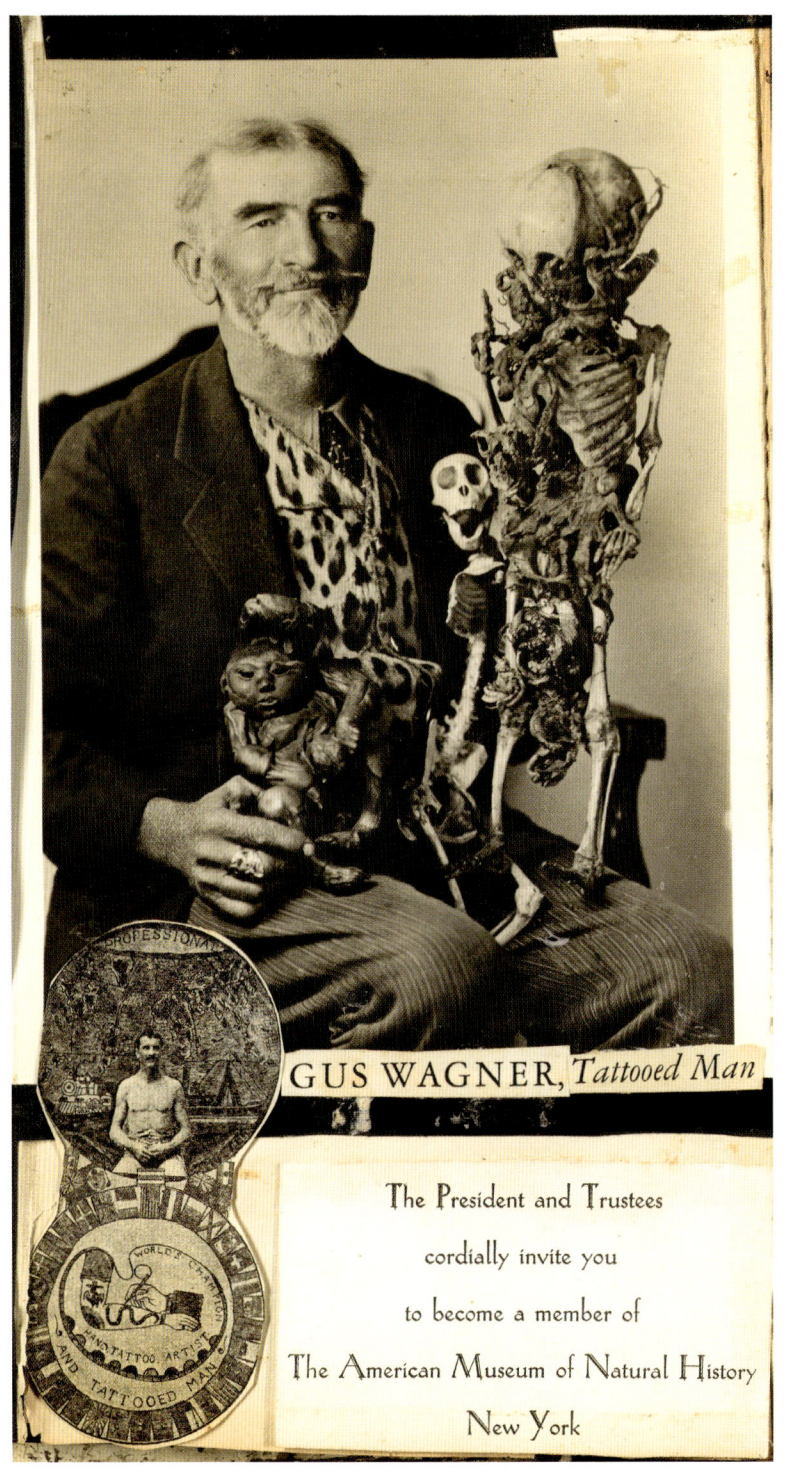

GUS WAGNER, *Tattooed Man*

The President and Trustees
cordially invite you
to become a member of
The American Museum of Natural History
New York

they would just say casually, 'Oh, that's Grandpa Snazzy.' Well, Grandpa Snazzy finally began to get pretty beat up, and they needed to dispose of him. They buried him in the hollow at their Chase County home. Gus said it really would make people wonder, if they ever dug up that assortment of bones."

Lotteva carried on the ingenuity of her family traditions, with a deep love for her work and the capacity to learn new skills. In a November 24, 1974, article in the *Plainview Daily Herald*, Lotteva told journalist Marie Harris that she was "inspired to paint when she saw Prairie Rose Henderson, famous cowgirl, and woman bulldogger, riding a white horse in a parade, resplendent in large white hat, green satin blouse embroidered on the back with a gold dragon, and white trousers. But she was 12 years old when she made her first good oil painting—of an Indian riding a pony down a mountain trail. Mrs. Davis opened her own art studio on the family ranch at Clements, Kansas, when she was 14 and there did banners, signs, and quite a few small canvases."[2]

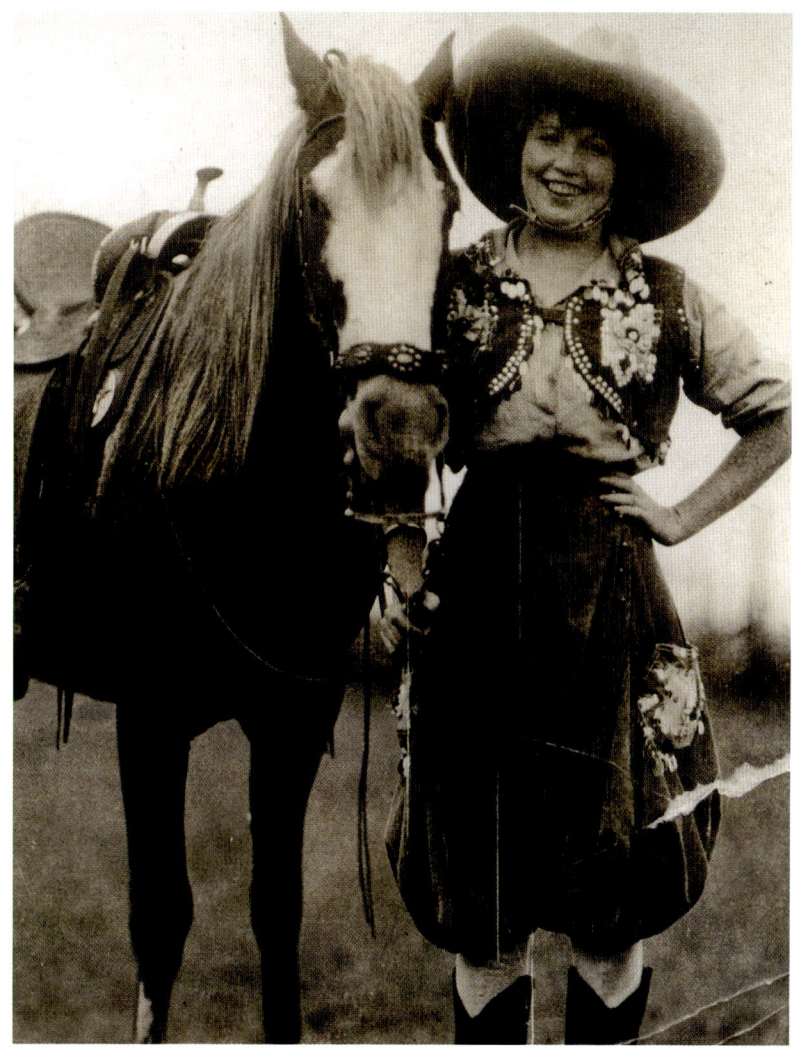

Prairie Rose Henderson, ca. 1910s

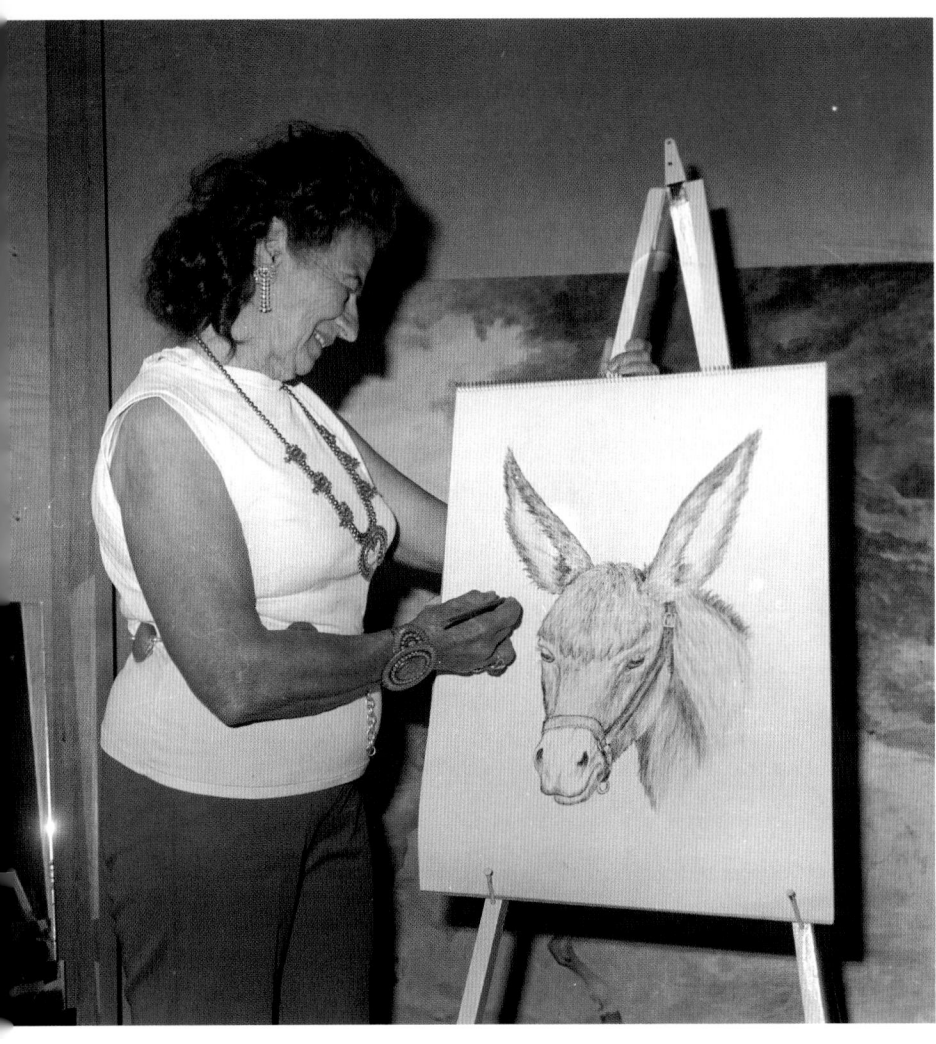

While sign painting provided significant income to Lotteva, she worked when she could as a tattoo artist, often setting up in the living room of her house and sometimes renting storefronts. Lotteva wanted to be tattooed, but Maud said, "Don't do it, because you will have to wear long sleeves and a high collar when you lecture, or people will be distracted by the tattoos." Lotteva lectured on voodoo and herpetology.[3]

In an interview with journalist Ellen Sweets, Lotteva said that she never got tattooed because of a "family feud. . . . Although we all knew how to tattoo—Papa taught her and me—Mama wouldn't let Papa tattoo me. I never understood why. She relented after he died and said I could get tattoos then, but I said that if Papa couldn't do them like he had done hers, then nobody would. And that was that. End of story."[4]

Despite never getting tattooed herself, Lotteva was a tattoo artist, nonetheless, eschewing electric tattoo machines for hand tools and utilizing techniques that were centuries old, practiced by her parents and the Indigenous cultures of the South Sea Islands, New Zealand, Australia, and elsewhere around the globe.

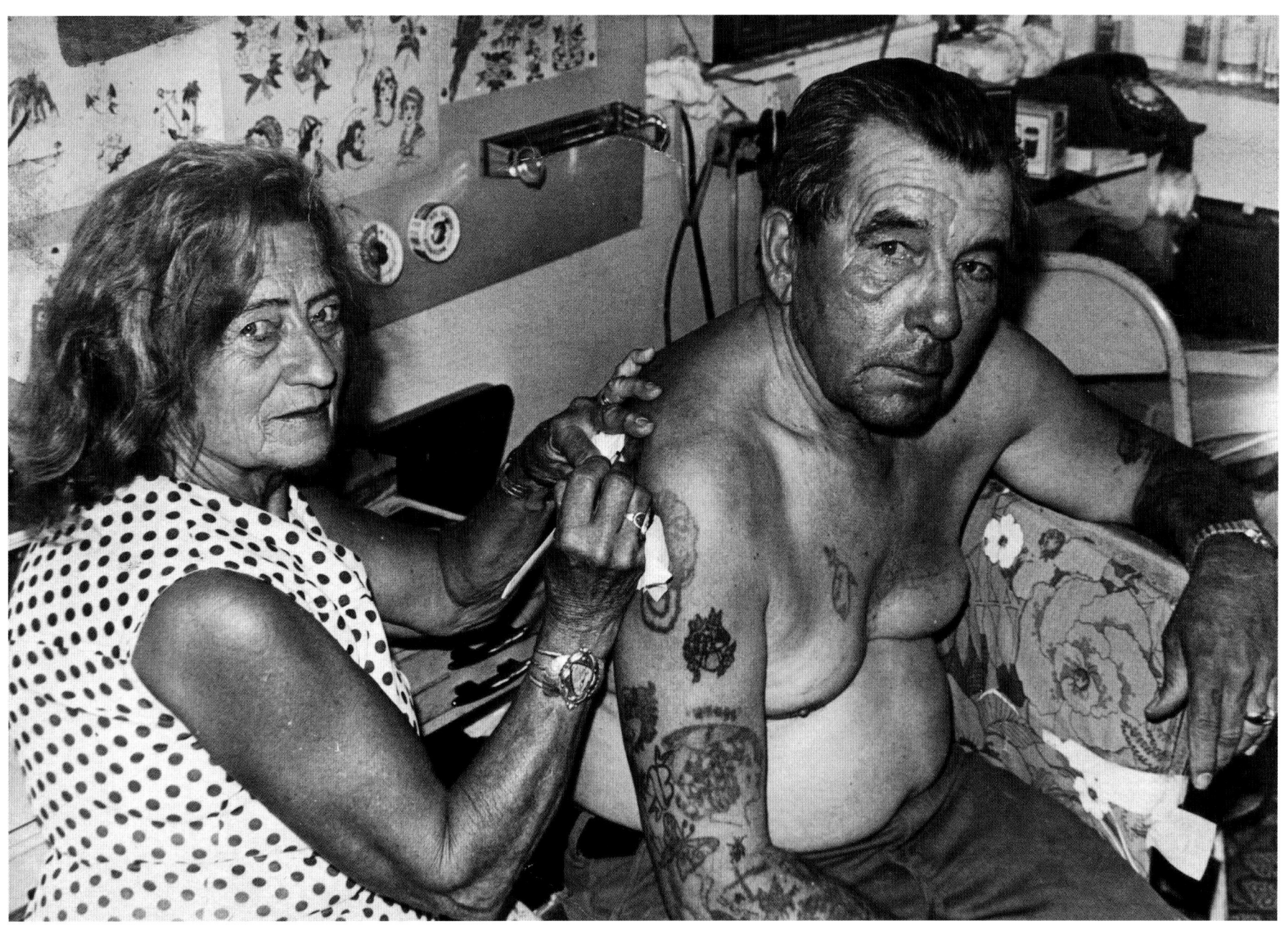

Lotteva tattooing her husband, Russell
Eugene "Tarzan" Davis, ca. 1970s

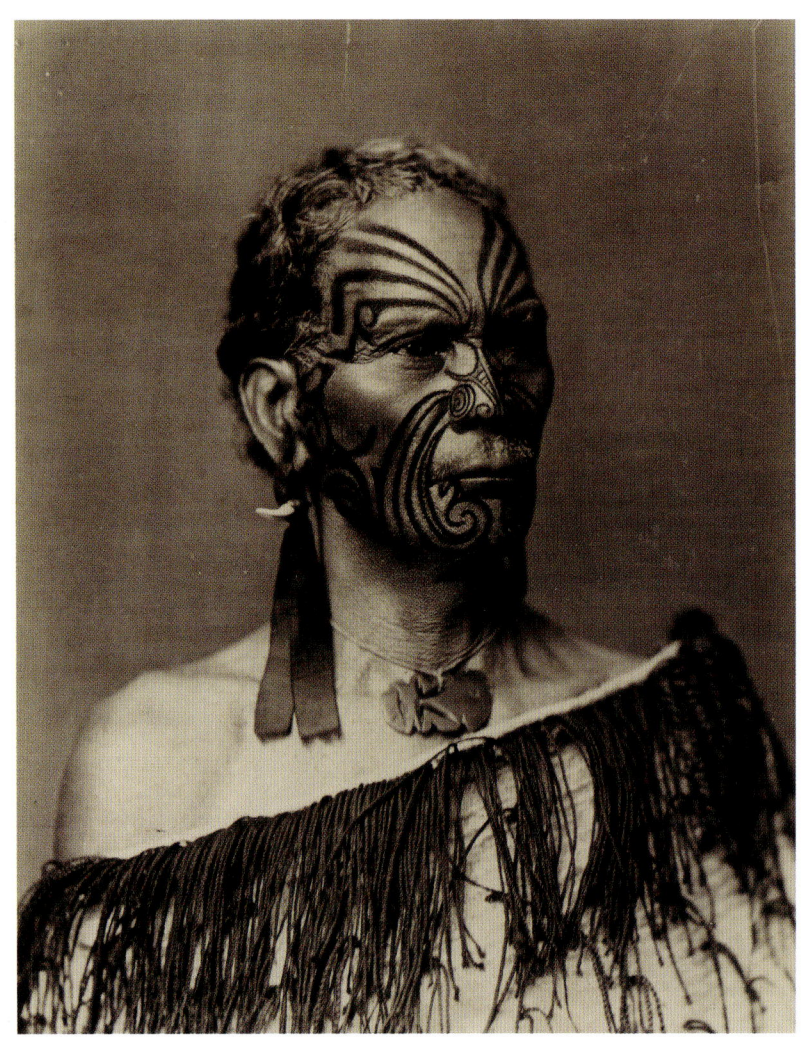

Tattooed Maori woman,
New Zealand, ca. 1880–90

Lotteva used a small paintbrush soaked with ink when she was tattooing, and as she worked, she ran the needles of her hand-made tattoo instruments through the bristles on the brush to pick up the pigment, which she would then push under the skin.

Virtually all her father's tattoos, Lotteva recalled, were made with hand tools, and he was especially proud of his Maori tattoos: "He had some that was, uh! I mean painful. I believe he said that the bamboo needle was worse than any of them. He said the fish needles and all of them things, they were bad enough. He said they would cut and go deep and bleed a lot. But the bamboo needles, you've seen a bamboo chopstick, and the end of it is cut off, and it looked like little needle points. Like a wire brush. Well, they split that; then they tie them [the needles] on to a piece of bamboo and they tattoo you with that. It's very, very painful. You might just stick them with a sliver, how it hurts. Well, this bamboo is like that, and it breaks off and you gotta keep diggin' it out. He said that was the most painful tattoos he got, bamboo work.

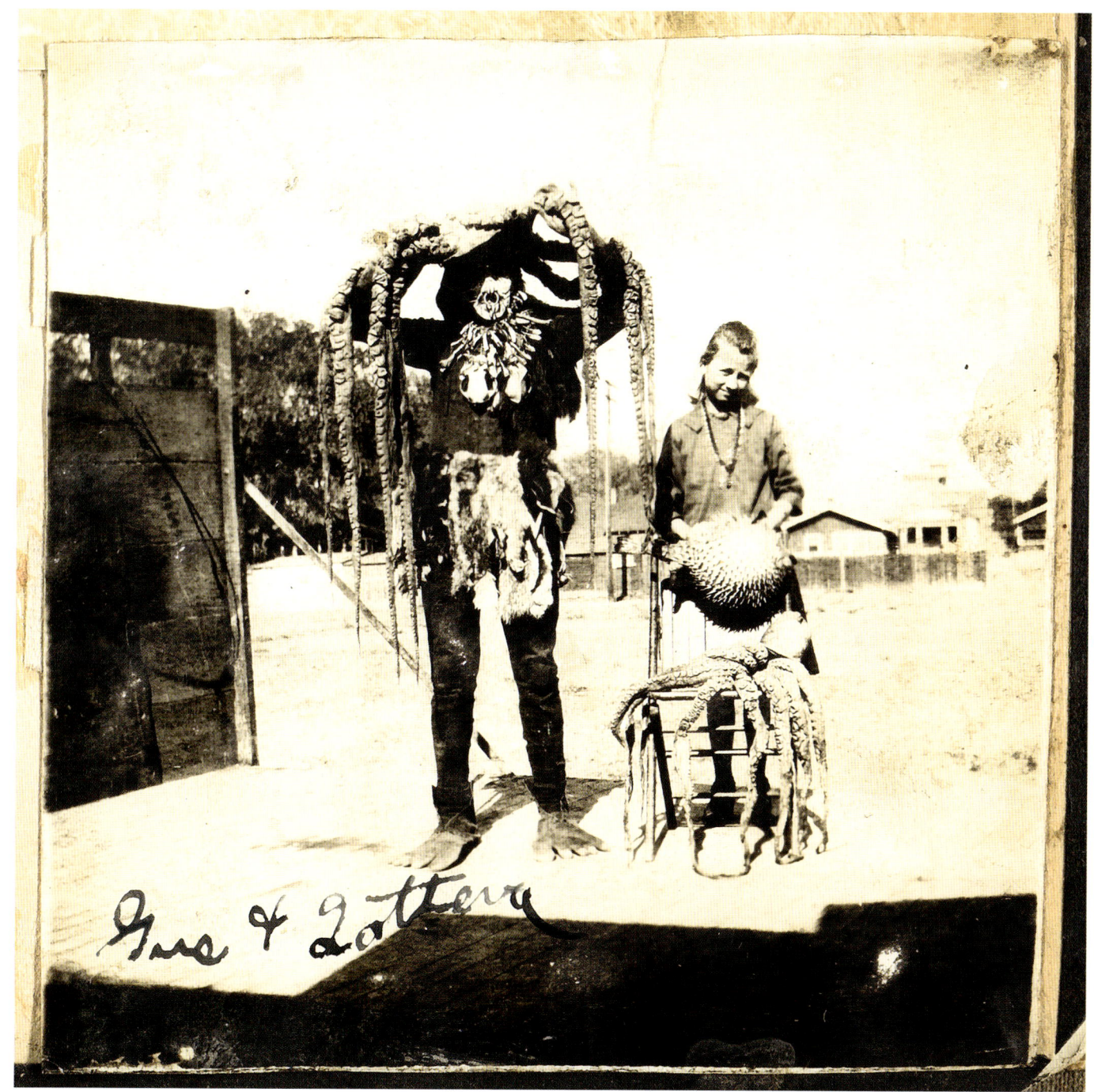

Gus and Lotteva. *Detail from Gus Wagner's scrapbook*

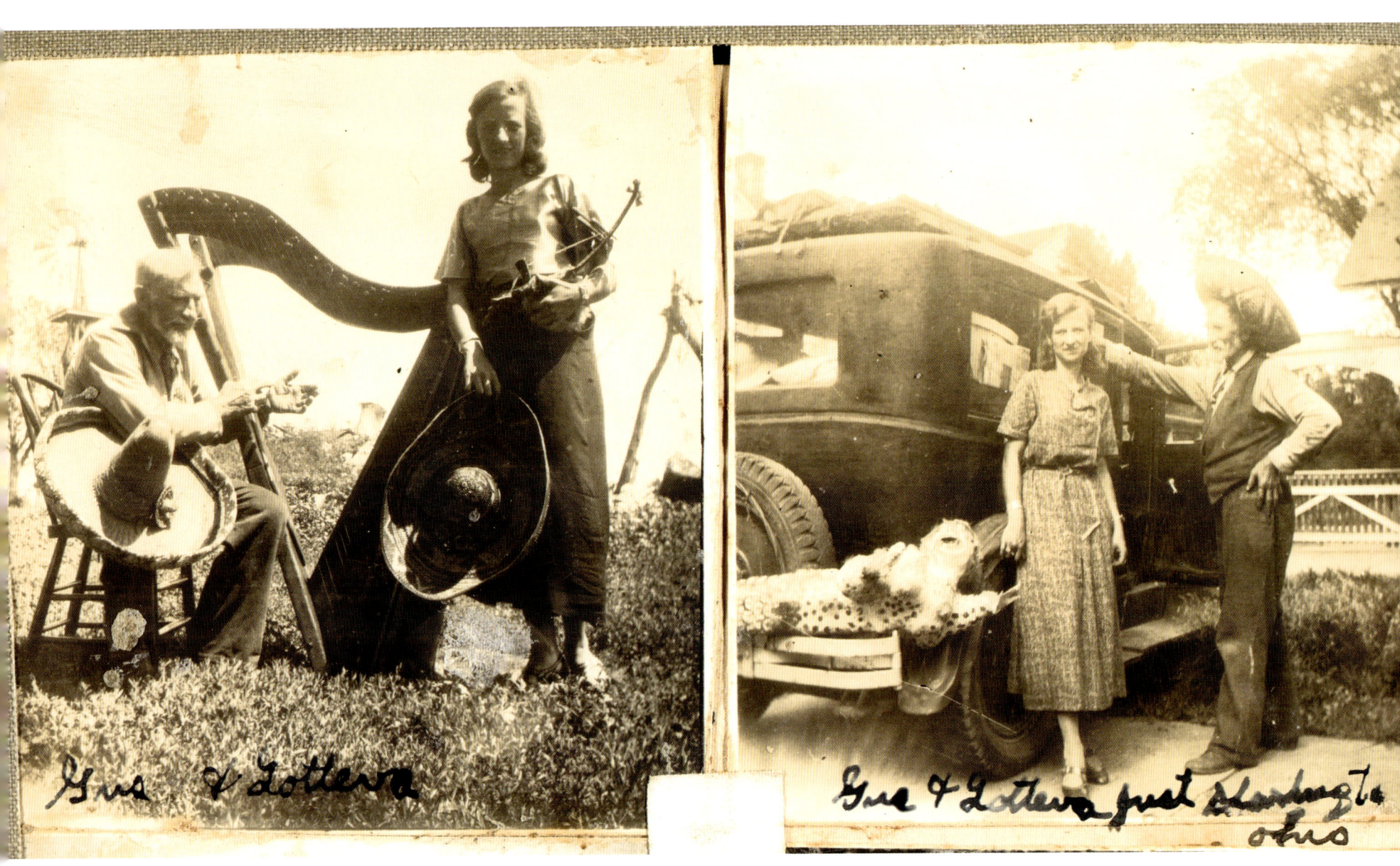

Detail from Gus Wagner's scrapbook

"I don't remember how many people Papa tattooed all over, but he tattooed one by the name of Jack Oilman. Well, Jack Oilman had been bitten on the hand by a rattlesnake, and his fingers was like that [shows how they were deformed]. Couldn't write, could barely move his arm at the elbow, and Papa started at the wrist. He went around and around and around and . . . by the time he got that snake's head upon his shoulders, he was writing with that hand."[5]

Lotteva was proud of her father; for her, he embraced the virtues of the Old West—the distinctly American ideals of independence and self-reliance. Lotteva treasured the vest her father "had when he was with Buffalo Bill's show—a beaded buckskin vest. He wore it to kind of dress up. And then he had two or three brown leather vests. He was great to wear leather. Oh, I remember the little kinda pinstriped shirts, and then he'd wear an armband here, kinda hold 'em up. He was great to wear them. He didn't particularly like to wear a dress coat to work. But he was always a little fussy about his work."[6]

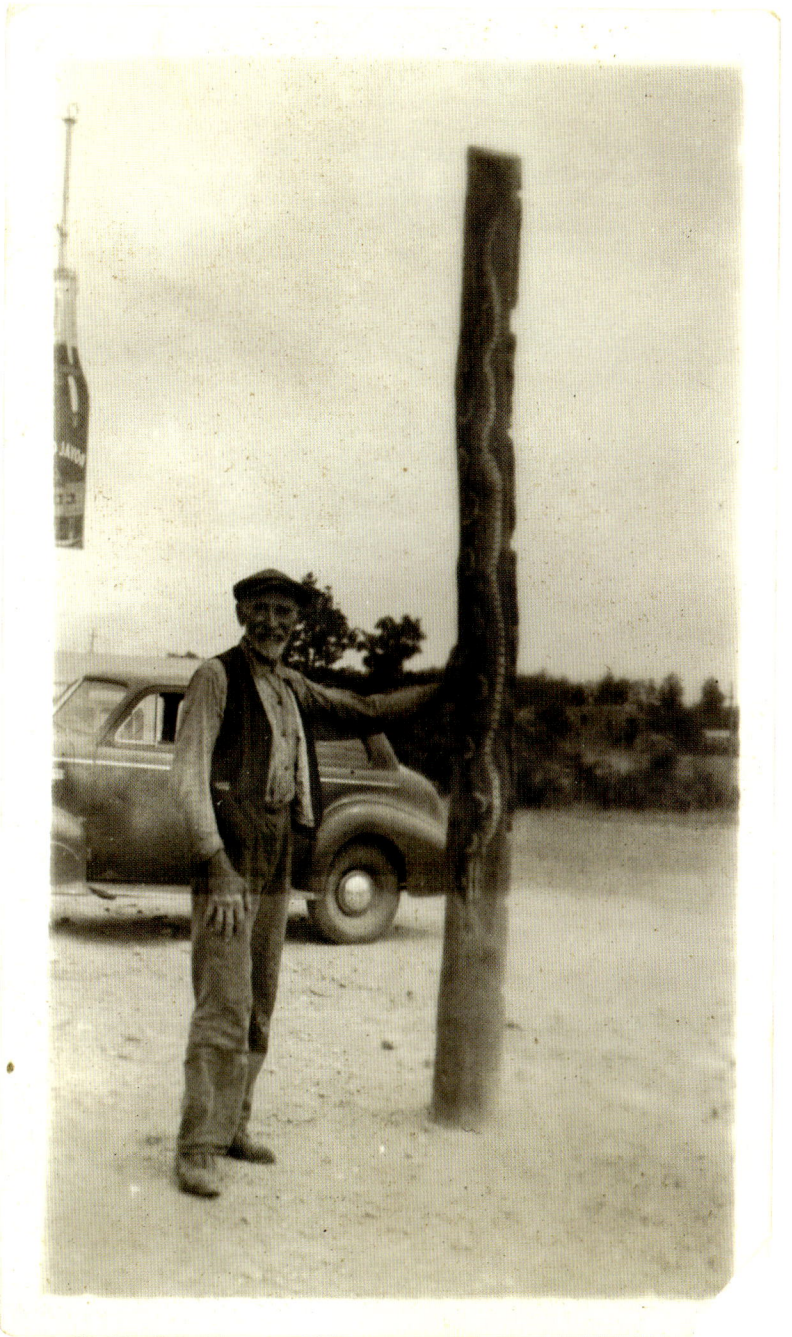

Gus at Hamlin's shop with a carved totem pole, 1937

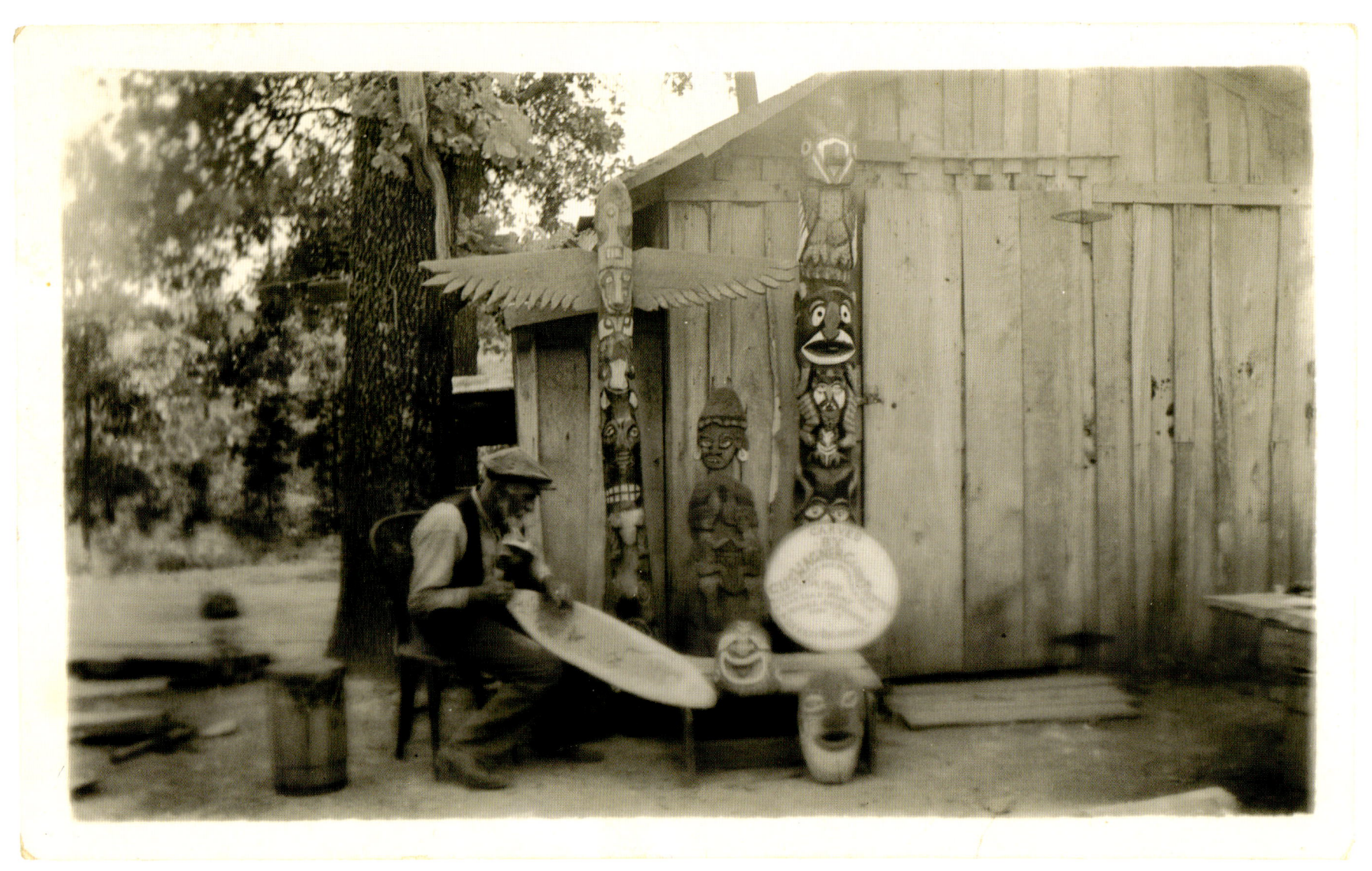

Gus carving in front of his cabin, ca. 1937

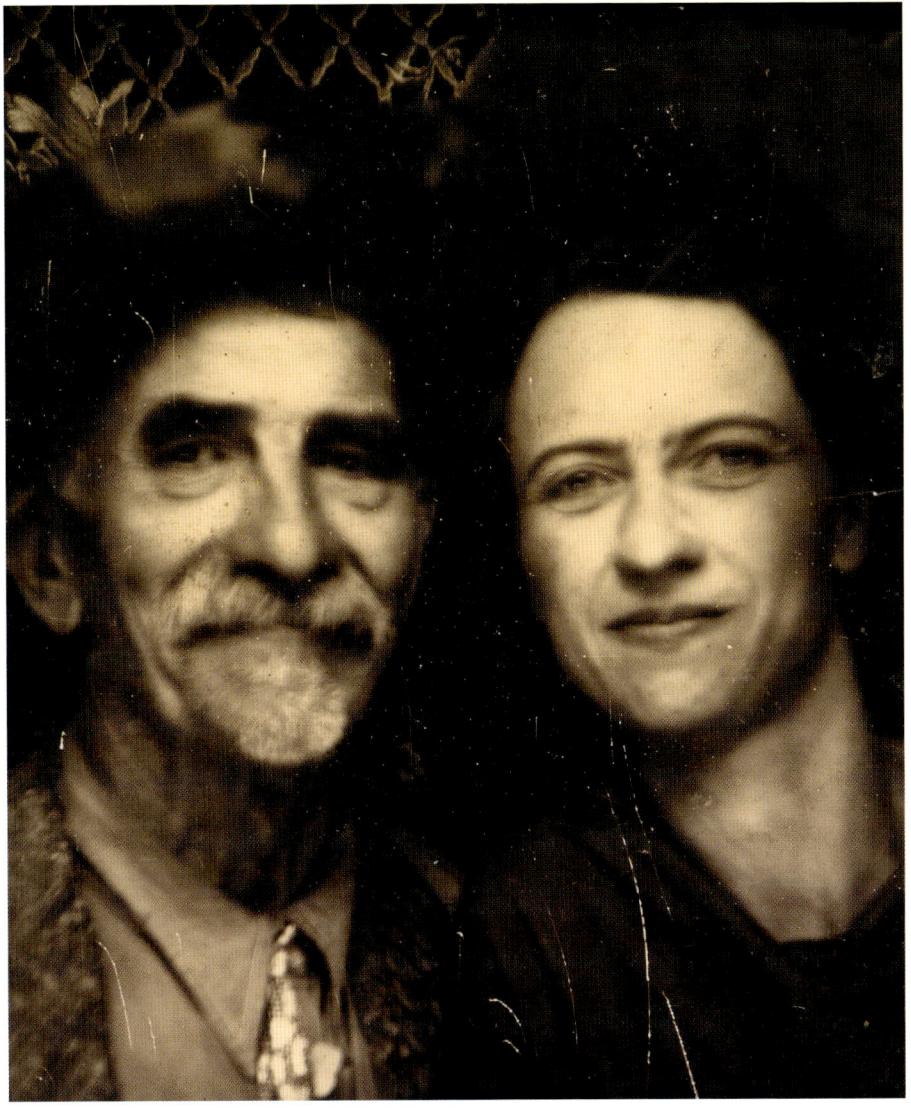

Gus and Lotteva, ca. 1930s

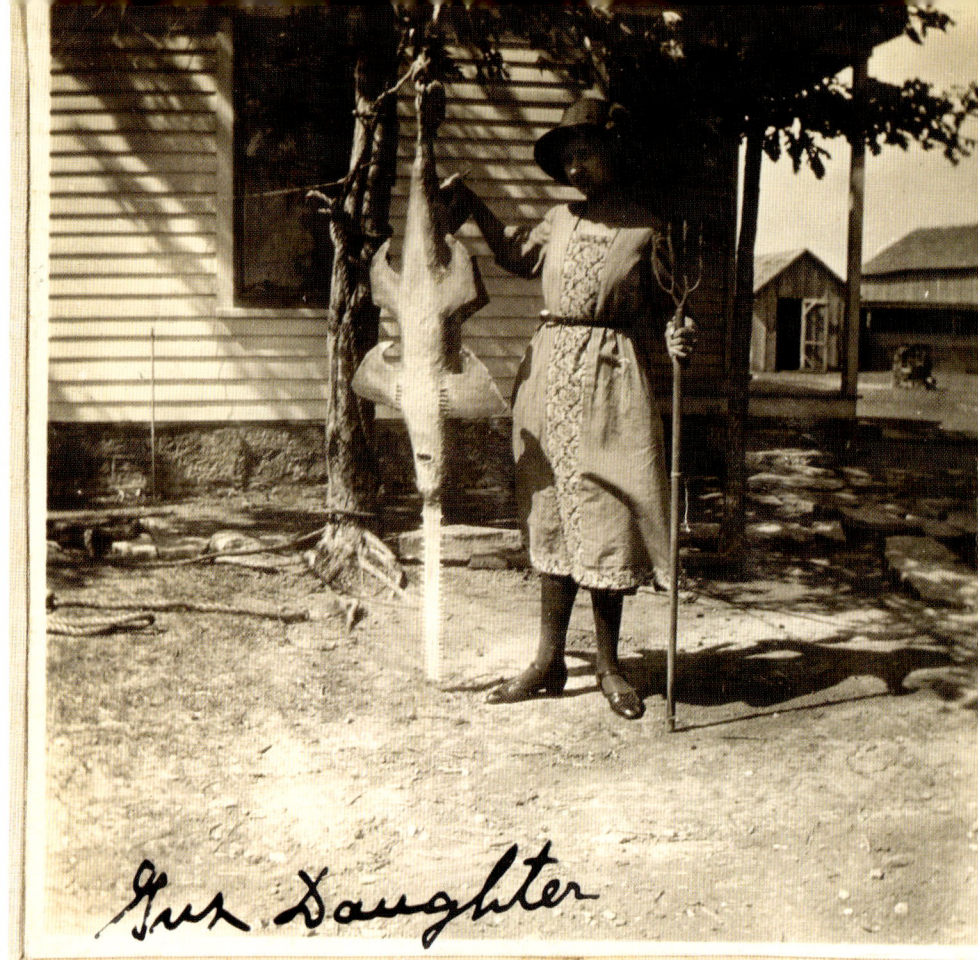

Gus Daughter

Detail from Gus Wagner's scrapbook

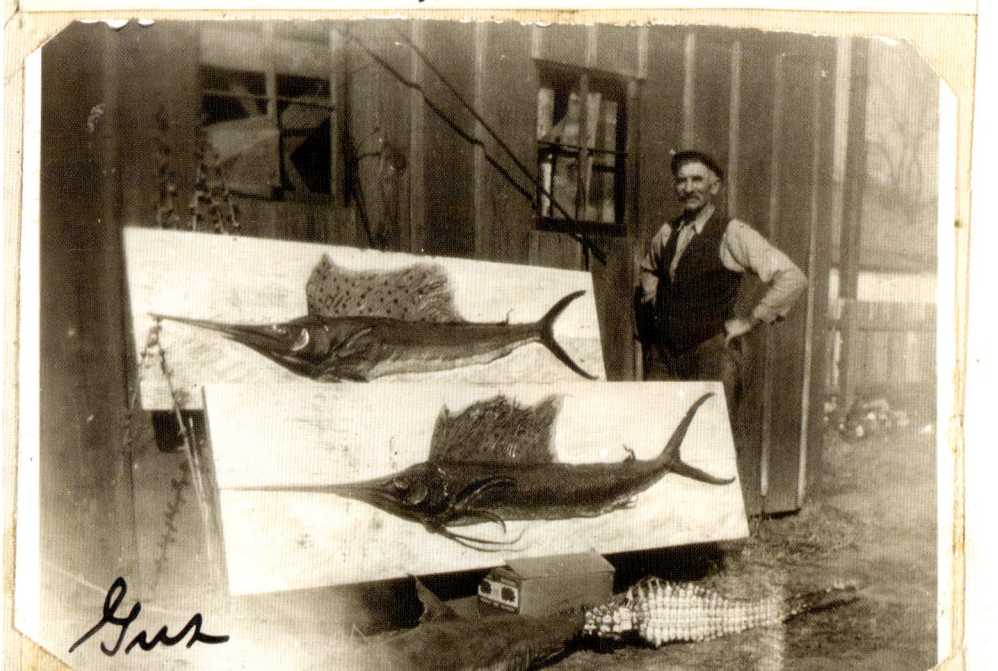

Gus

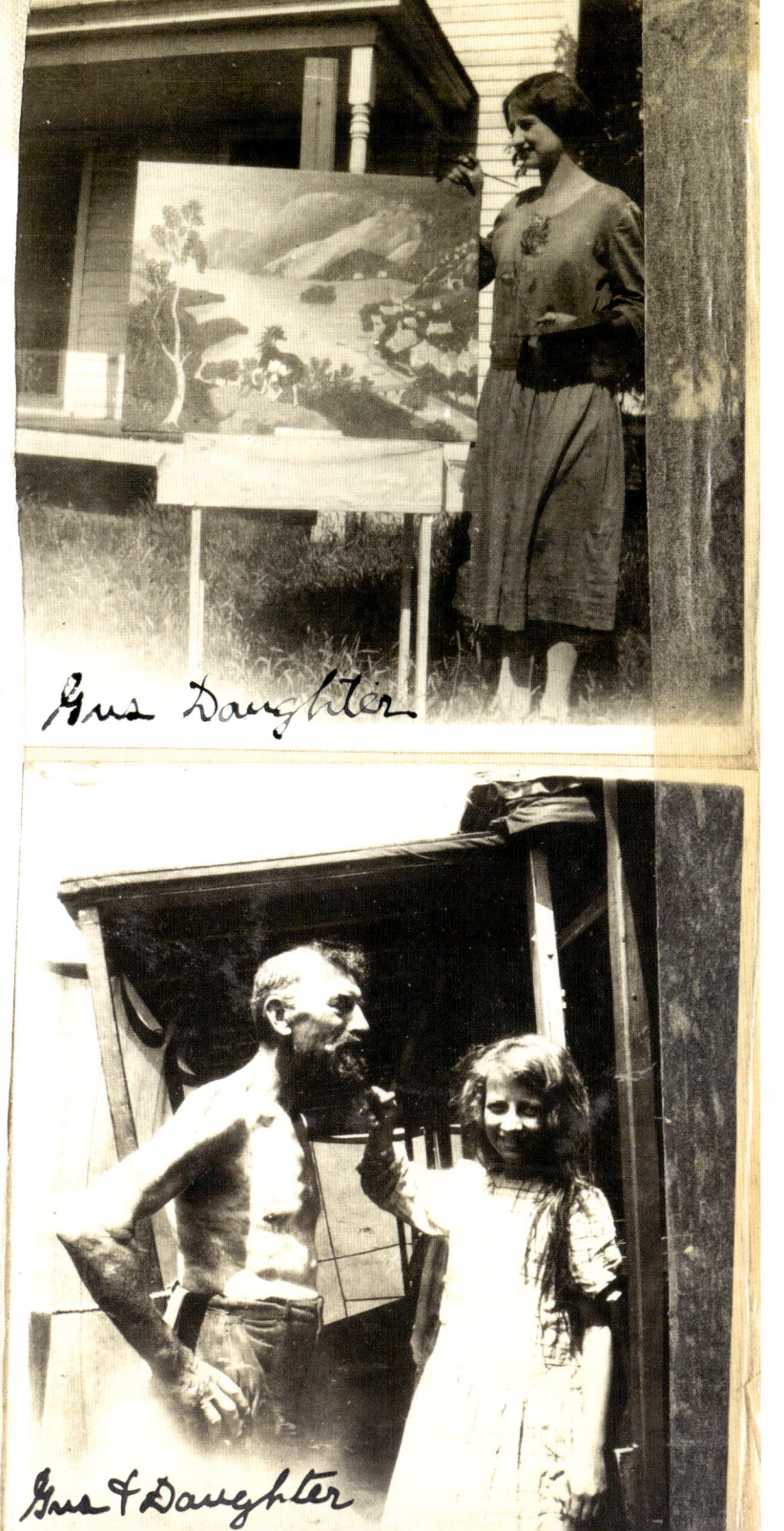

Gus Daughter

Gus & Daughter

While Gus Wagner knew how to handle snakes, lizards, and wild animals, there is no evidence of him ever being a horseman, while one can only imagine that Lotteva's mother, Maud, who grew up in rural Kansas, was very familiar with ranch life. Lotteva loved to rodeo because she loved horses, whether she was painting them on paper or canvas or on the windows of storefronts in little towns in Texas and Oklahoma, or tattooing them on people's arms and legs, backs, and chests, or featuring them in "color books" she published,[7] or scaling them up in three-dimensional forms for the merry-go-rounds of the ragtag circuses and carnivals her parents toured with and staged themselves.

Pat Hook said that Lotteva "started drawing horses when she was very little. She saw a show horse go by and drew it because it was beautiful. She had been sick and saw the horse from a window.

Detail from Gus Wagner's scrapbook

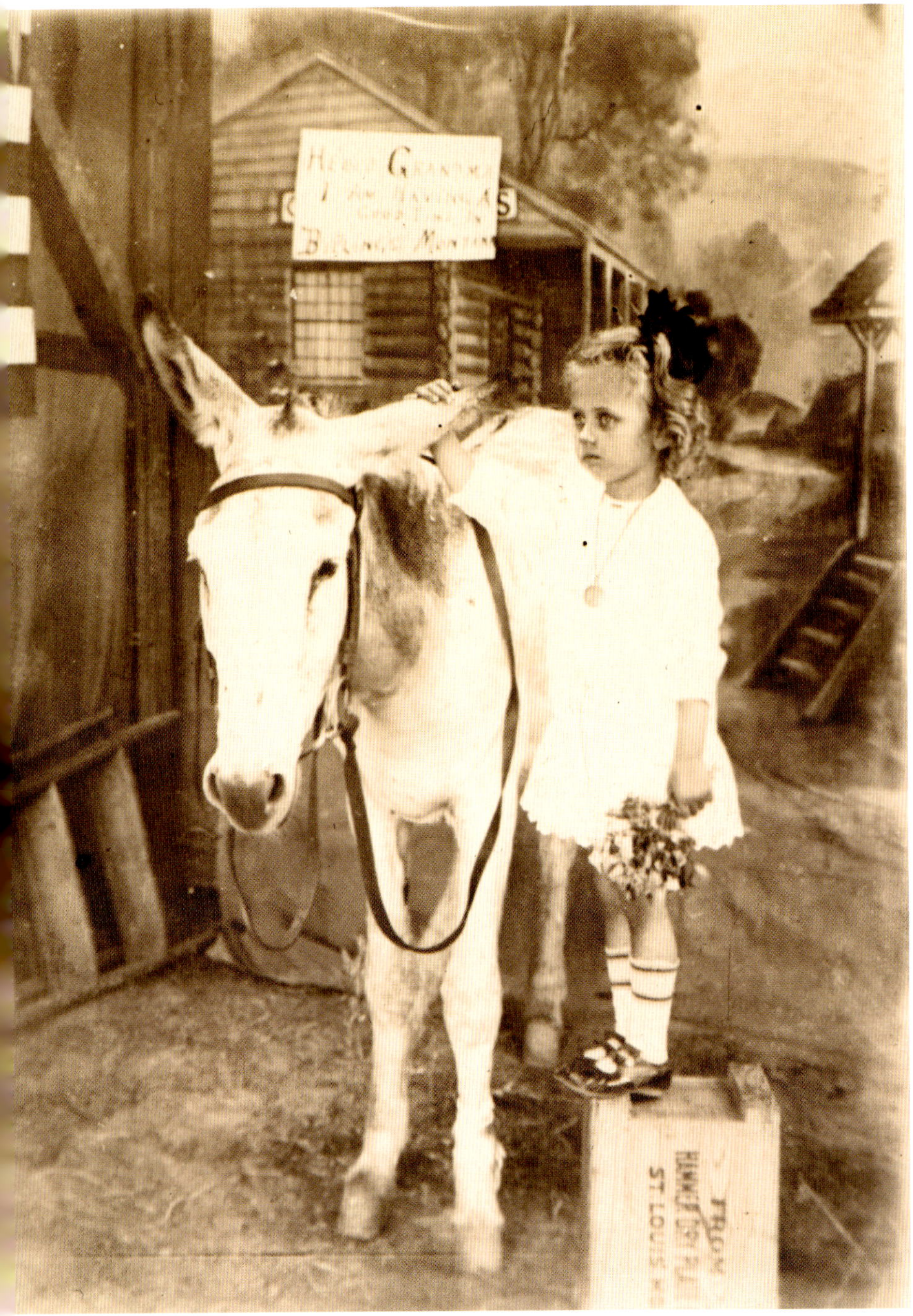

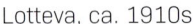

"The family didn't want Lotteva to ride a horse because it was too dangerous. She rode anyway, but not too well. A man asked, 'Who taught you to ride?,' and she admitted no one had, so he taught her how to ride. He said, 'Wrap the reins around the hand that you don't write with, and hold on to the saddle horn with that hand.' She learned to pull the horse's head around and get it down on its side [to get her foot out of the stirrup before it went down].

"Lotteva rode her horse into Cottonwood Falls to paint windows for the rodeo. She liked the rodeo best of the many things she had done. She painted windows in many towns—100-plus windows in a town—and then slept on the bus. No two windows were alike in a town."[8]

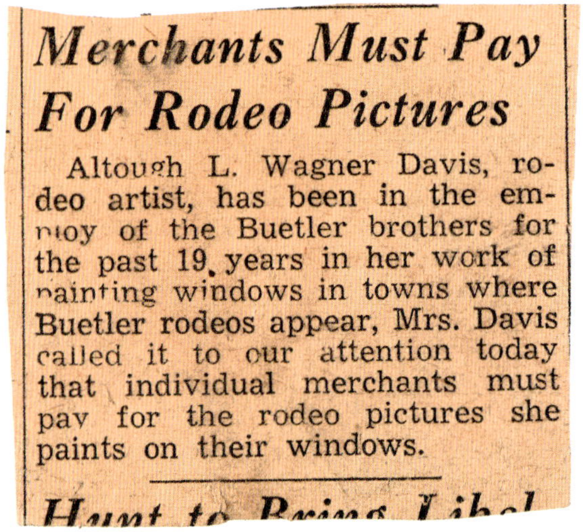

Merchants Must Pay For Rodeo Pictures

Altough L. Wagner Davis, rodeo artist, has been in the employ of the Buetler brothers for the past 19 years in her work of painting windows in towns where Buetler rodeos appear, Mrs. Davis called it to our attention today that individual merchants must pay for the rodeo pictures she paints on their windows.

Hunt to Bring Libel

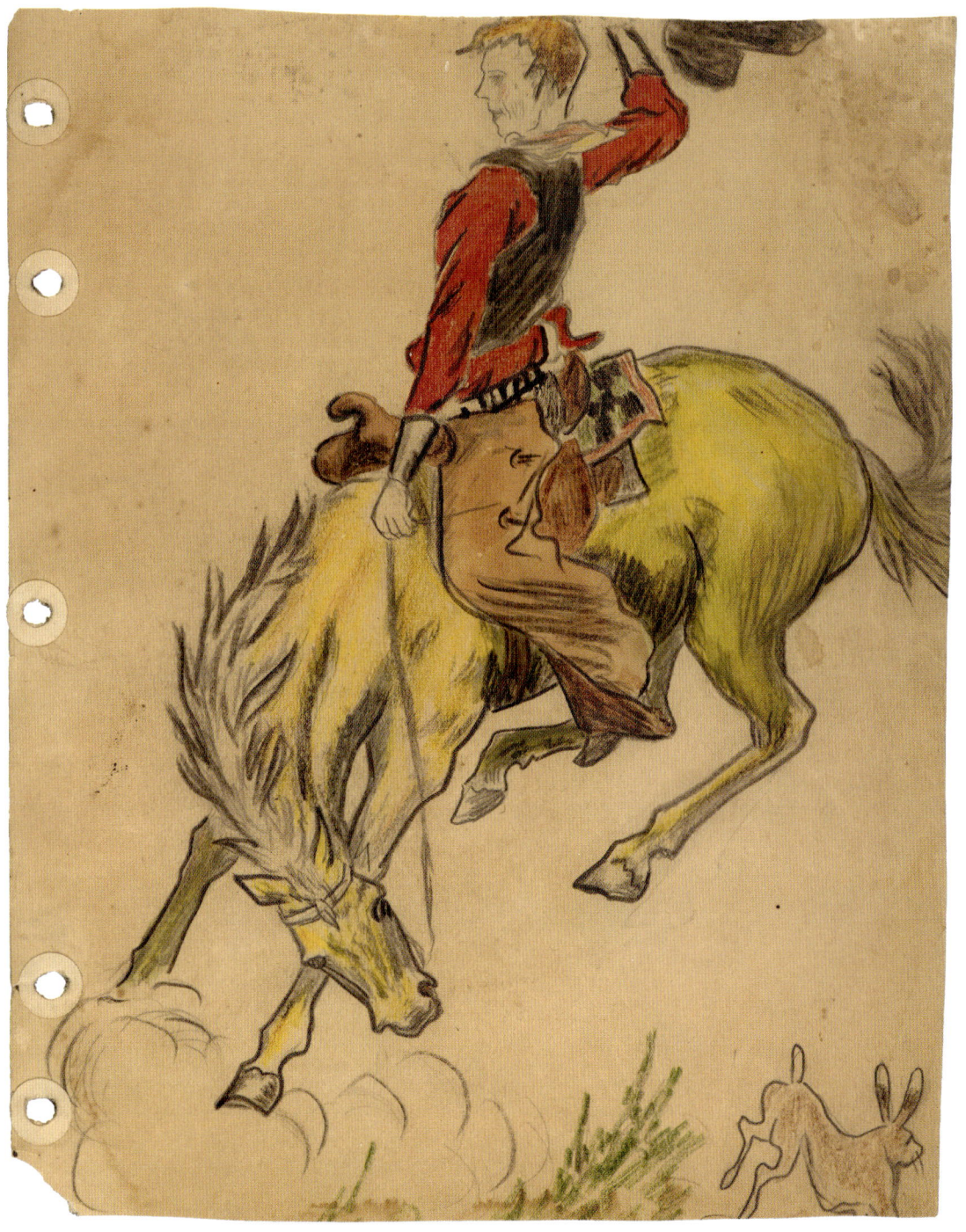

Illustration by Lotteva

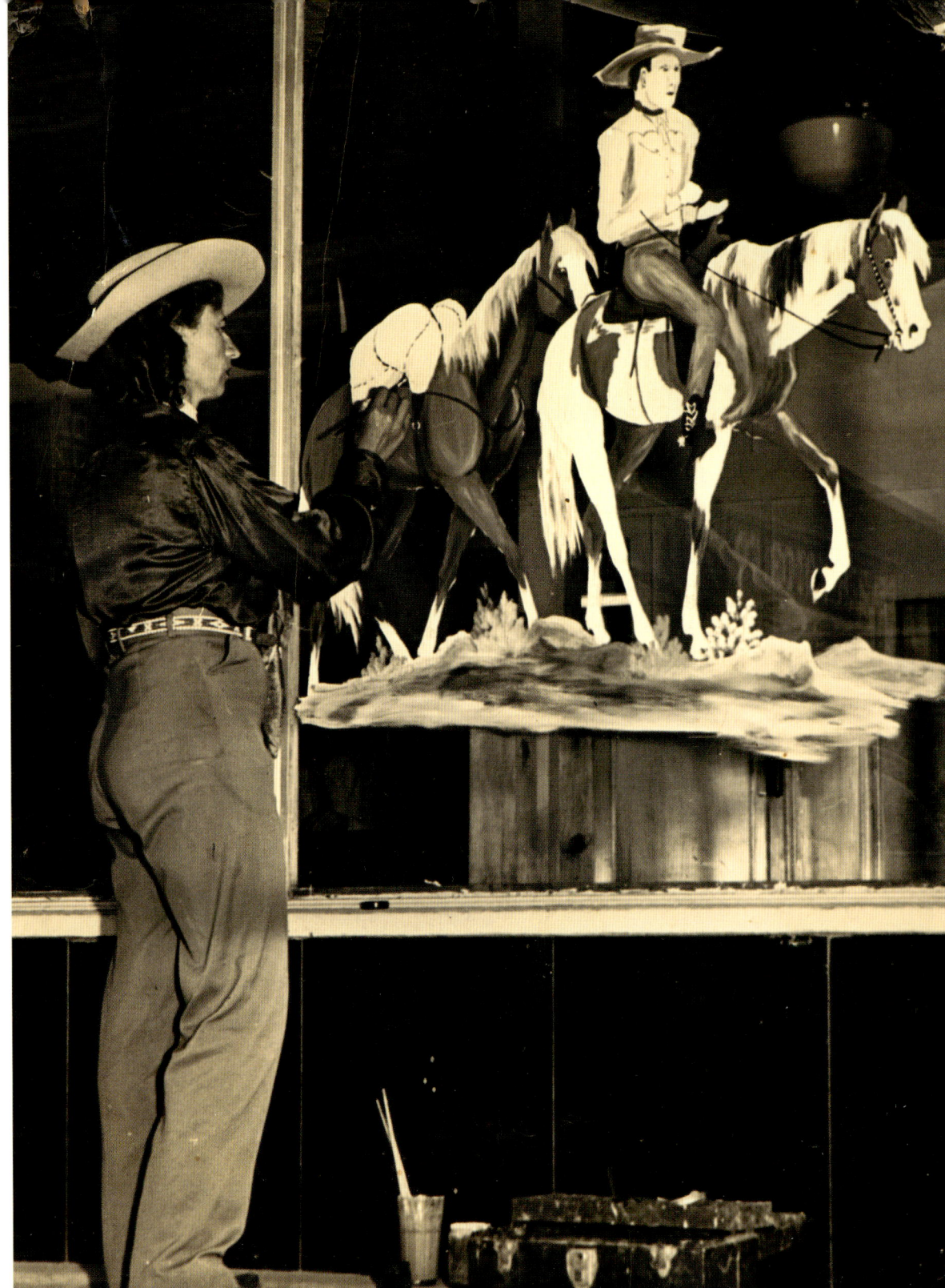

Lotteva painting a store
window, ca. 1950s

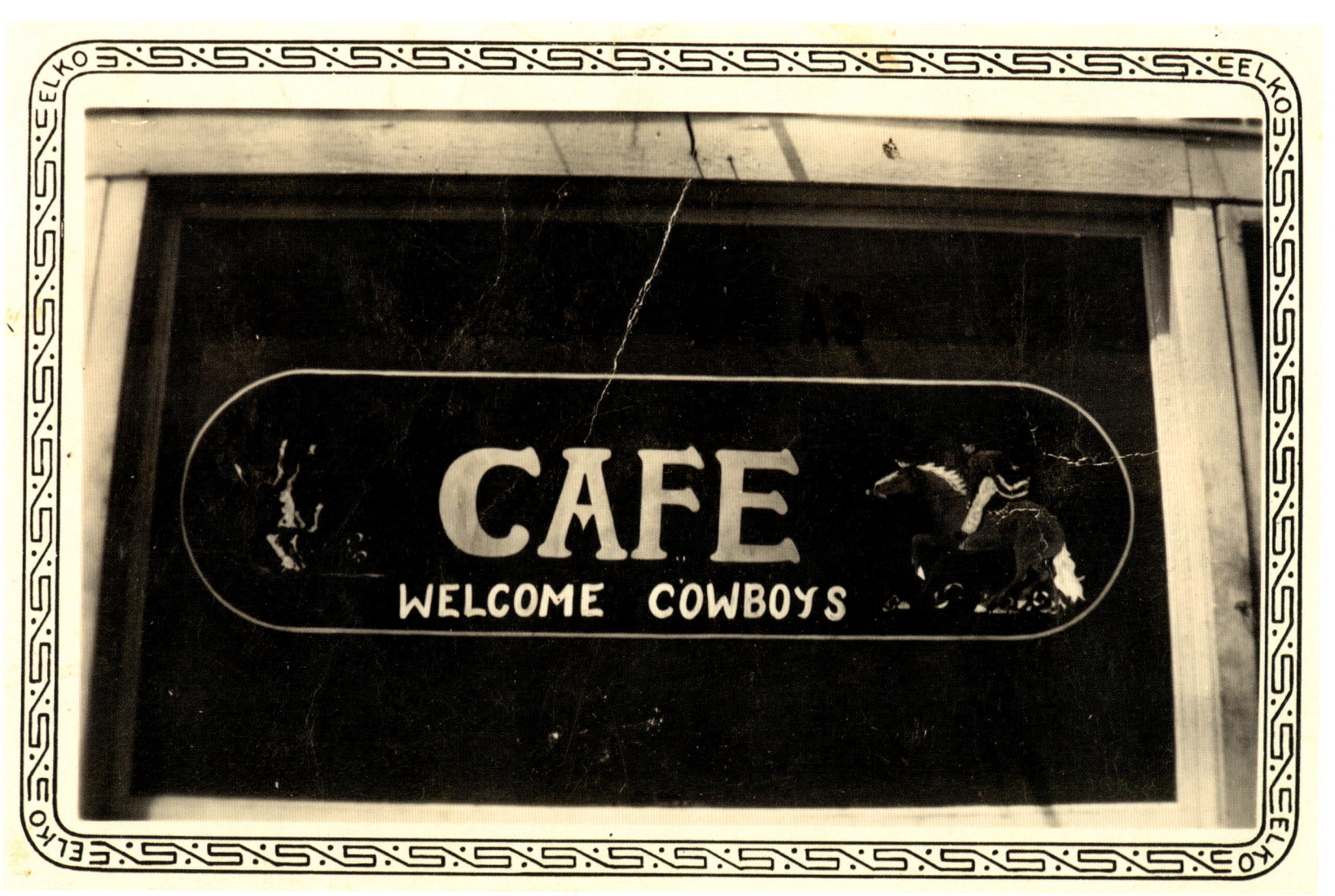

Café window painting by Lotteva,
ca. 1950s

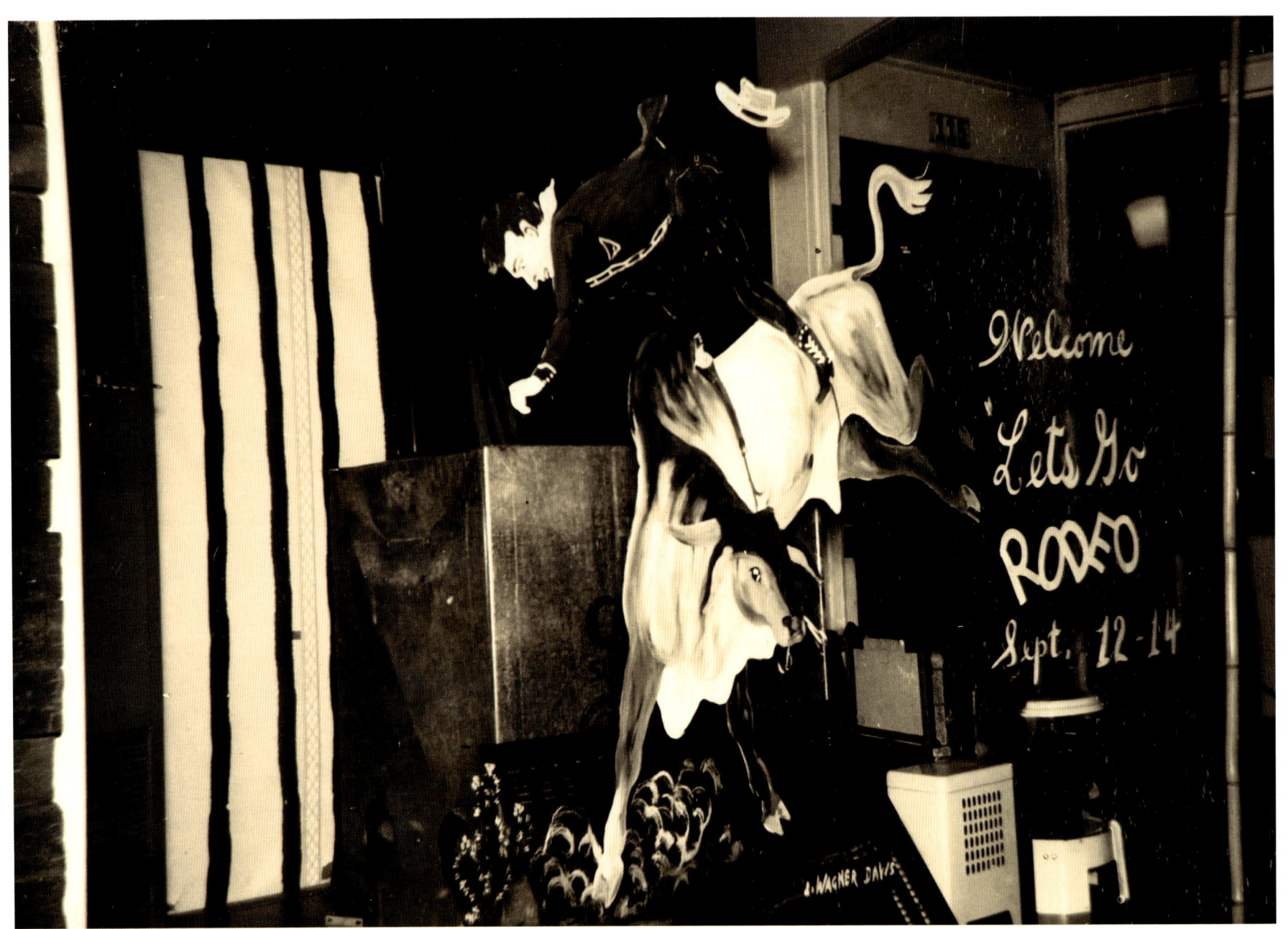

Store window painting by Lotteva, ca. 1950s

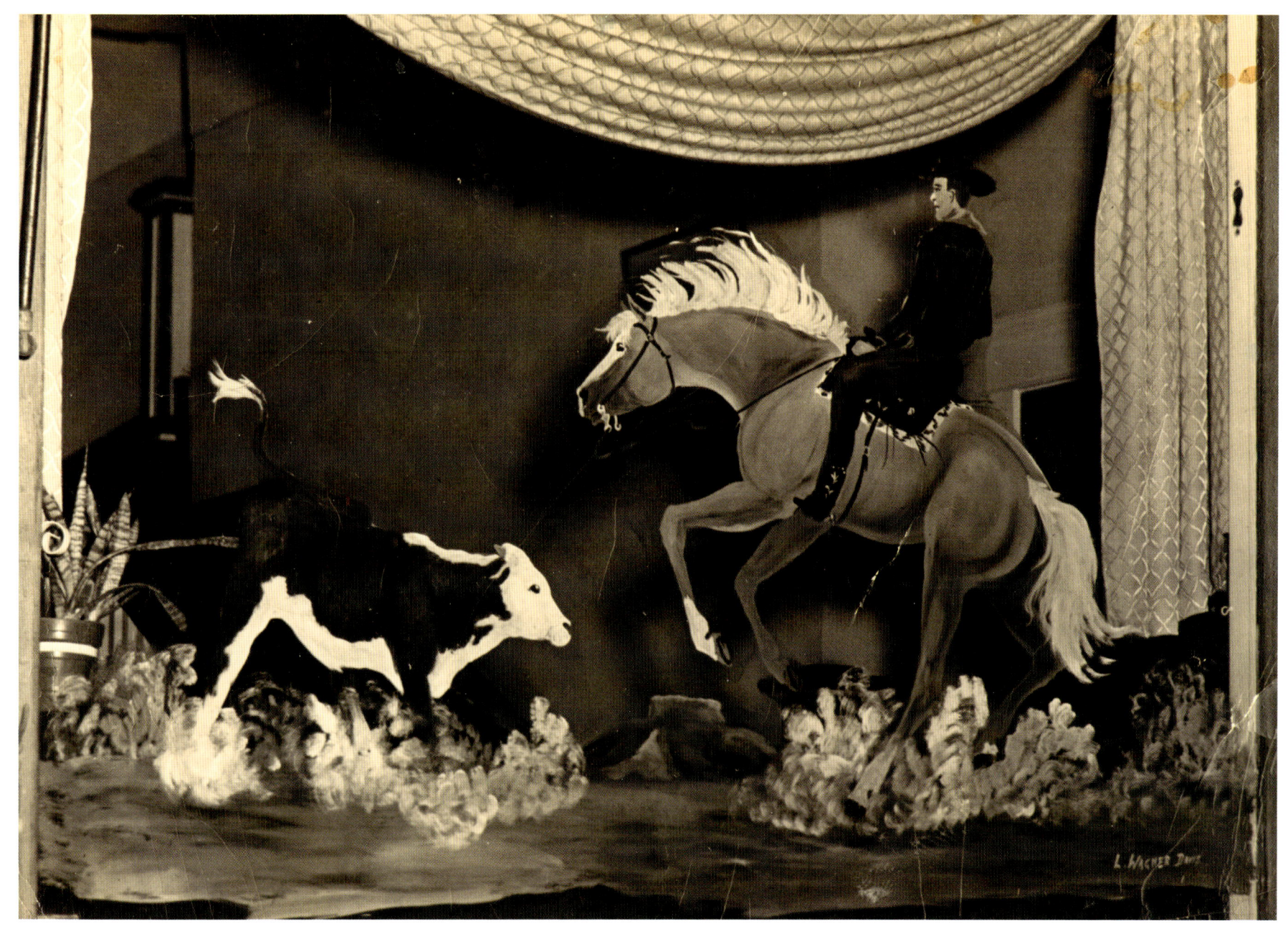

Store window painting by Lotteva, ca. 1950s

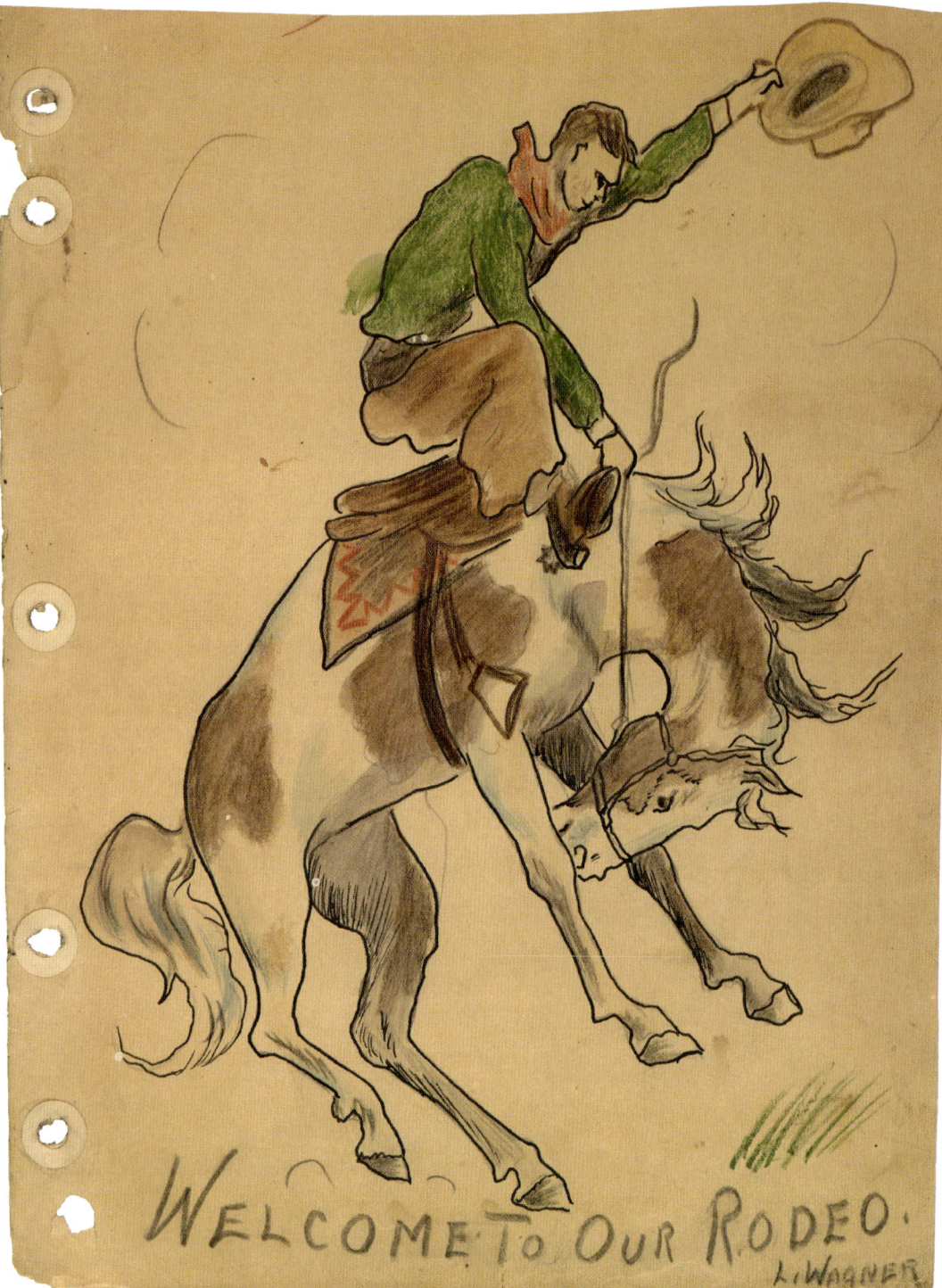

Illustration by Lotteva

In 1941, Lotteva married Russell Eugene "Tarzan" Davis of Oklahoma. "He was known as 'the Oklahoma Plow Boy.' Maud nicknamed him Tarzan. She may have had a crush on him. He could pull a car with his teeth. Lotteva could do it too—a matter of leverage." She had known Tarzan for a long time (since 1927) but had turned him down on marriage. Then when Gus was dying, he said he wished he could have seen her married to Tarzan. Tarzan said much the same thing later in the day, and she accepted. They were on the way to El Dorado when they decided to get married and went to the courthouse."

After Gus died in 1941, Lotteva did her best to earn a living by painting signs and windows, advertising rodeos, where her husband, Tarzan, often competed. While working with famous fan dancer Sally Rand and her husband, bronc rider Turk Greenough, Lotteva saw an empty storefront that she thought might make a good tattoo studio.

"I said to Tarzan, 'You see down there on the corner from where you're sitting. There's a little building down there; I'd like to have it and put a tattoo shop in it.' Well, Papa had just passed away and my mother was just down, that's all. Couldn't get her to pull out of it. I said, 'Let's rent it.' So I went in and got it for 10 dollars a month. Went in and hung a bedsheet up across there; I got a couple of nail kegs, and pasteboard boxes to throw trash in, put a board in the window to set my stuff on, hung the designs on the bedsheets."

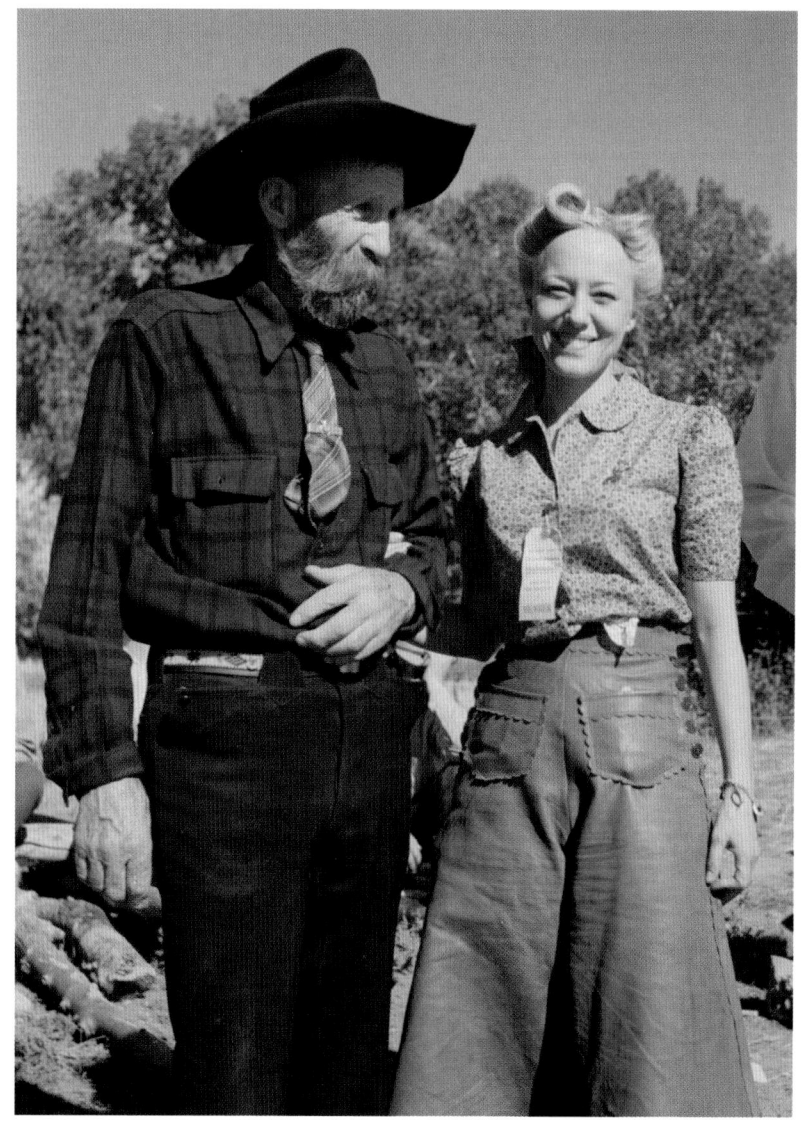

Sally Rand and Turk Greenough's father at a stockmen's picnic and barbecue, Wyola, Montana, 1941

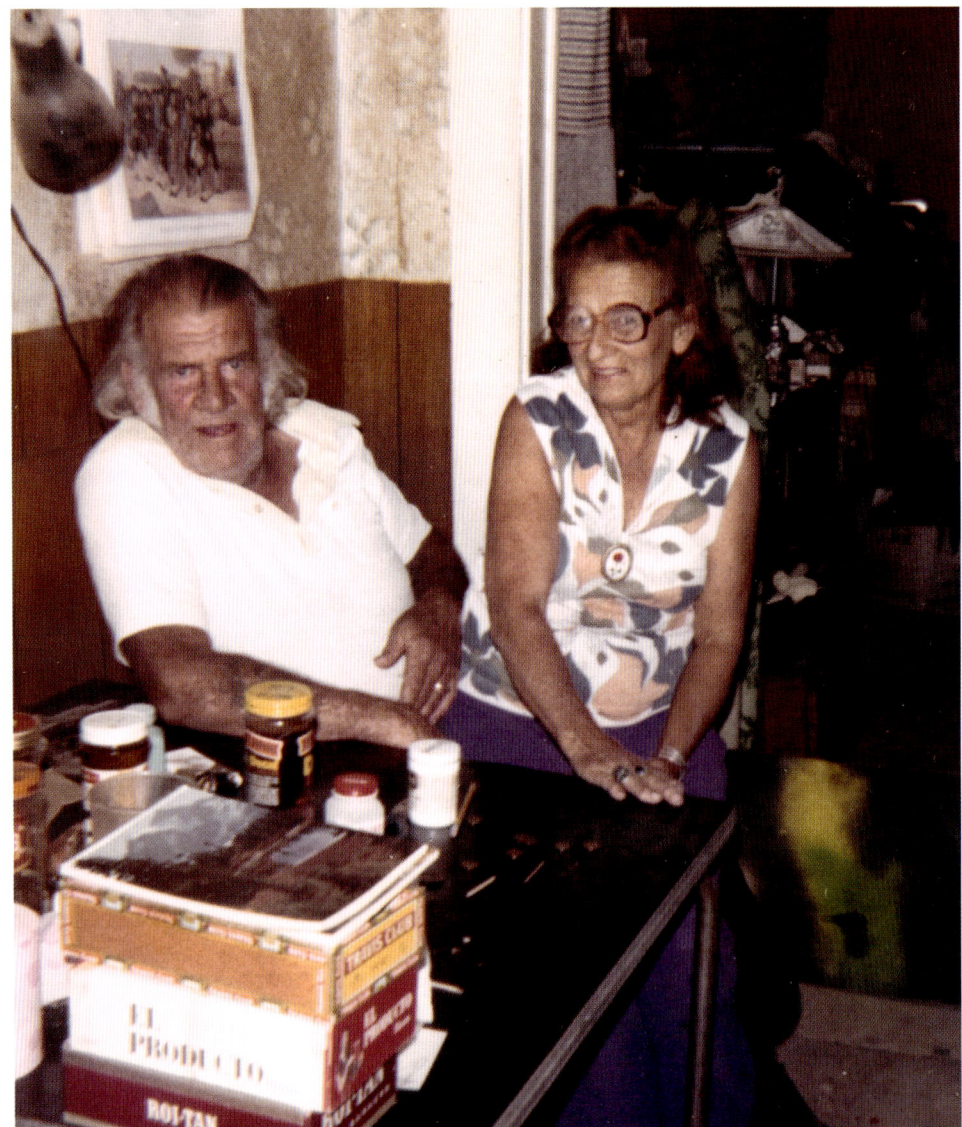

Russell Eugene "Tarzan" Davis
and Lotteva, ca. 1970s

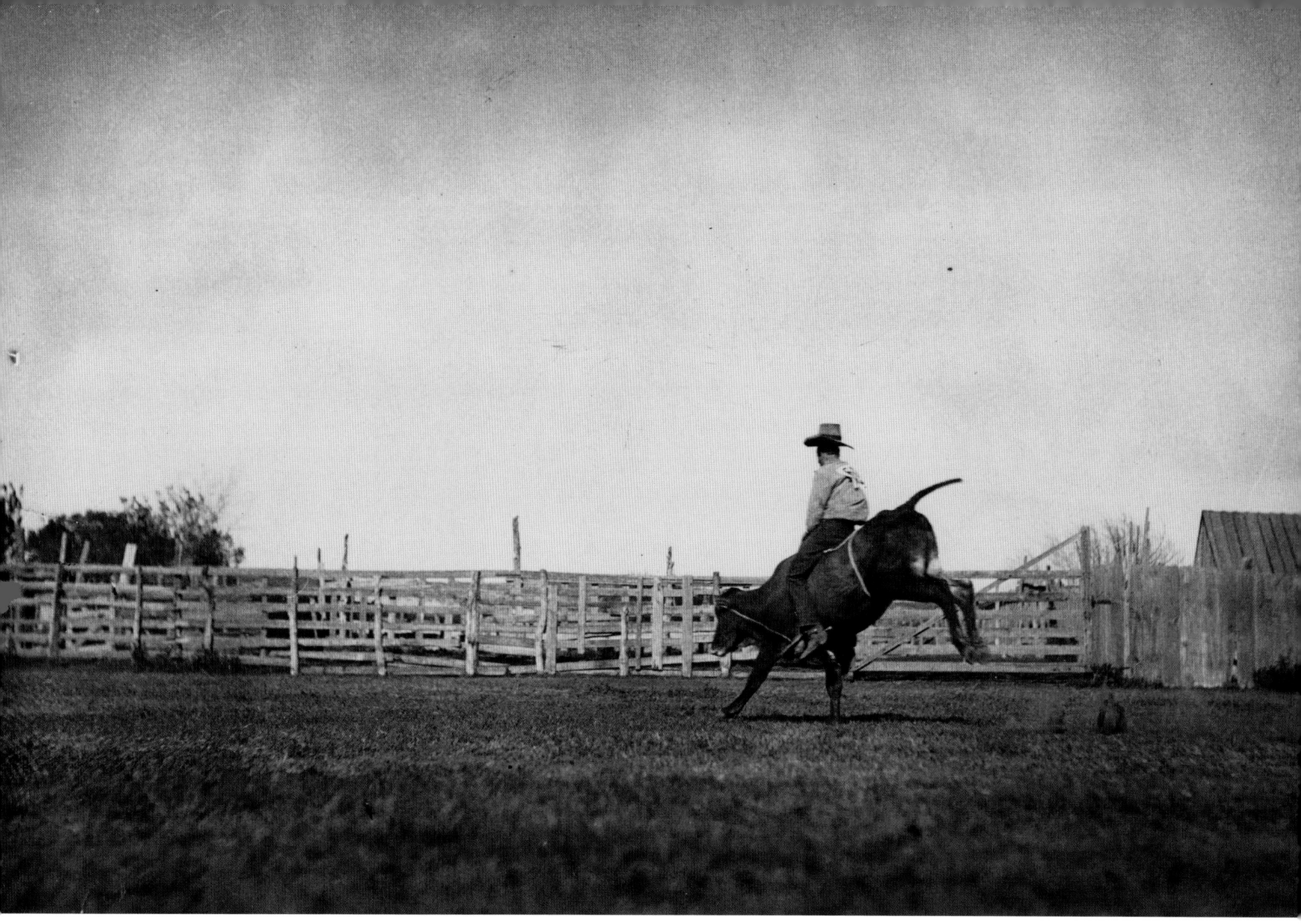

Tarzan, Canadian, Texas, ca. 1930s

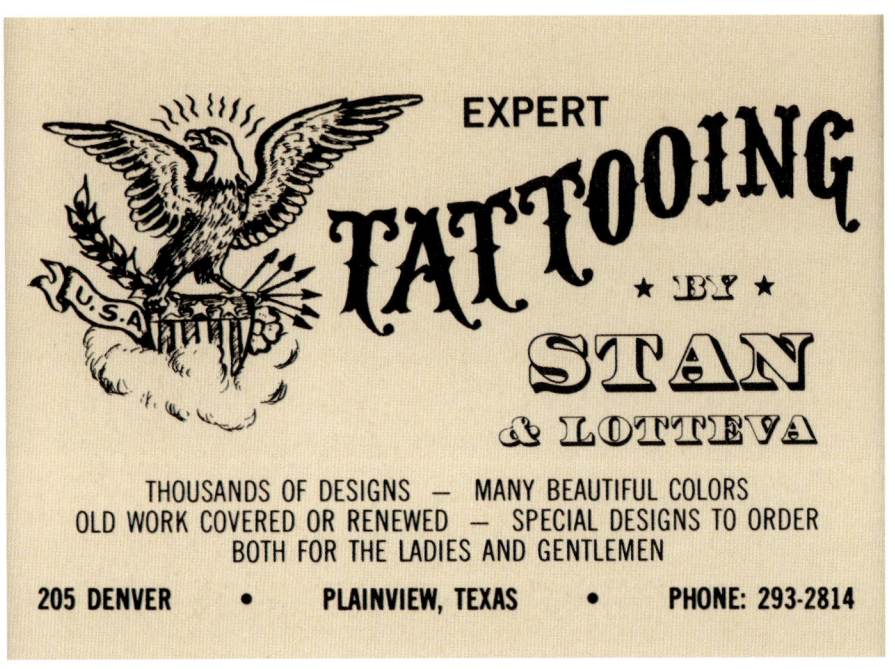

EXPERT

TATTOOING

★ BY ★

STAN

& LOTTEVA

THOUSANDS OF DESIGNS — MANY BEAUTIFUL COLORS
OLD WORK COVERED OR RENEWED — SPECIAL DESIGNS TO ORDER
BOTH FOR THE LADIES AND GENTLEMEN

205 DENVER • PLAINVIEW, TEXAS • PHONE: 293-2814

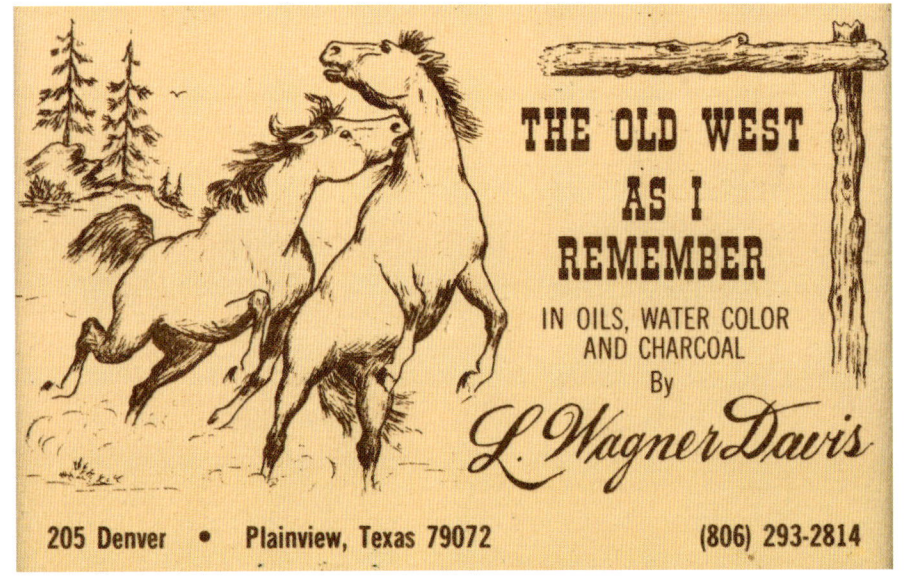

THE OLD WEST
AS I
REMEMBER

IN OILS, WATER COLOR
AND CHARCOAL
By

L. Wagner Davis

205 Denver • Plainview, Texas 79072 (806) 293-2814

As a tattoo artist, Lotteva was endeared to her clients and those who knew and loved her. Lotteva's career as a hand tattooist marked the end of an era.

According to Ellen Sweets, Lotteva made her last tattoo in 1990. "But it wasn't the last her fans heard of her. In the underground subculture of true tattoo aficionados, Lotteva Wagner Davis's name is known from coast to coast."

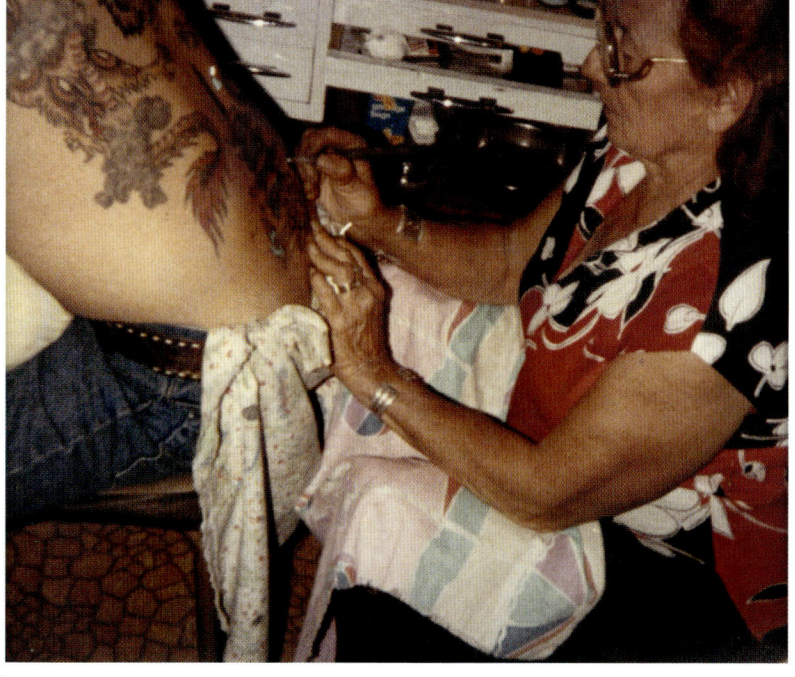

Lotteva tattooing, ca. 1970s

Lotteva told Sweets that although she "had her own tattoo business when she was twelve," she seemed to focus more intently on another love—painting—creating signs and banners with scrollwork and flowing-scrip themes that ultimately served her well in tattooing. According to Sweets, "She did not have to look for inspiration. The offspring of circus gypsies . . . she lived a life in which, as a rule, there were no rules. But the colorful lifestyle that permeated so much of Davis's daily existence is gone, save for the samples of tattoo art and prices in her front room and the antiquated tattooing machine built for her by her father that sits covered in a corner, a dirty, dusty reminder of better days. What remains now are the vivid memories: of an aviation show that her mother promoted and featured Wilbur and Orville Wright; of her father tattooing a man named George Gobel ('I was never sure if he was related to the comedian or not,' she says), of her own paintings done while working with the world-famous clown Emmett Kelly.

"'Between train wrecks, windstorms, and business deals and the Depression, I don't know how much money we made and lost,' Davis says.

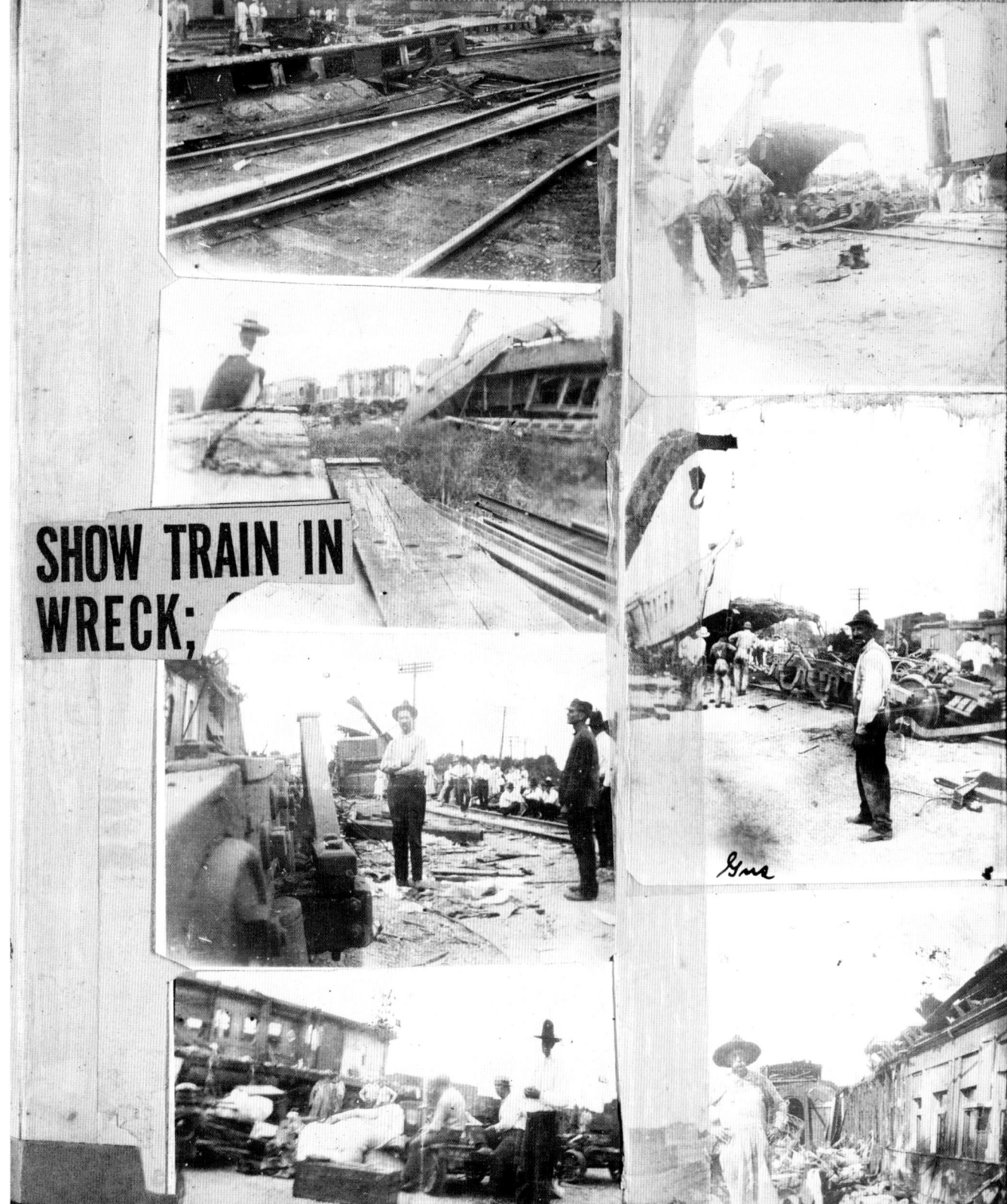

Page from Gus Wagner's scrapbook

"'But I have my memories, and no one can take those away. I remember Pancho Villa used to cross over into Laredo [Texas] for the bullfights, when we were there doing a show. Villa's nephew and I grew up together.'"

Lotteva confided to Sweets that it was "puny" health that shaped her life's work. Over the years, she suffered bouts with typhoid fever, whooping cough, scarlet fever, and measles. At age four, she contracted measles, and it was during her recovery that she started drawing: "All I did was lie in bed. We were with Papa's circus, somewhere in South Dakota in a hotel, when I saw a horse across the street. I grabbed up a pad of paper and started drawing as fast as I could."

By the time Lotteva was fourteen, she was selling her own custom-ordered paintings of lions, tigers, and bears. She signed her works on paper and canvas simply with the letter "L," because she worried that people might not do business with a female.

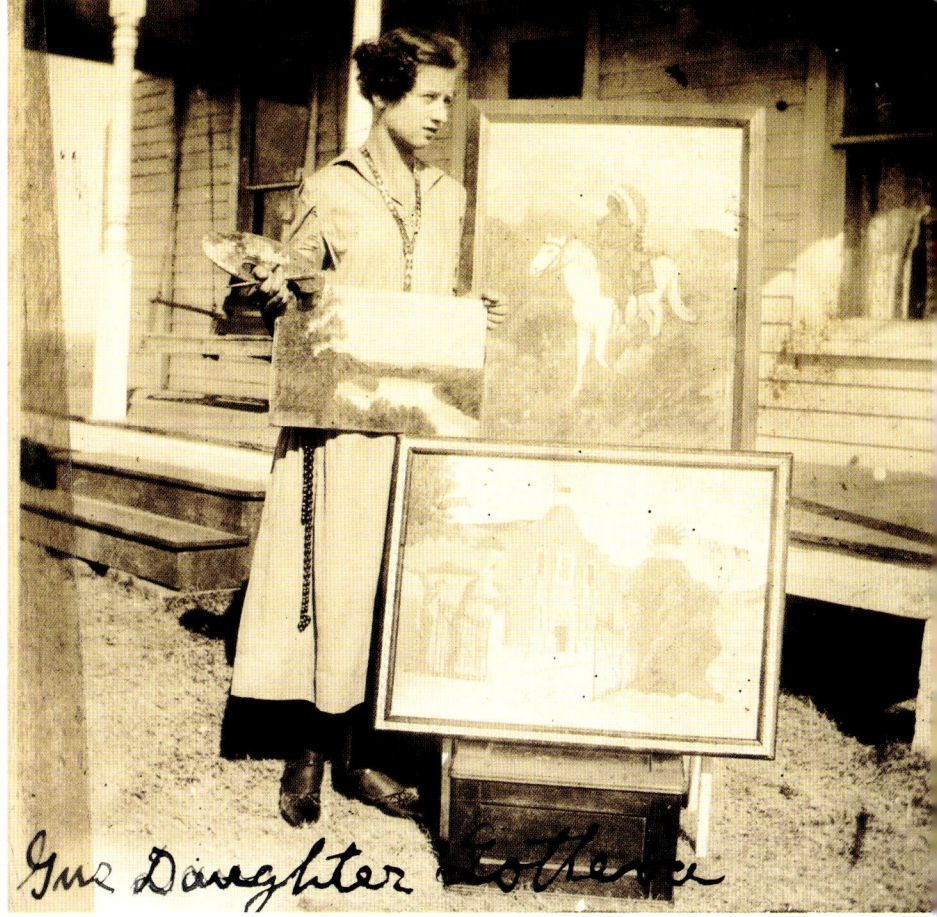

Lotteva with her paintings, ca. late 1920s.
Photo from Gus Wagner's scrapbook

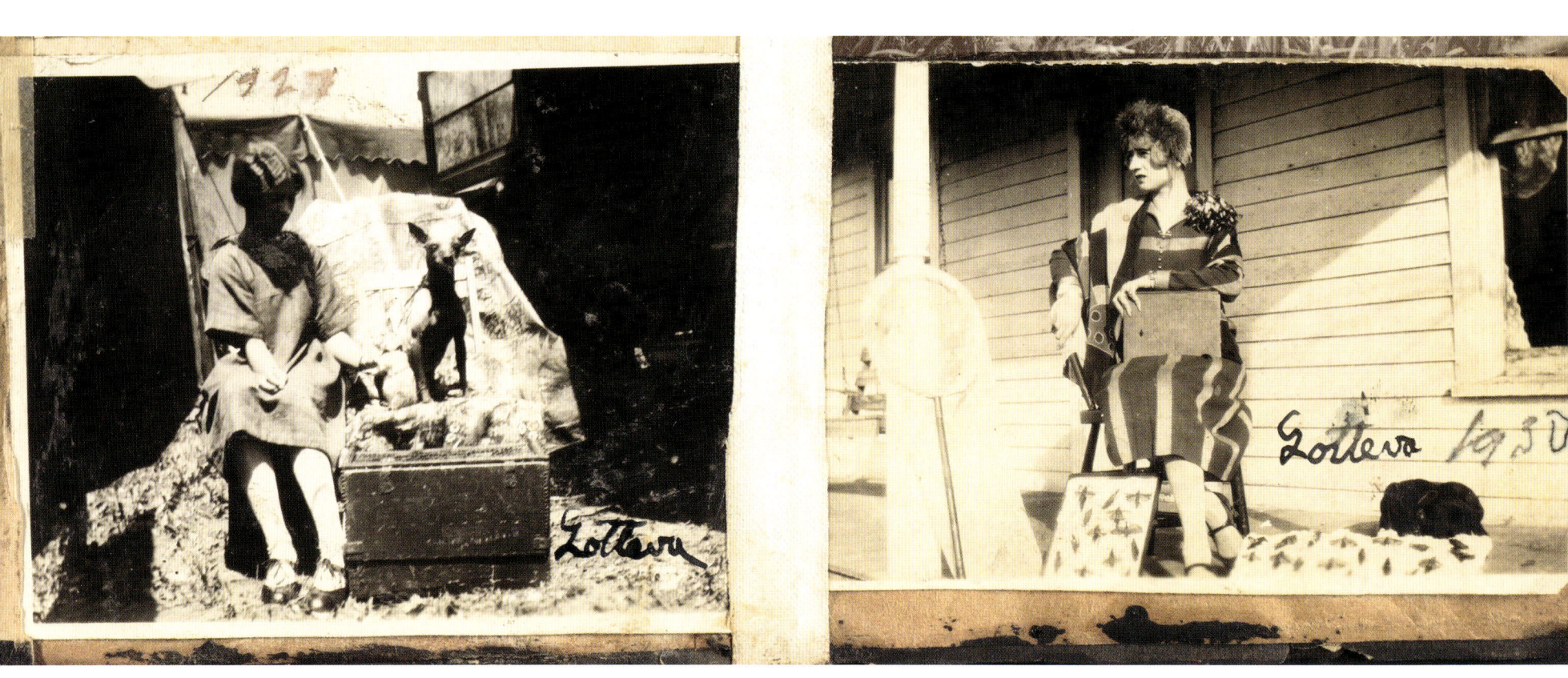

Detail from Gus Wagner's scrapbook

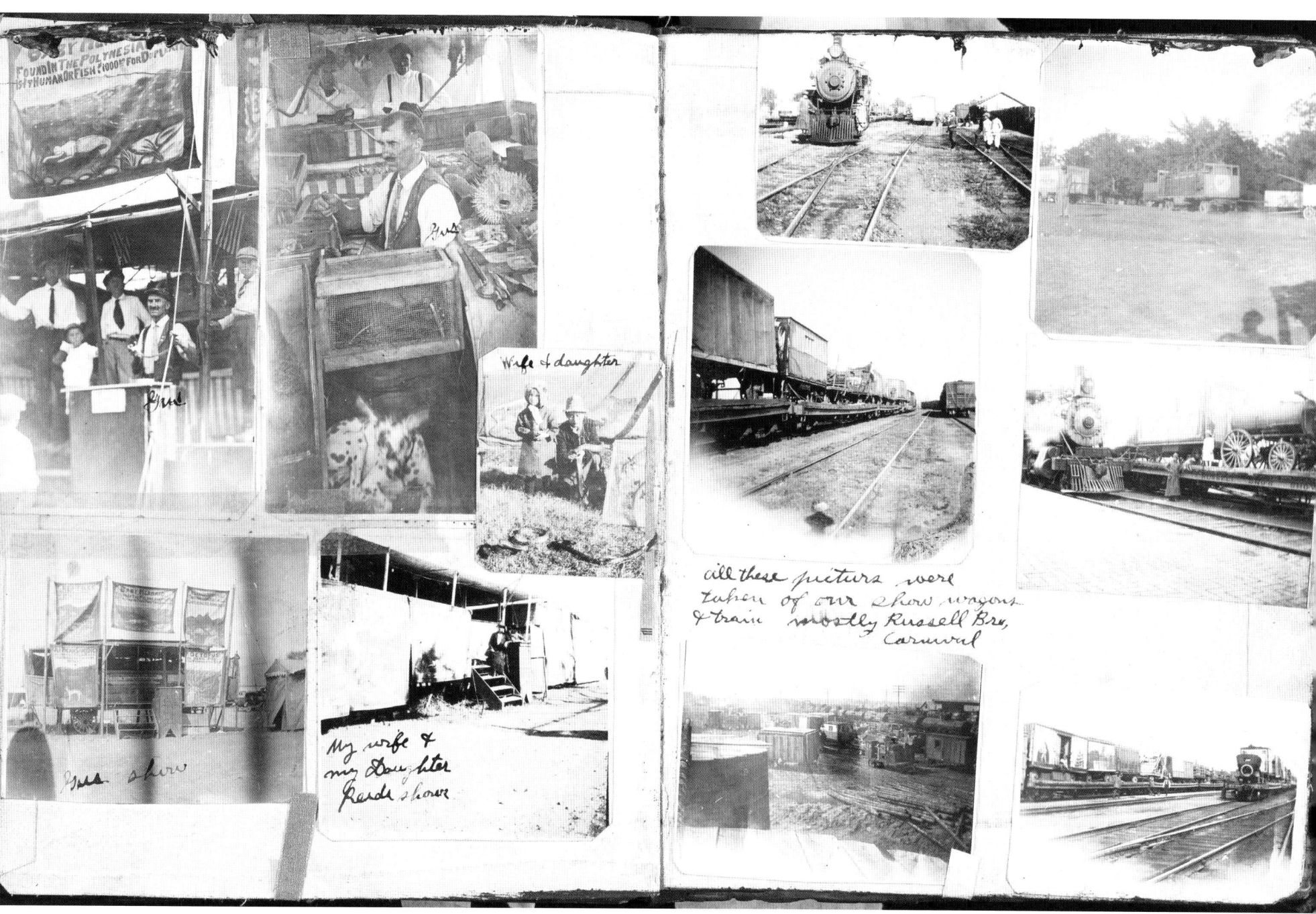

Pages from Gus Wagner's scrapbook

In addition to painting, Lotteva did anything and everything she could to eke out a living on the road. When she was twenty-eight, she began restoring merry-go-round and carousel horses. In an interview with Nicki B. Logan, Lotteva said, "The Gooding's Million Dollar Midway show had a Herschell-Spillman merry-go-round, moving wooden horses from town to town in wooden crates. The truck carrying the crates drove under a tree limb, knocking a crate off and breaking the head on a dappled gray horse. Mrs. Gooding had a cabinetmaker repair the horse but planned to ship the horse back to the factory for repainting, since it was almost impossible to match the paint sprayed on at the factory with a brush."[9]

Lotteva told Mrs. Gooding that if "she could find her three tubes of paint, including Persian Blue, she would duplicate the dappled gray—but if she didn't like the finished horse, she didn't have to pay her. Mr. Gooding encouraged his wife to let Lotteva try, saying, 'Can't lose at that rate; why don't you let her try?' Lotteva's success at matching the original appearance of the carousel horse led to more work, and before long, she had established a reputation for 'authentic restoration of horses.'"

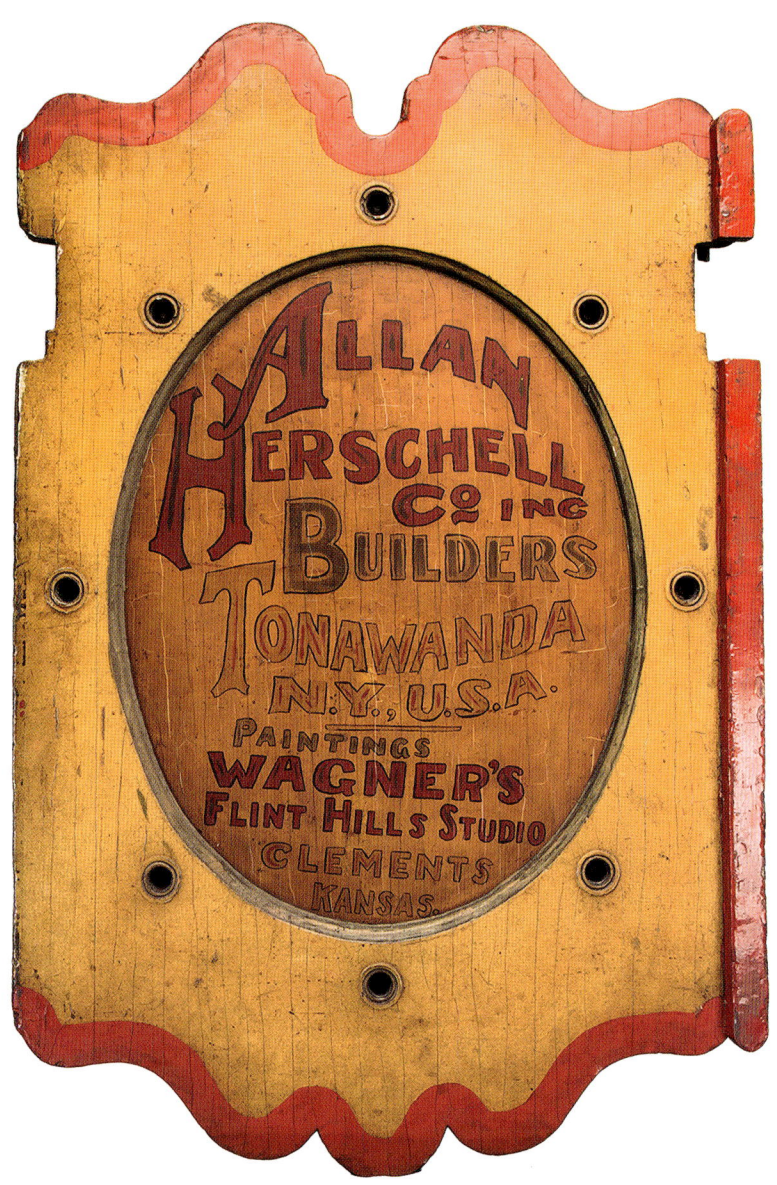

The classic Allan Herschell carousel sign, repainted by Lotteva Wagner Davis

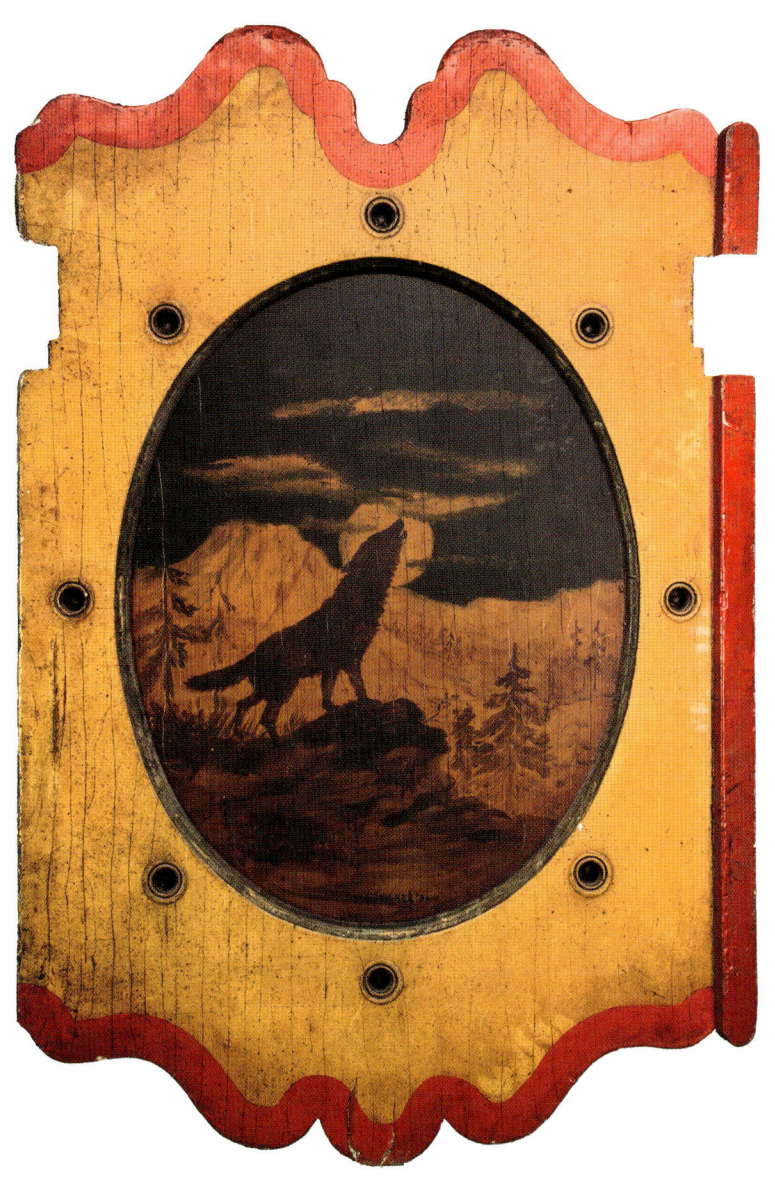

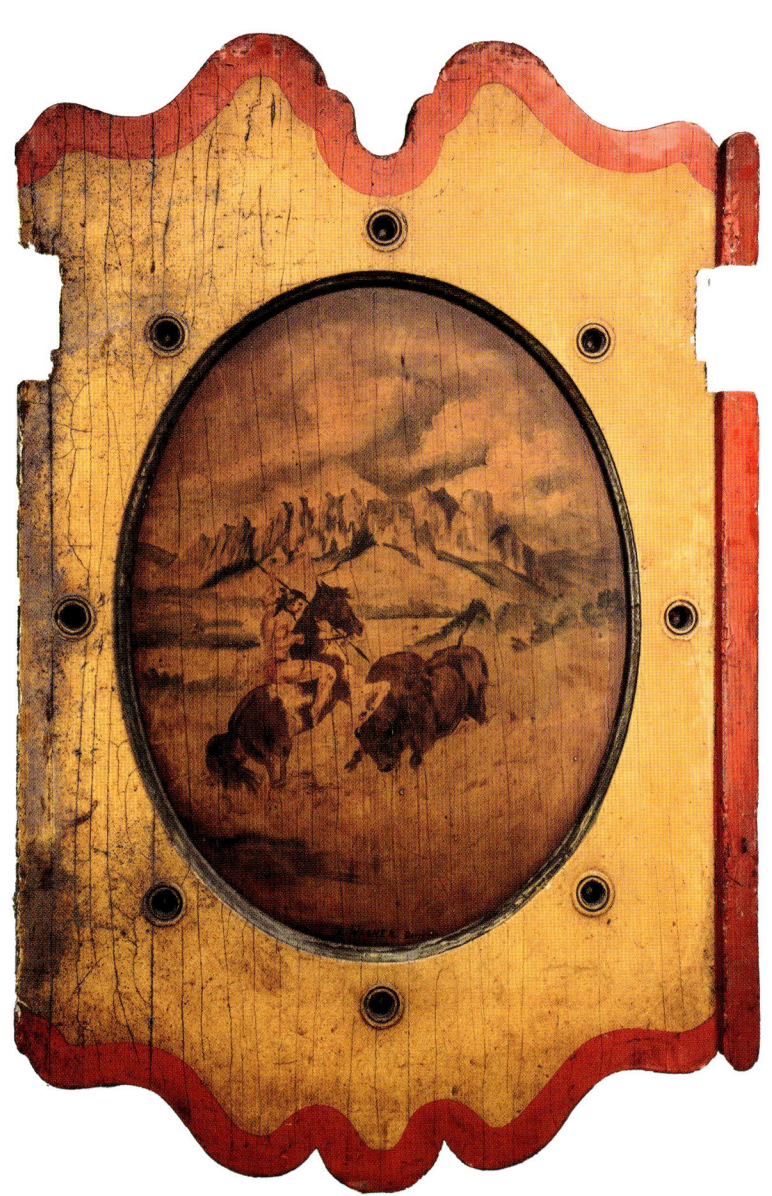

Howling at the Moon, painted by
Lotteva Wagner Davis

Buffalo Hunt, painted by
Lotteva Wagner Davis

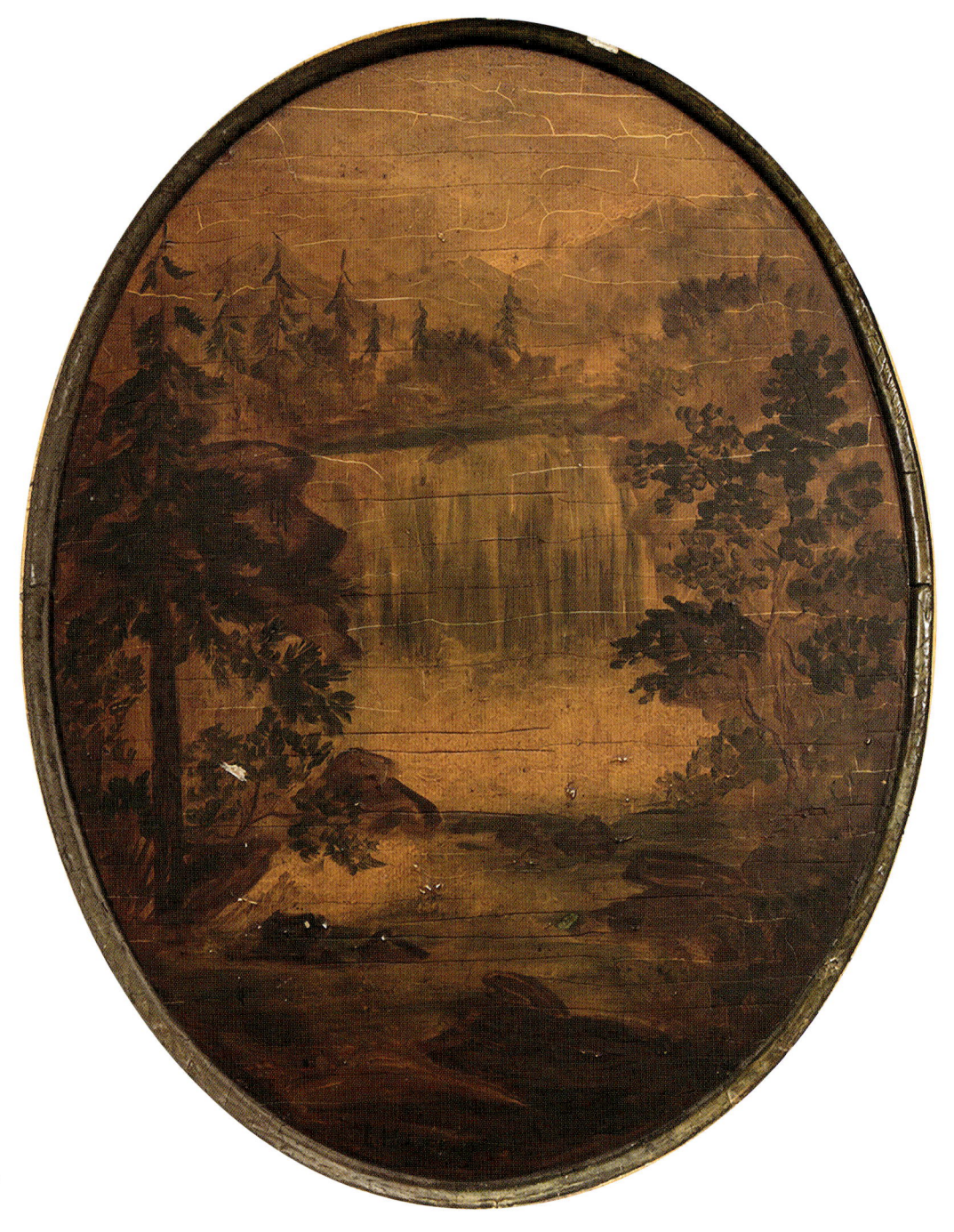

The Waterfall, painted by Lotteva Wagner Davis

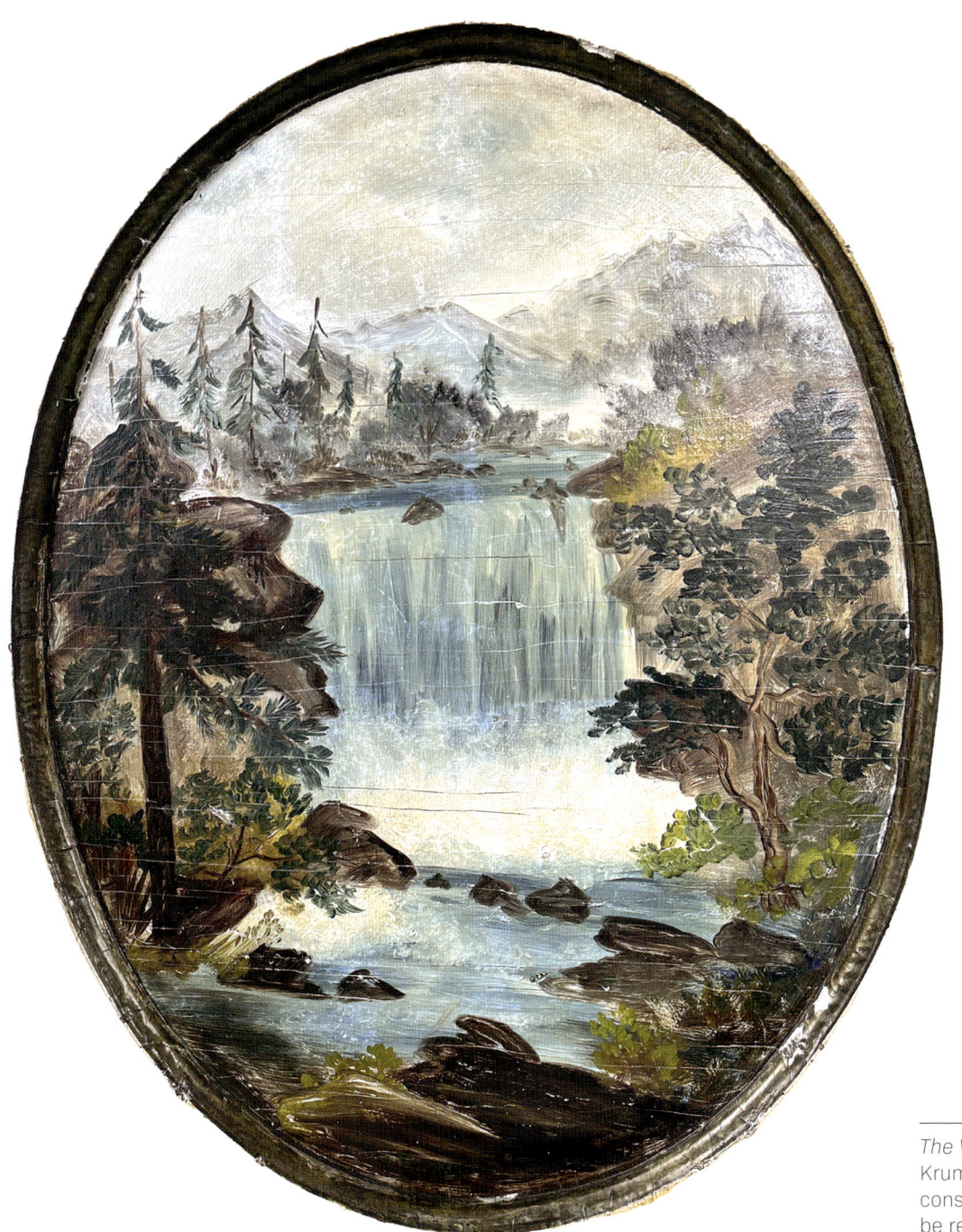

The Waterfall, professionally conserved by Christina Krumrine in New York City. An exact and time-consuming task, multiple layers of varnish had to be removed without degrading the actual paint.

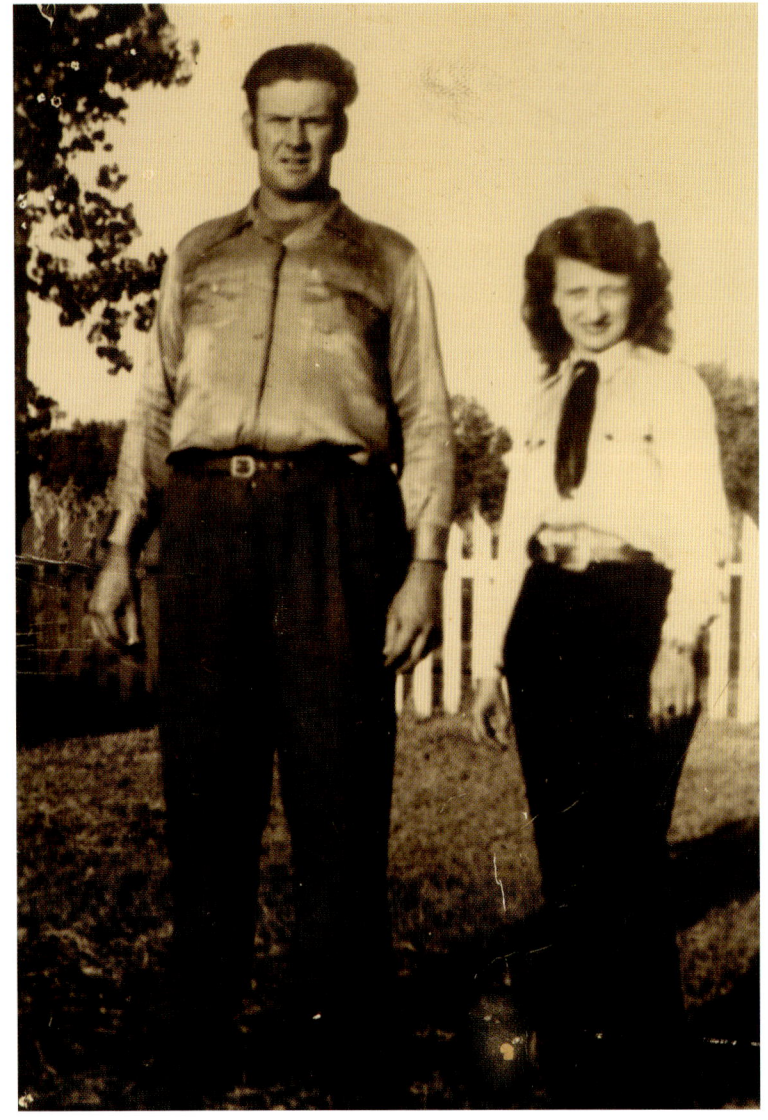

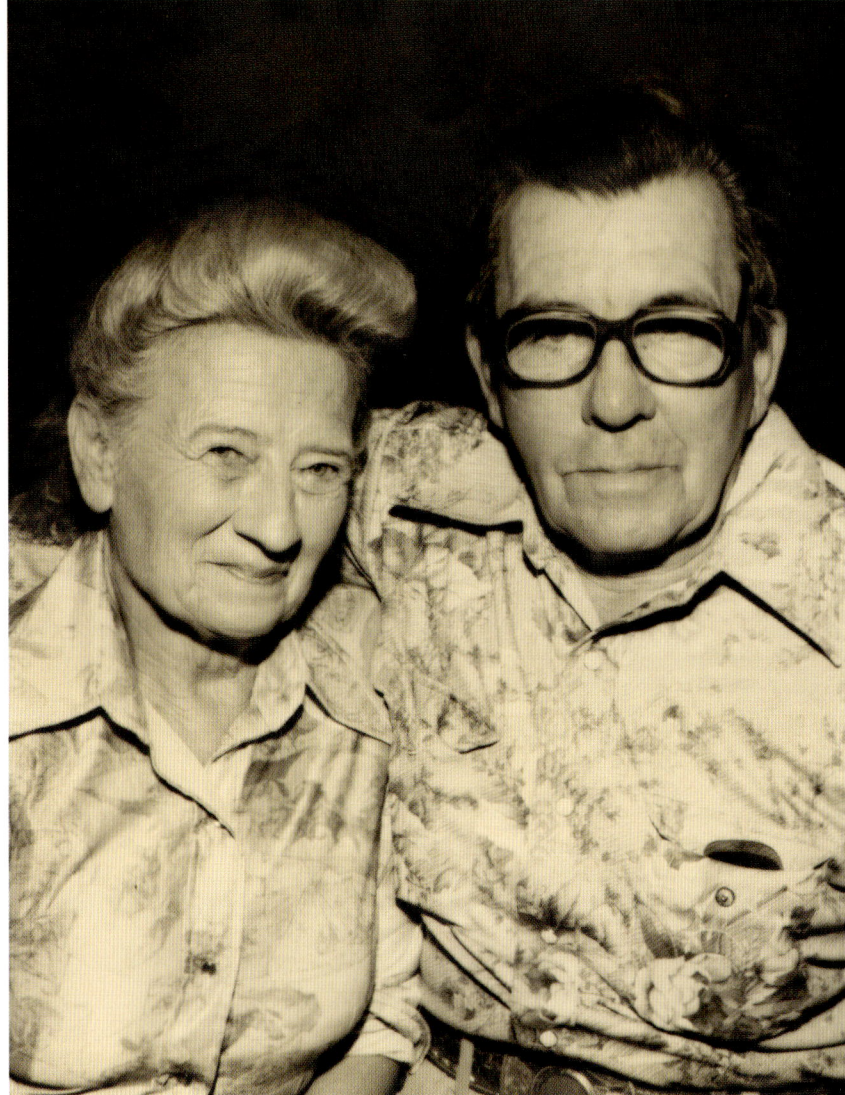

Tarzan and Lotteva, ca. 1940s

Lotteva and Stan Allen, ca. 1980s

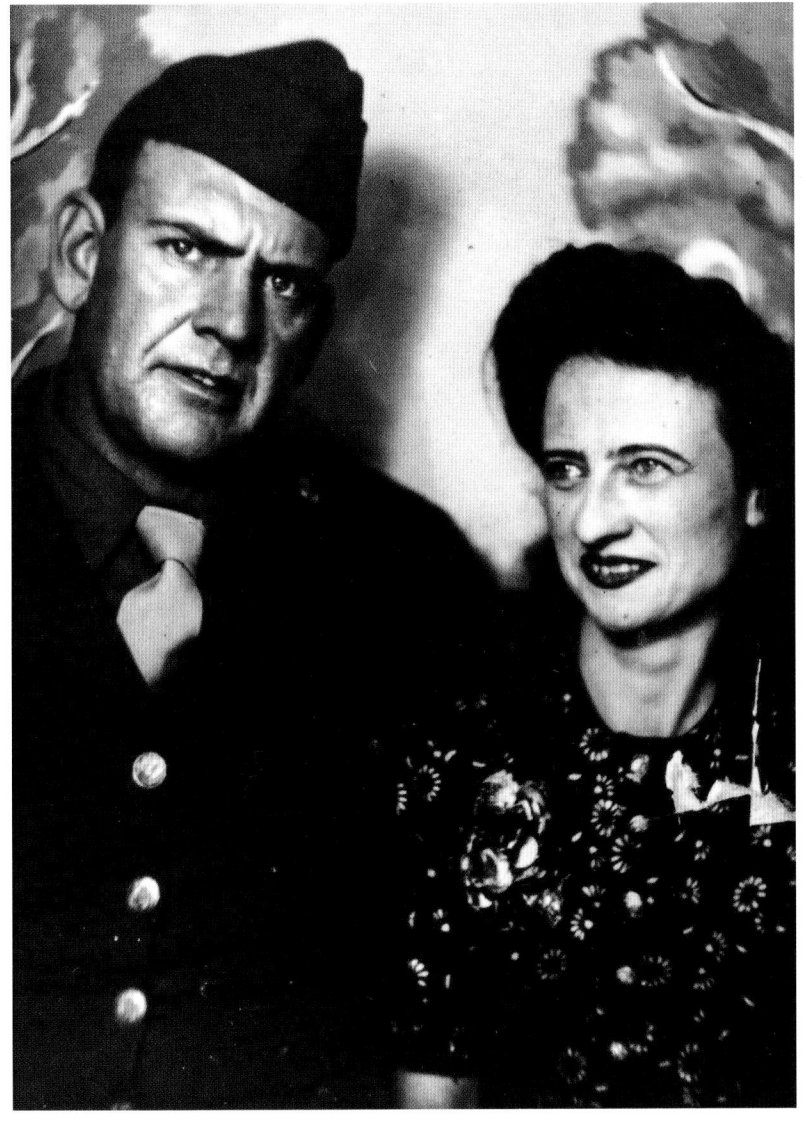

Tarzan and Lotteva, ca. 1940s

During the last years of her life, Lotteva had to slow down, plagued by diminished eyesight, an injured hip, knee problems, and arthritis. But she never gave up painting her beloved horses and her imaginings of Native American life. She survived three husbands, who Lotteva said were Native American—"a Cheyenne, a Chippewa, and a Cherokee."

While there are no records of Lotteva having her own biological children, Robert "Rockey" Carl Reisner, who inherited the Wagner family collections, said that he was her "son." The details of Rockey's life are sketchy, although it is clear from one of the business cards in Lotteva's personal papers that Rockey was also a sign painter in Plainview, Texas, working with her and her husband, Tarzan, owner of Cactus Signs.

According to Pat Hook, "Lotteva and Tarzan wanted to have children but were not able to. Lotteva did have one son from an early marriage that her mother forced her to annul. It only lasted about eight days. She never told the family about the pregnancy. They thought she was out with a show. She had the baby in Iowa and left it with the woman who had cared for her. She stayed with the woman for about two weeks after the birth and then went home. And didn't tell anybody.

"When she let it be known that she wished she could find her son, someone said he thought he knew who it was. The young man he brought over was Rockey Reisner, who is a fire chief in a small town to the south of Plainview, Texas. I don't know what proof she has that he is the one. She says she doesn't know whether he knows she is his mom. He calls her mom, but so do lots of other people. Most of her belongings are stored at his house."

Rockey and Lotteva were close. An article in *The Rising Star* (Texas, August 13, 1987) noted that "Most everyone from here attended the De Leon Peach and Melon parade Wednesday evening. The float of Mr. and Mrs. Rockey Reisner took second place on out-of-town float. Mrs. Lateva [*sic*] Davis of Plainview is visiting her son and wife, Mr. and Mrs. Rockey Reisner."

When Ellen Sweets interviewed Lotteva in September 1993, Lotteva said that her only living relatives were her son, Rockey Reisner, who at the time lived in Sipe Springs in west-central Texas, and a cousin, Pat Hook, in Manhattan, Kansas. Her eyes tearing up, Lotteva said she was "scared to make friends with anyone. . . . At my age, death is a next-door neighbor."

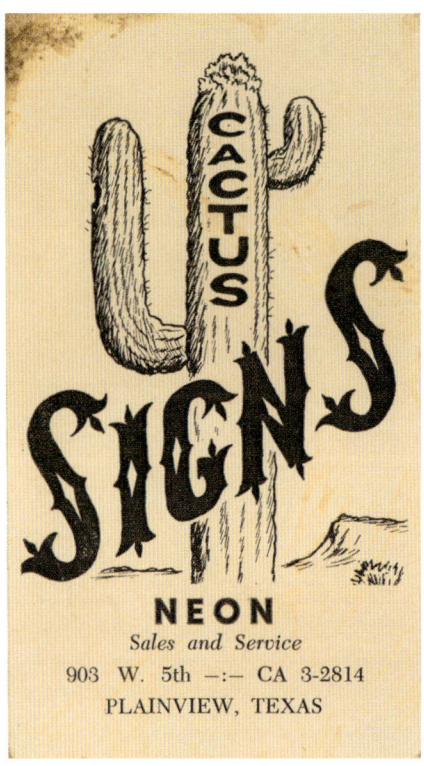
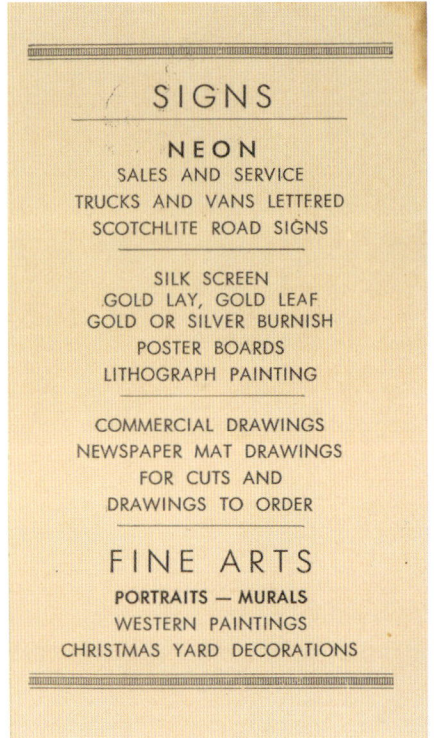

Cactus Signs business card, front and back

Reisner's business card

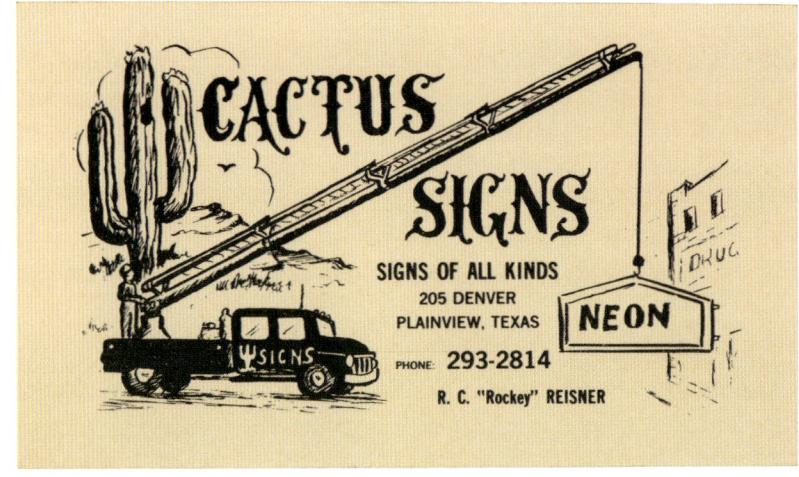

Lotteva's husband, Tarzan, died on April 24, 1977. A year later, on January 10, 1978, Lotteva married Stan Allen in San Antonio. Stan "traveled with Hill's Greater Shows and Byers Brothers Shows for many years and was a tattoo artist for forty years. He was associated with Cactus Signs." Stan passed away at age sixty-eight on October 1, 1984.

Pat Hook had written to Lotteva after getting her address from Chuck Eldridge at the Tattoo Archive in North Carolina. Pat read about Gus, Maud, and Lotteva and wanted to meet her, because they had the same paternal ancestor, Roswell Stevens.

Pat traveled to Plainview, Texas, in June 1992 and spent a couple of days with Lotteva, taking notes during and after their conversations.

Lotteva loved to talk about her parents but focused mostly on Maud and their many relatives in Kansas. "The house," Pat said, where Lotteva lived in Plainview was "an ordinary-looking house, but when you went in the front door, she had a tattoo parlor that probably had at one time been the living room. Everything was very meticulous—she had an autoclave and had lots of pictures on the walls. If you went to the back house, there was a kitchen, a couple or three bedrooms, and a storage area, where she had a merry-go-round horse that she had restored, a sign she had painted for a couple of her kids, as she called them, who were wanting to open a bird store, and who helped to take care of her. Behind Lotteva's house was a tornado shelter. It was a small trailer that had been buried in the backyard. And there were little steps that went down to it."

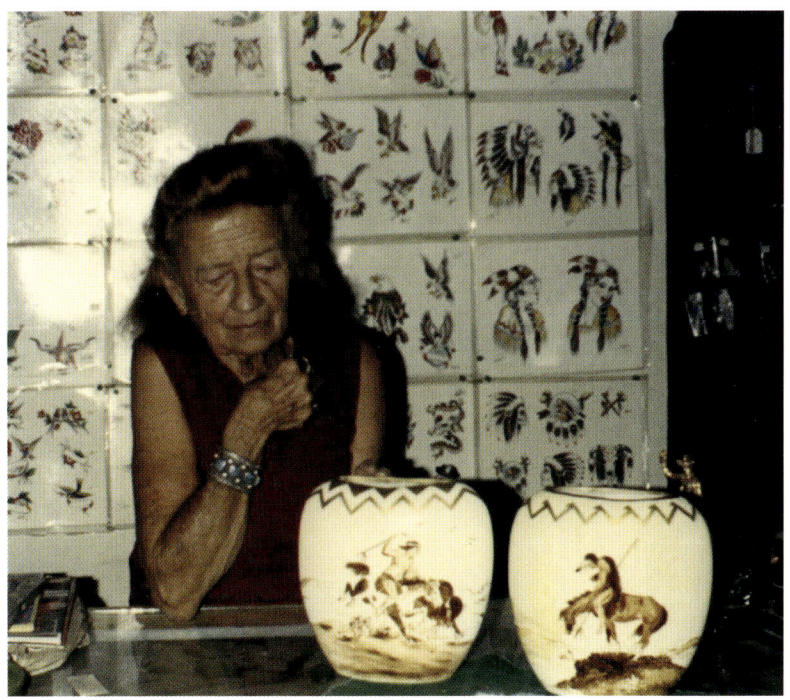

Lotteva and vases she painted at her tattoo studio in Plainview, Texas, 1992

In one conversation, Lotteva told Pat that her parents, Gus and Maud, were buried "side by side in Homestead Cemetery, and on each of their gravesites was a small piece of concrete that was unidentified, because Maud had sold her skin to somebody, and Lotteva was afraid that somebody would try to come and dig up her mom. To distinguish between Gus's and Maud's gravesites, the initials M.W. were carved into one of the pieces of concrete."[10]

Given what Lotteva explained to Pat, one can only wonder if Gus's grave marker was blank for the same reason that Maud's was essentially anonymous. Unknown to Pat, tattoo artist Ron Dolecek went looking for Gus's and Maud's graves on his own nearly two decades later: "In 2011, I found a nephew of Gus Wagner on the internet, and he emailed me an obituary for Gus that I hadn't seen before. Being from the area in Kansas where Gus and Maud lived, I went looking for their gravestones in Homestead Cemetery in Chase County but couldn't find them. So, I left a note in the guest registry that was in a metal box near the entrance, and six or seven months later, I was contacted by an old woman named Bernice O'Dell, who contacted her cousin, who used to be a caretaker at the cemetery. Together, they located the gravestones and had groundskeepers clear away a bush that had concealed what was nothing more than two concrete slabs.

Gus's was a blank, and Maud's was indicated just by an 'MW.' I again contacted Bernice and asked her how we could provide headstones. And she said that it had to be approved through her. So, I pooled my money and had designs drawn, and she approved them, and I had them made and placed them alongside the existing concrete stones with a small group of friends."[11]

By all accounts, Lotteva adored her parents and was grateful to her closest friends, who became her extended family over the years. According to Pat Hook, "Lotteva told [me] that she had cared for two husbands in their terminal illnesses, and she said she would never marry again. During the last years of her life, some carnival friends introduced her to a man named Dennis, who lived in her house and was supposed to be her protector. But Dennis was an alcoholic, and he was mean when he was a drunk. And he often got into fights after he was drinking. One time, he was in fight with another man, and Lotteva tried to intercede, and she got knocked over and broke her hip. So, she had a hip replacement, and it was very successful. So, she decided to get a knee replacement also, and she was staying with a young couple who wanted a bird store, but she got sick with pneumonia."

Lotteva Wagner Davis died on December 29, 1993.

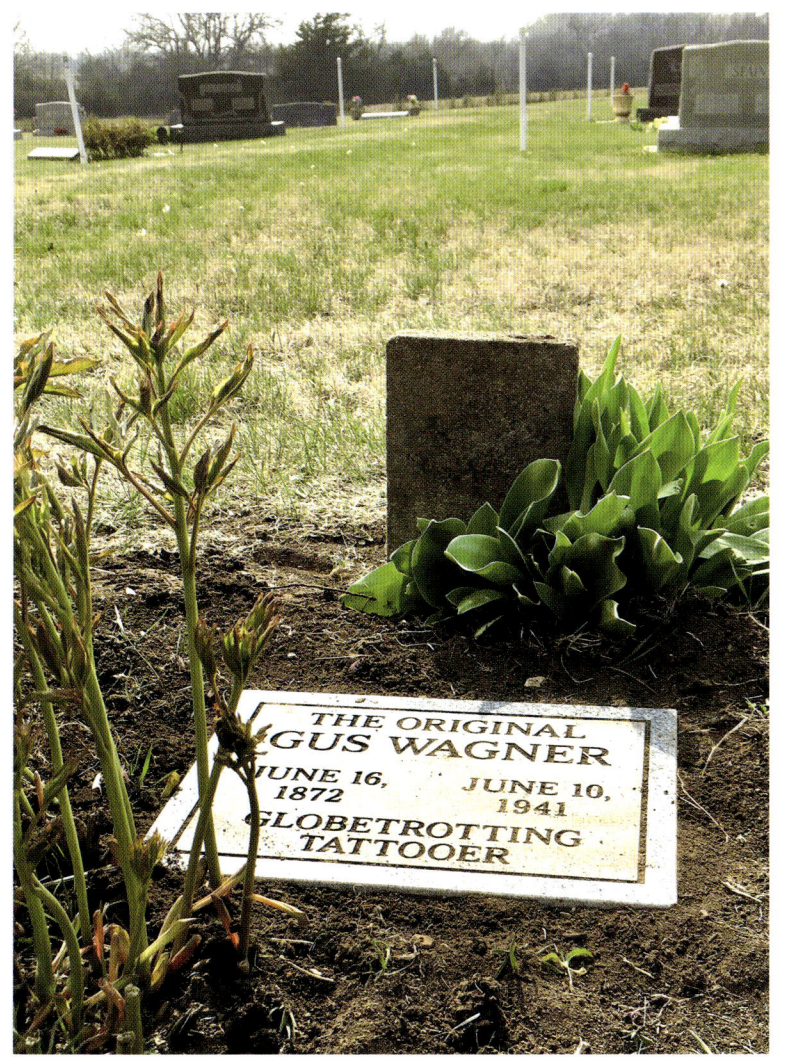

Gus Wagner's gravestone, 2016

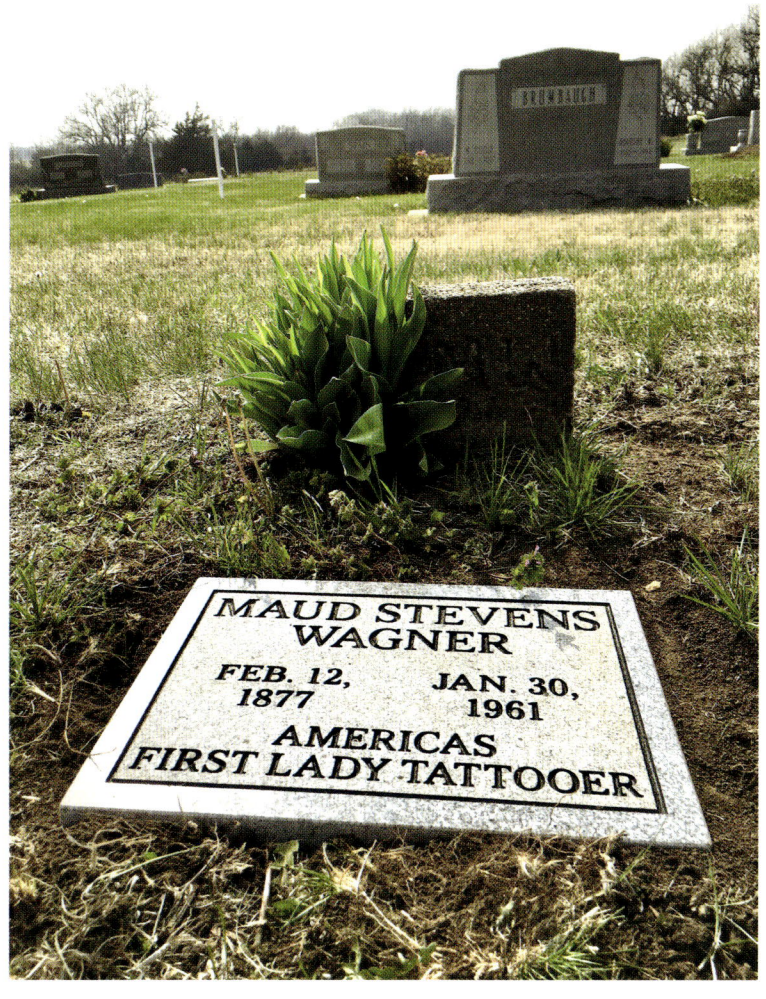

Maud Wagner's gravestone, 2016

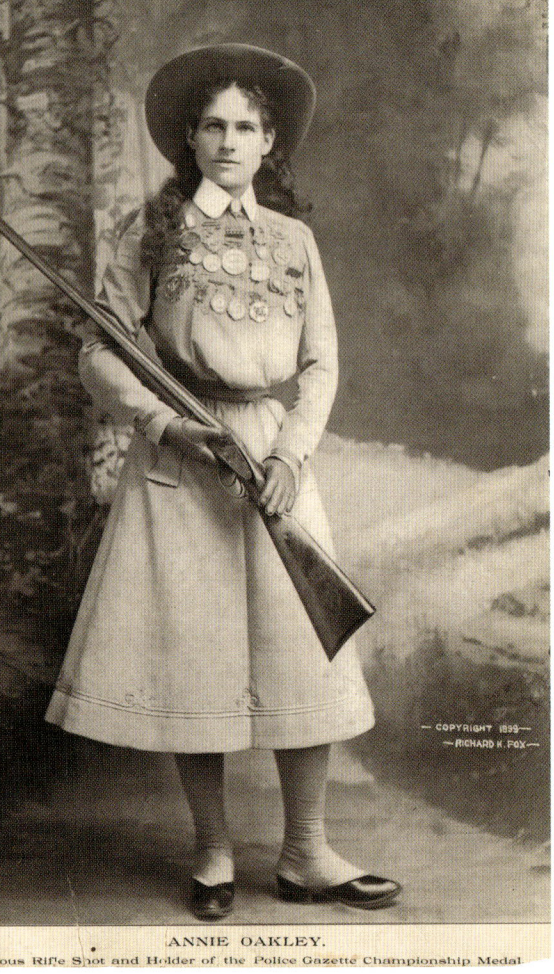

Annie Oakley, ca. 1899

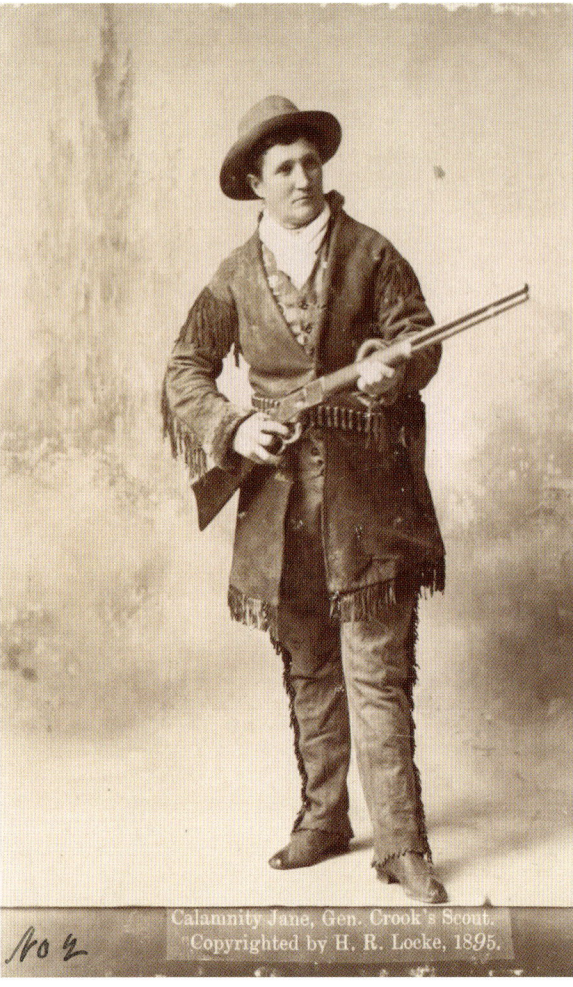

Calamity Jane, ca. 1895

Lotteva was a woman of her own making, embodying the spirit of women of the Old West who preceded her, women who defied the norms of the day and were determined to assert their individuality and ingenuity—women such as Annie Oakley and Calamity Jane, whom she may have seen in Wild West shows when she was a girl growing up. But she never lost sight of the small-town values of her mother and father. She was, as Pat Hook observed, "a person with one foot grounded in the ordinary world, and the other in this crazy carnival world. Most people would never dare to do the stuff she did."[12]

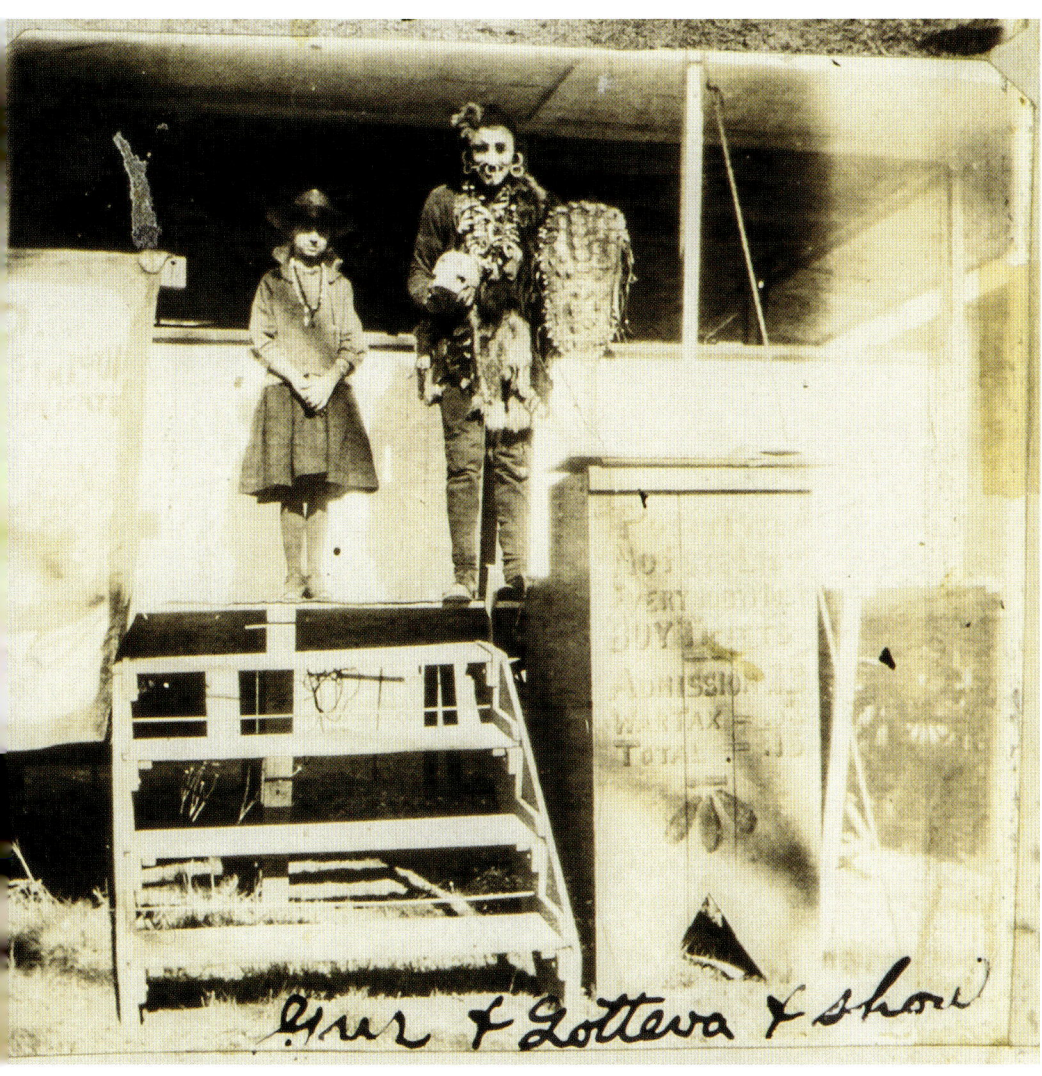

Lotteva and Gus, ca. early 1920s.
Detail from Gus Wagner's scrapbook

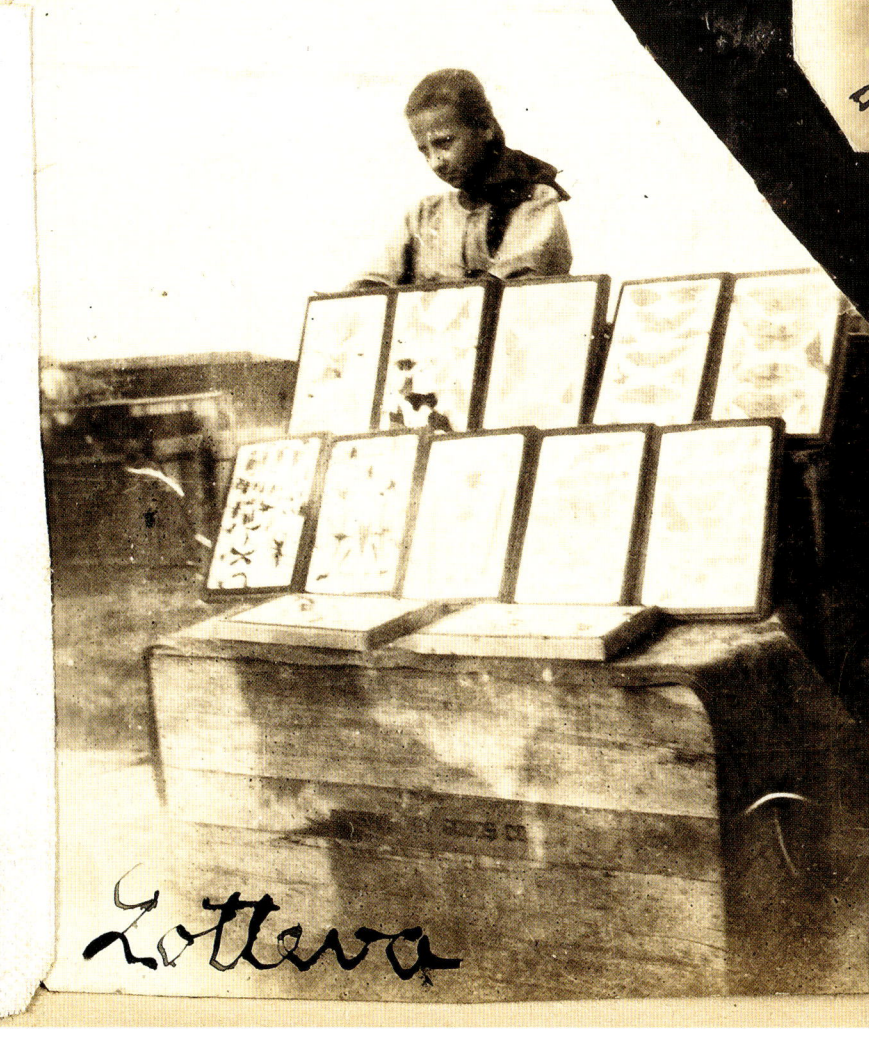

Lotteva, ca. 1920s. *Detail from Gus Wagner's scrapbook*

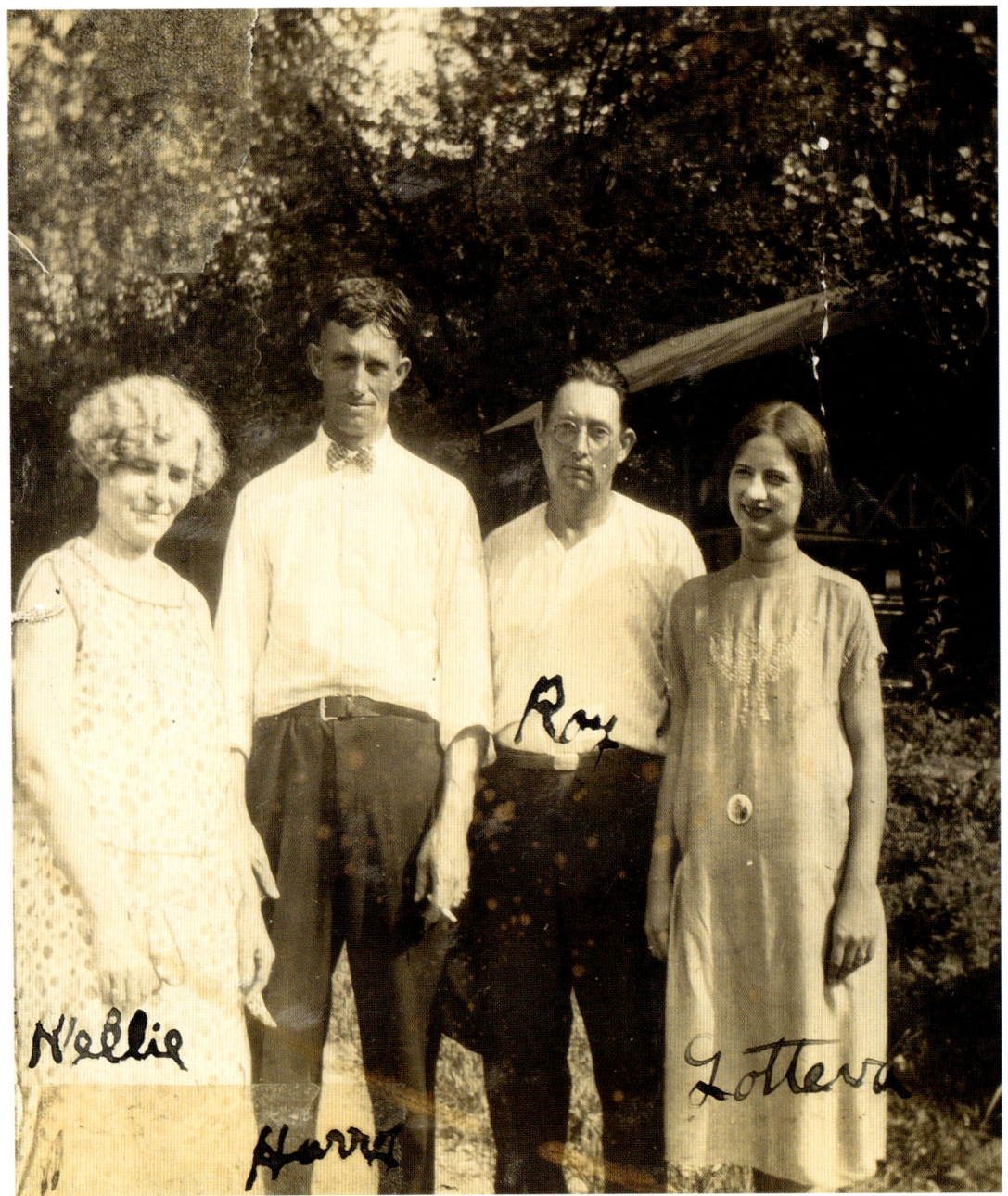

Lotteva on right, ca. 1920s. *Photo from Gus Wagner's scrapbook*

Opposite: Lotteva and Maud (*center right of group*) on the back of a train, ca. 1920s

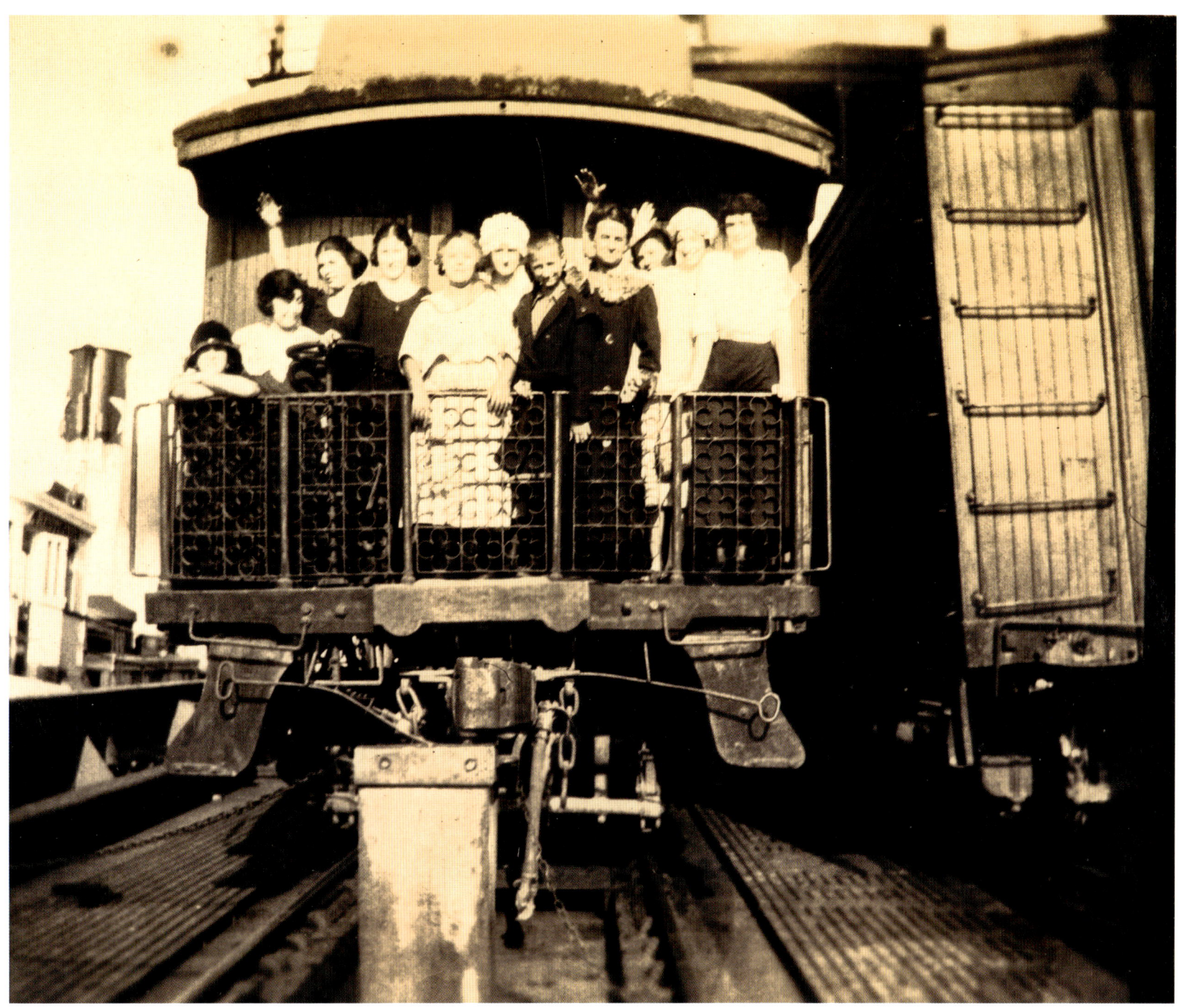

ORAL HISTORY: LOTTEVA WAGNER DAVIS

INTERVIEWED BY CHUCK ELDRIDGE
EDITED BY ALAN GOVENAR

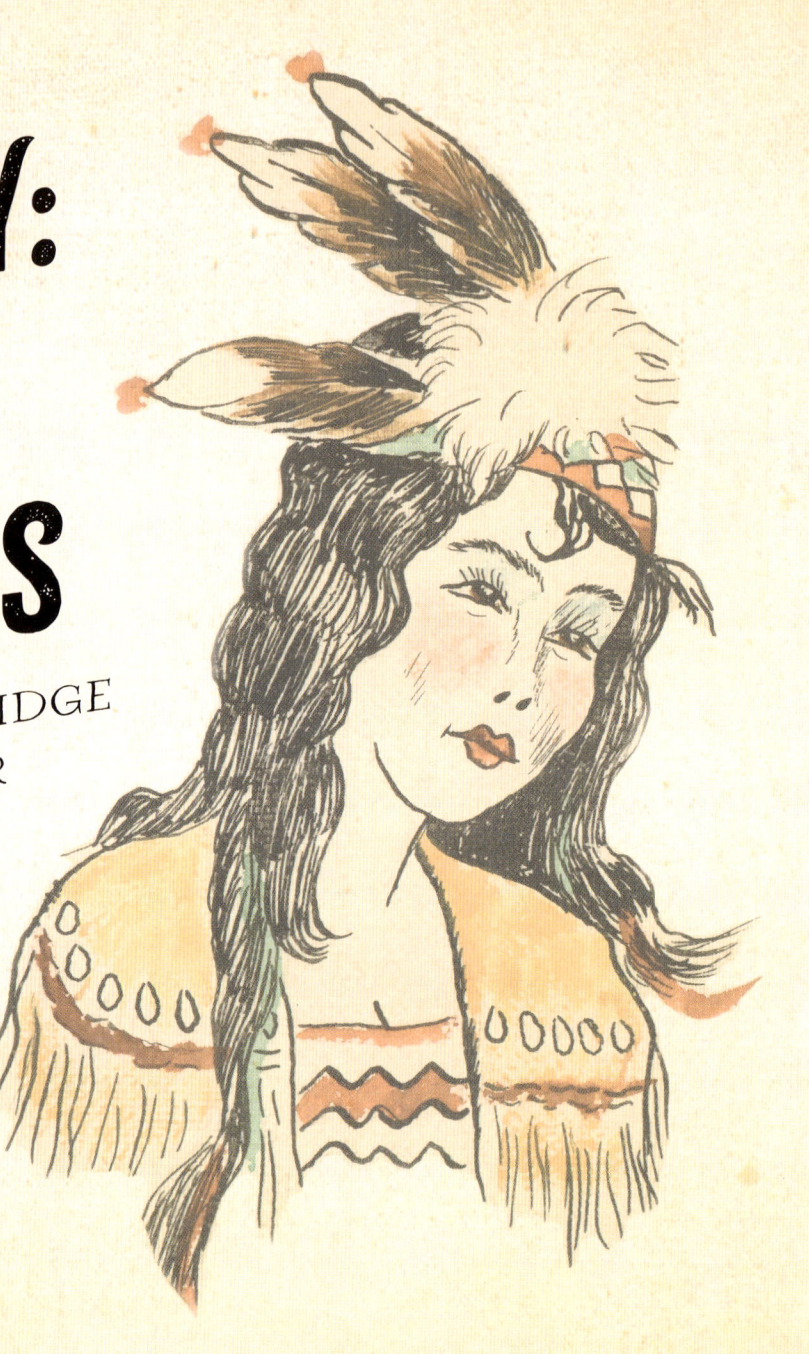

When I started tattooing, I was nine. Now, I had been practicing on oranges and on slick magazines. Papa would have me work with the hand needles on these slick magazines, cut through two pages and not cut the second one out. Might perforate it, but it wouldn't come out. But cut through the first two pages. That's how I learned.

One day Papa said, "I want you to put a design on me." I did. And one of the Wright boys, Joe Miller, was there. The night before, I had drawn a tattoo design, just my own idea, of a racehorse and a wreath of flowers, and he said, "I want you to put that on me."

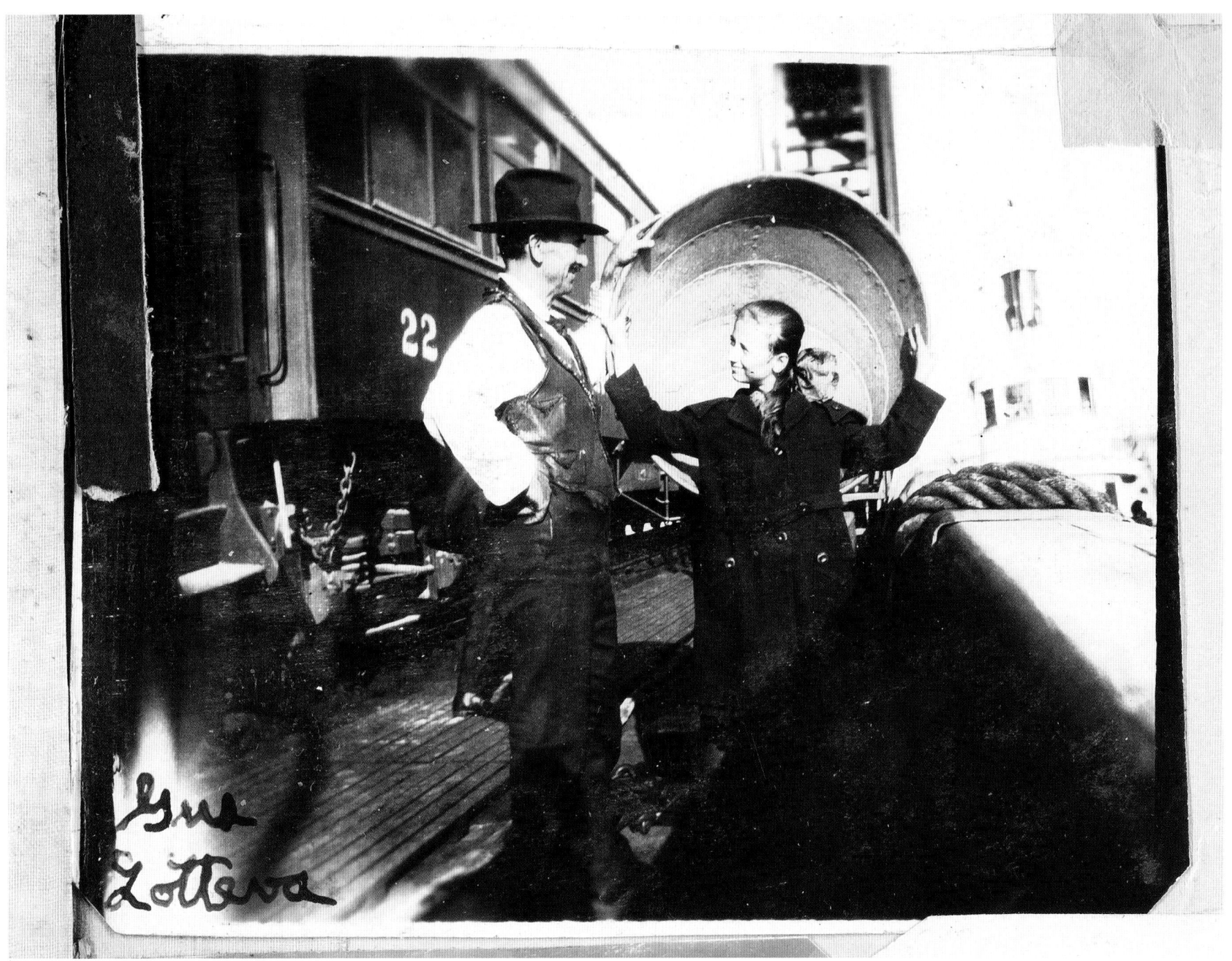

I said, "I can't tattoo."

He said, "But you just tattooed your father."

I said, "But I can't tattoo."

And he kept fussing, and Father said, "Tattoo him."

I said again, "But Pa."

"No buts," he said. "The man wants you to put the tattoo on him. But it's too late this evening."

He said, "Wait till tomorrow, and Joe can come in, and you can start. Just don't do it in one day. Put the outline, the shading on; the next week when it heals, color it. Only one thing I'm gonna tell you. You make it right because I'm not going to retouch it. I'm not gonna do it over. You've got to do it right." And you know, well, I did. Well, from then on, I was tattooing the Wright boys just about every week until I was twelve.

Detail from Gus Wagner's scrapbook

Opposite: Gus and Lotteva, ca. 1920s.
Detail from Gus Wagner's scrapbook

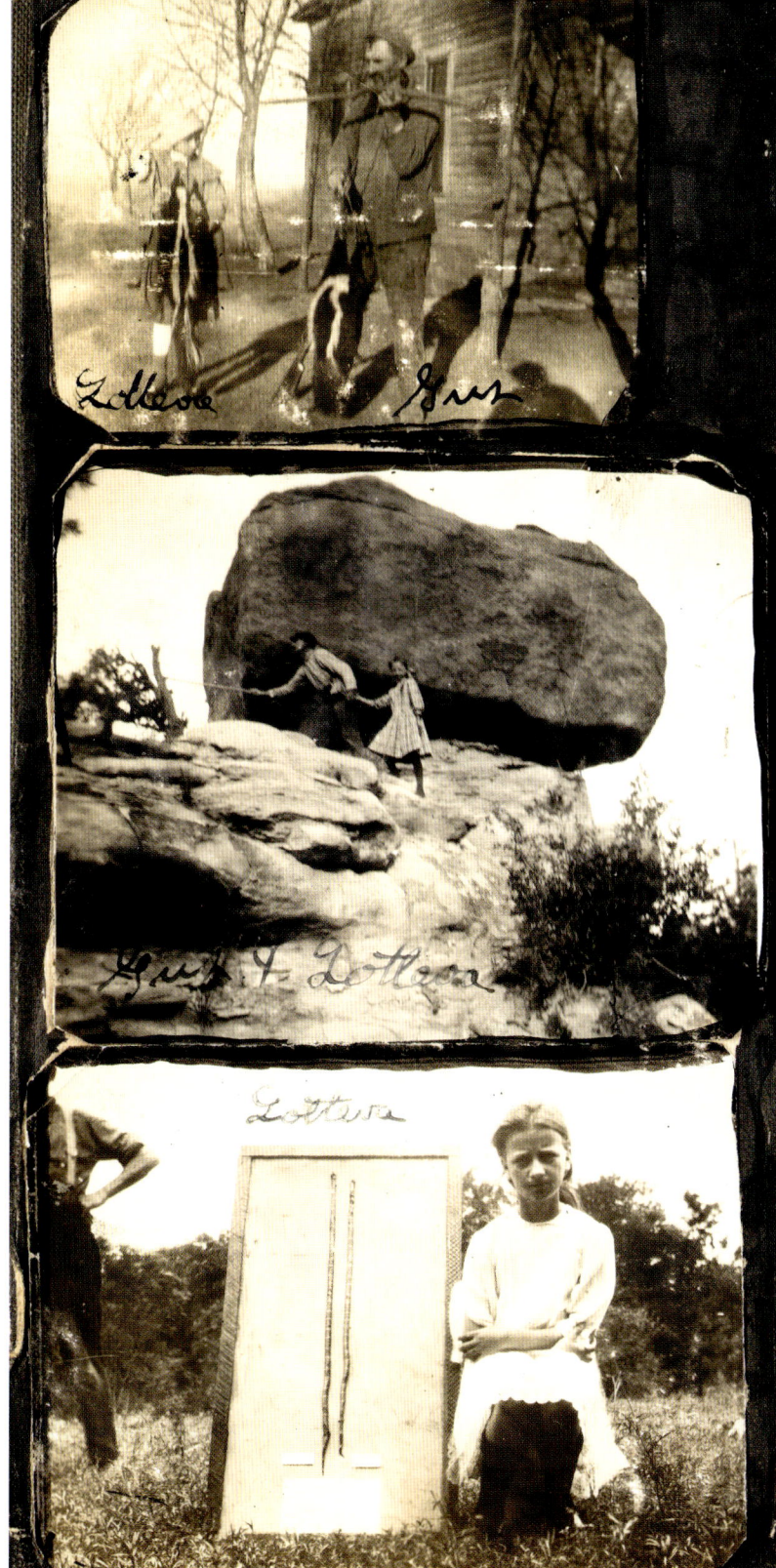

67

One day Papa was fixin' up another table for tattooing. He said, "That's yours. You can go to work for money. You've given enough work away."

So, that's when I professionally went to work. But I really went to tattooing when I was nine, tattooing every week on them Wright boys.

I'm still using the same tools as I did back then. I've even got the needles Papa tattooed Mama with. They're chopsticks, and they're sloped. They have a little notch on them, so the thread doesn't come off. Filed off here, and they're different widths according to how many needles you want on them. You put the needles on there, wrap them with number eight thread. They got a slight slant to them. They're two deep, and I use anywhere from six to 25.

And I've got more than a set of ivory needles made in Japan. And I got a new set of chopsticks that are gorgeous things. They're like black lacquer, with all colors on them, and I'm gonna make me a set of tattoo needles out of them just for fun. But, for now, I go to any old Chinese joint and get me some chopsticks; they're all made out of chopsticks; they're just perfect things to use.

Lotteva's tattoo instruments

Even my liners are two deep. That way it carries the ink between the needles. If you use a single needle, there's no way for the ink to go in. You've got not less than three needles. But if you use five needles, you got a good carrier then. Now you don't need to get all the needles in at once. They're set with a slight slope, and you go according to the flesh where you're working, and you keep them at a certain depth. Now ordinarily, a hand tattoo artist can tattoo the average person without drawing a drop of blood. You've got the ink at the surface. Right at the surface. You cut through the first layer of skin. You're right there where the blood is, but you don't cut deep enough that it's gonna bleed.

Tattoos by Lotteva

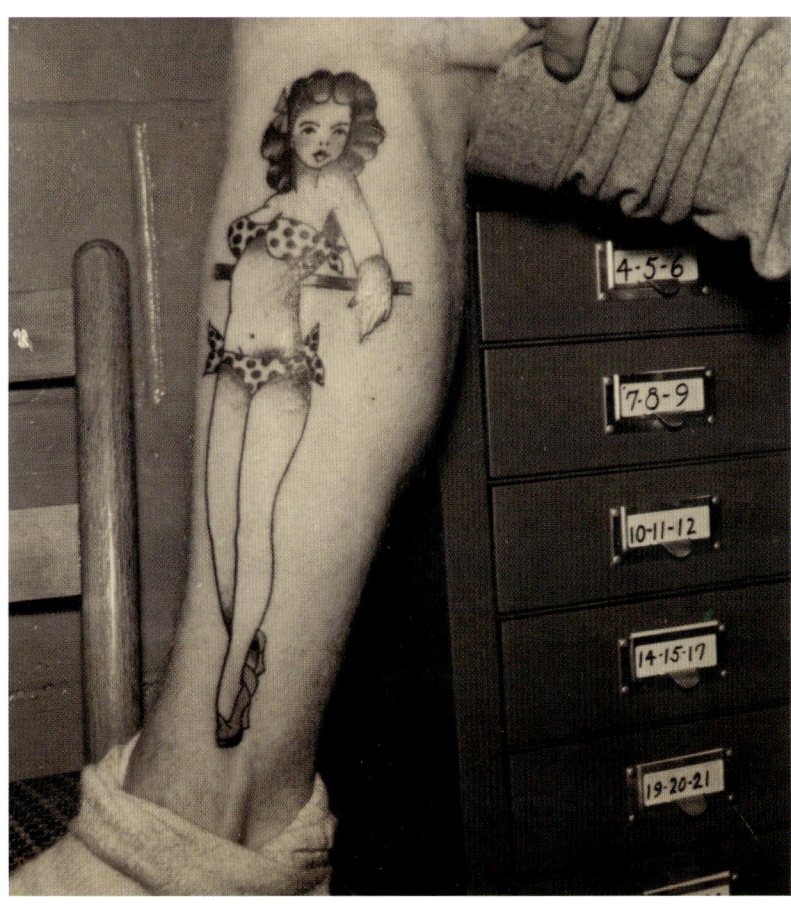

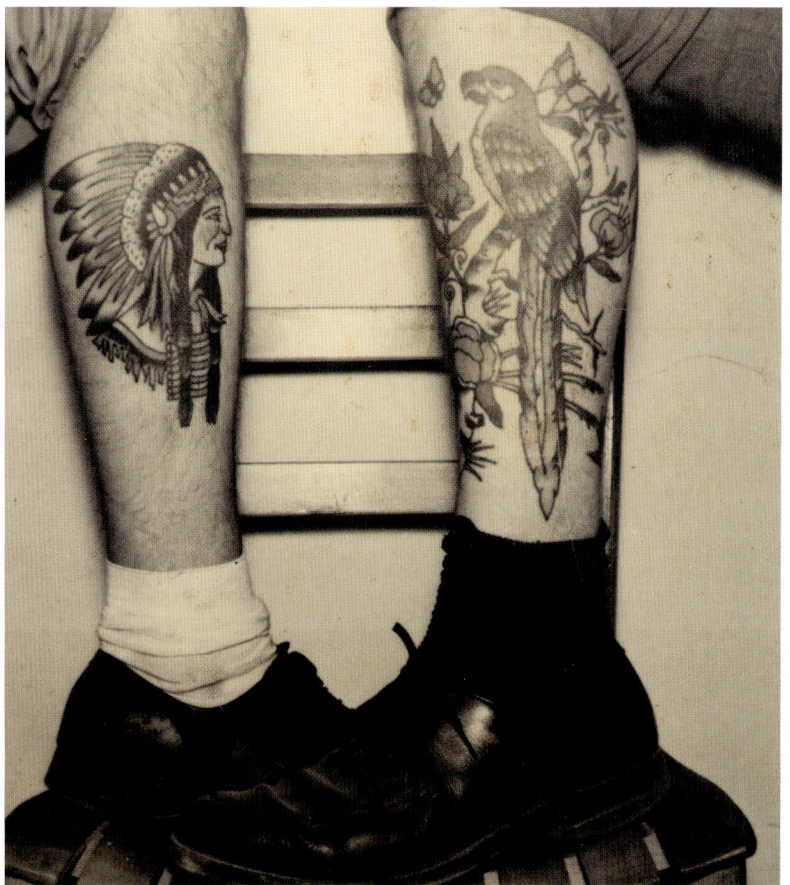

Now you get bleeders. I tattooed a man in Junction City, Kansas. He was in the Army, and I put big roses, cross flags, and an eagle on his chest. And he was a bleeder. I had to keep towels here, and my fingers would be stuck together with the blood. I had to constantly wash, wash, wash, to see my design. There was no way you could tattoo any more. Well, he went overseas. He got all shot up. He said the doctor said that was the first time he ever appreciated a man being tattooed. He said he could use that as a jigsaw puzzle to put him back together. But a good fourth or third of that design was missing! And he'd just come out of the hospital and had come back for me to fix it. I said, "Man, you bled like a stuck hog with this to start with; you're gonna bleed twice as hard, and it's gonna hurt twice as much." He said, "I don't care. I've gotta go back. I've come to get it fixed; I want it fixed." I did it. But that was working under much difficulty.

We used to have the old celluloid stencils that'd burn up. Then they had some made out of some kind of plastica. You put black powder on them, and you got it all over you, and then you go to wipe it and you'd lost your design. And if I freehand, I use a good pen with ink that don't come off. I freehand an awful lot. I had hundreds of designs on my walls. And I'd say over half of them I don't use. They ordered me to draw something else. They'd want me to draw. My husband used to say, "They just want you to draw, that's all."

Lotteva flash

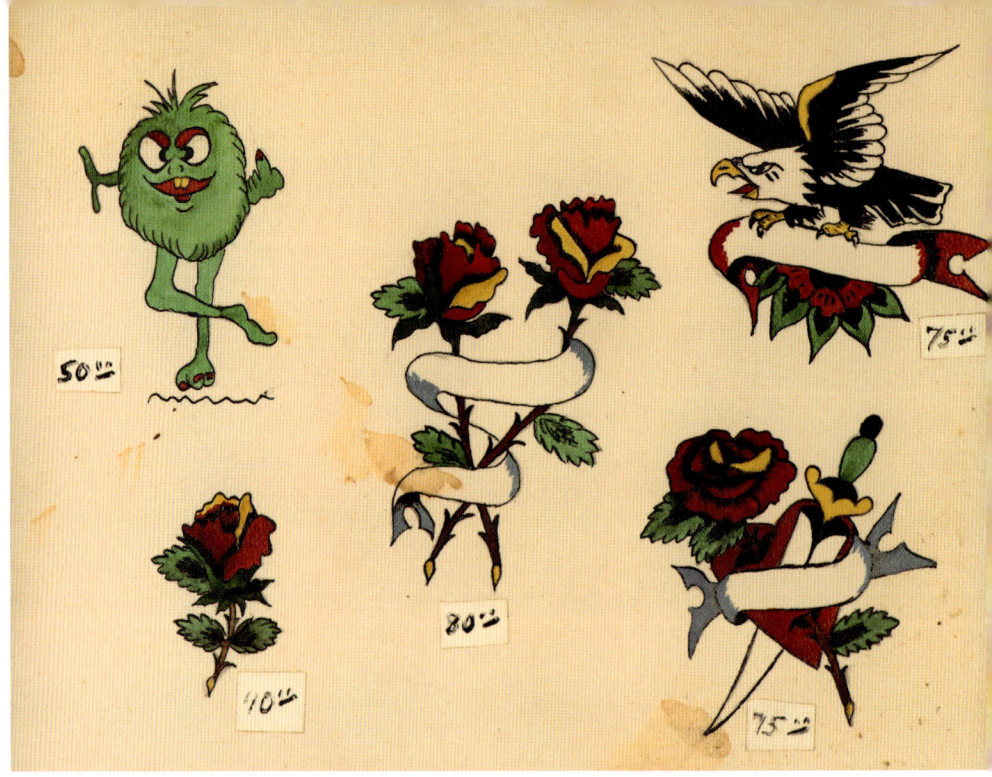

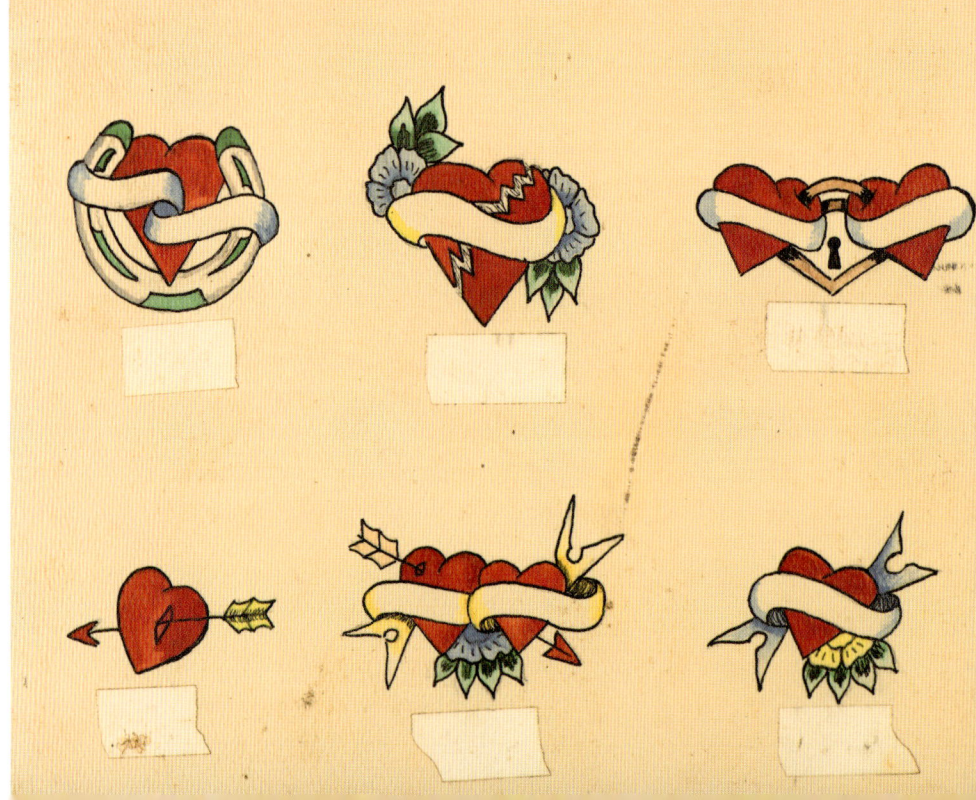

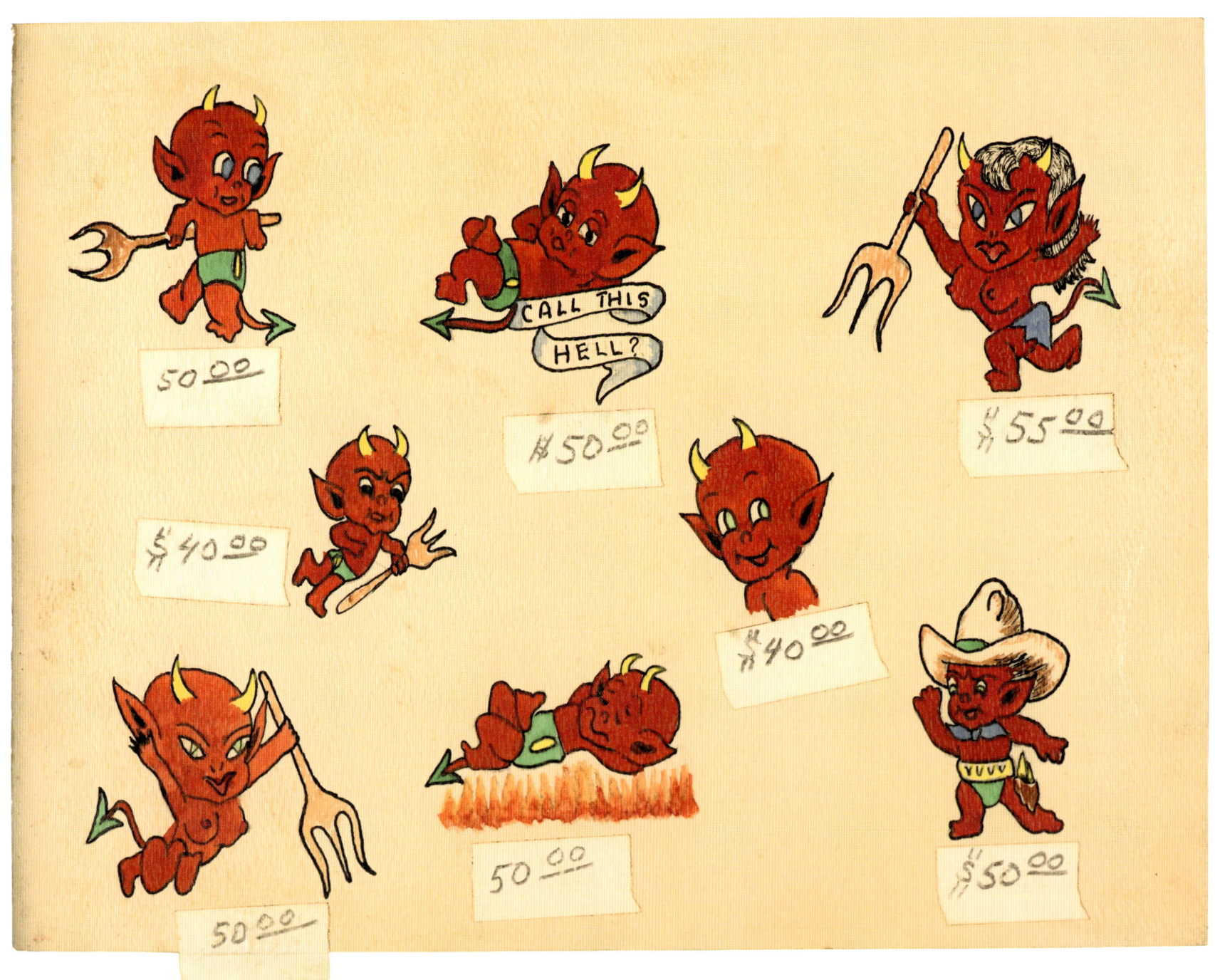

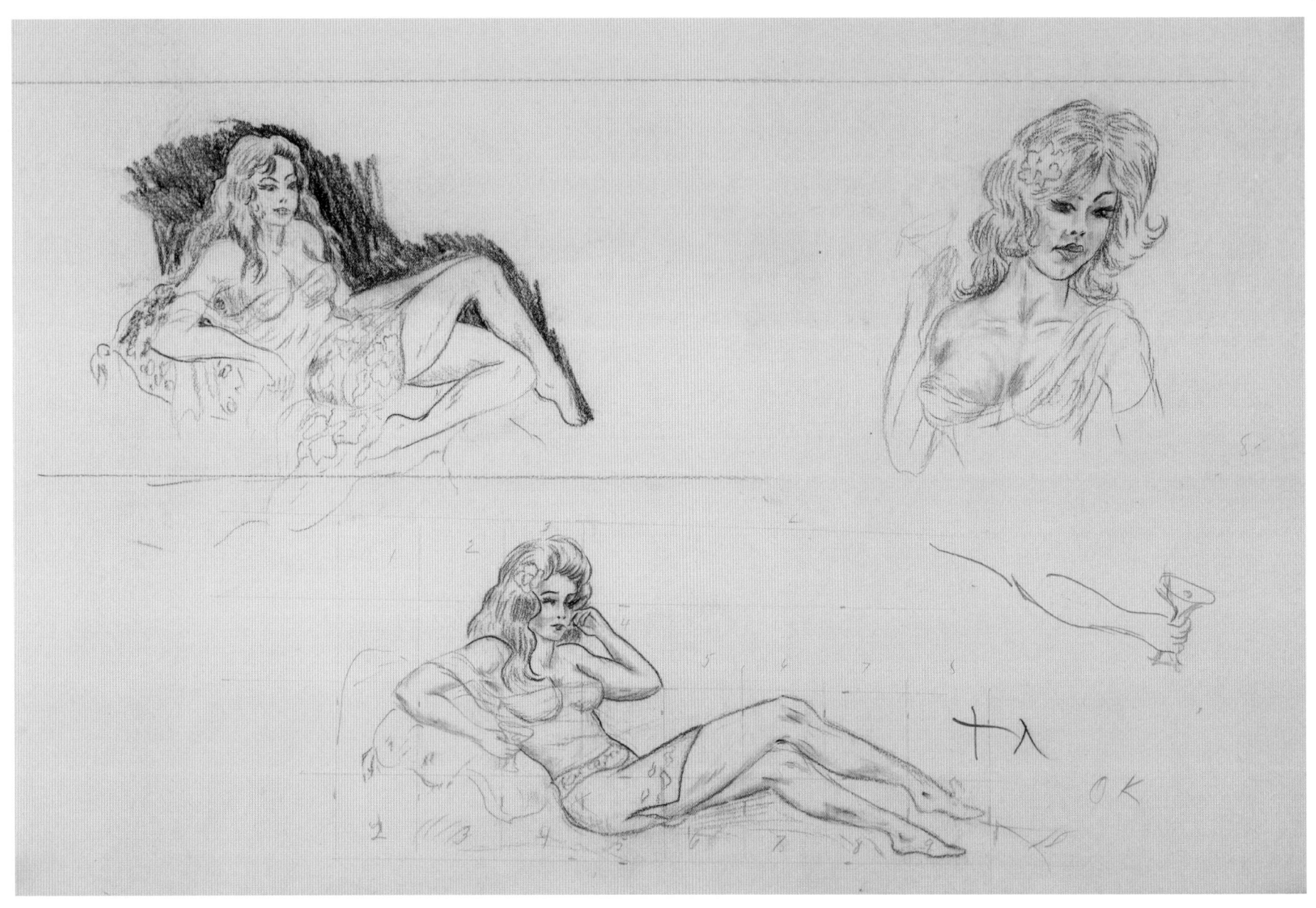

Sketches by Lotteva

I said, "I don't care so long as they get tattooed."

So, now, I make a stencil with old-fashion indelible pencils. I think they call them *hectographs*. And when I get ready to use them, then I turn them over and put the hectograph pencil on them. Wet the arm, put it on. You can wash them, wash them; they don't come off. It's just a little bit more work, but you don't lose your design.

There are so many shortcuts you can use. During the war, I did quite a few portraits of the GIs' wives and sweethearts. That's hard. It's good, real good money, but it's hard. It's such delicate work, and you can't make a mistake. You know what I mean? One little variation in an eye, or the corner of an eye or mouth or something, and you've lost it. You can't fix it. So, you just don't dare make that mistake.

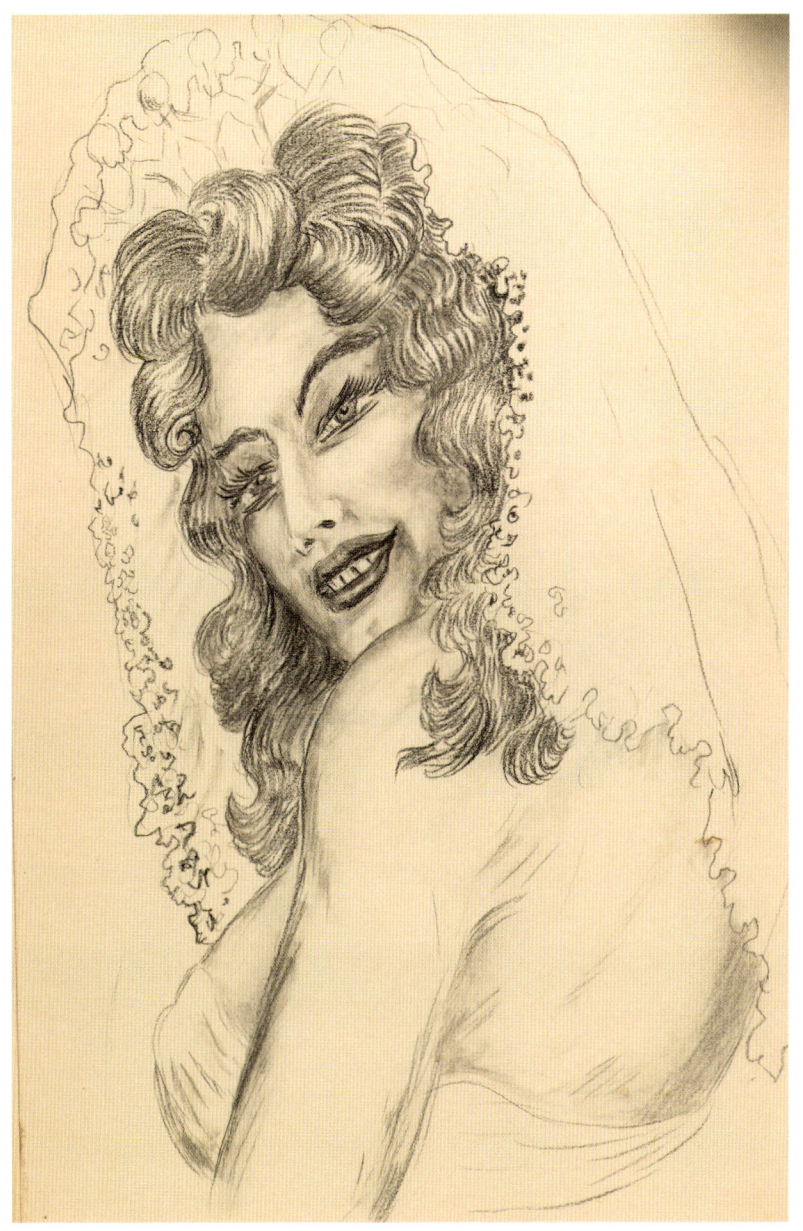

Sketch by Lotteva

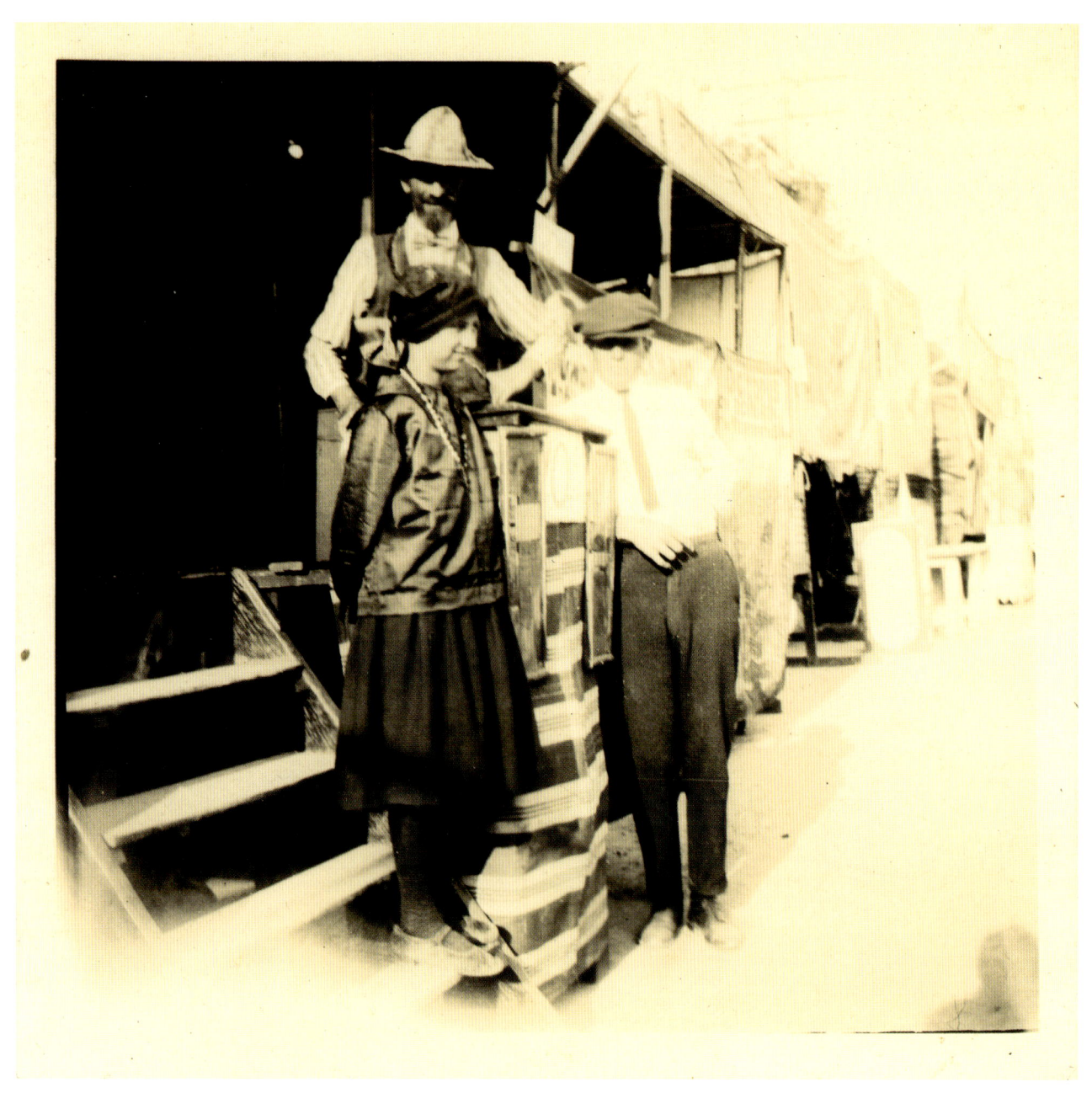

Gus and Lotteva, San Antonio, April 1922

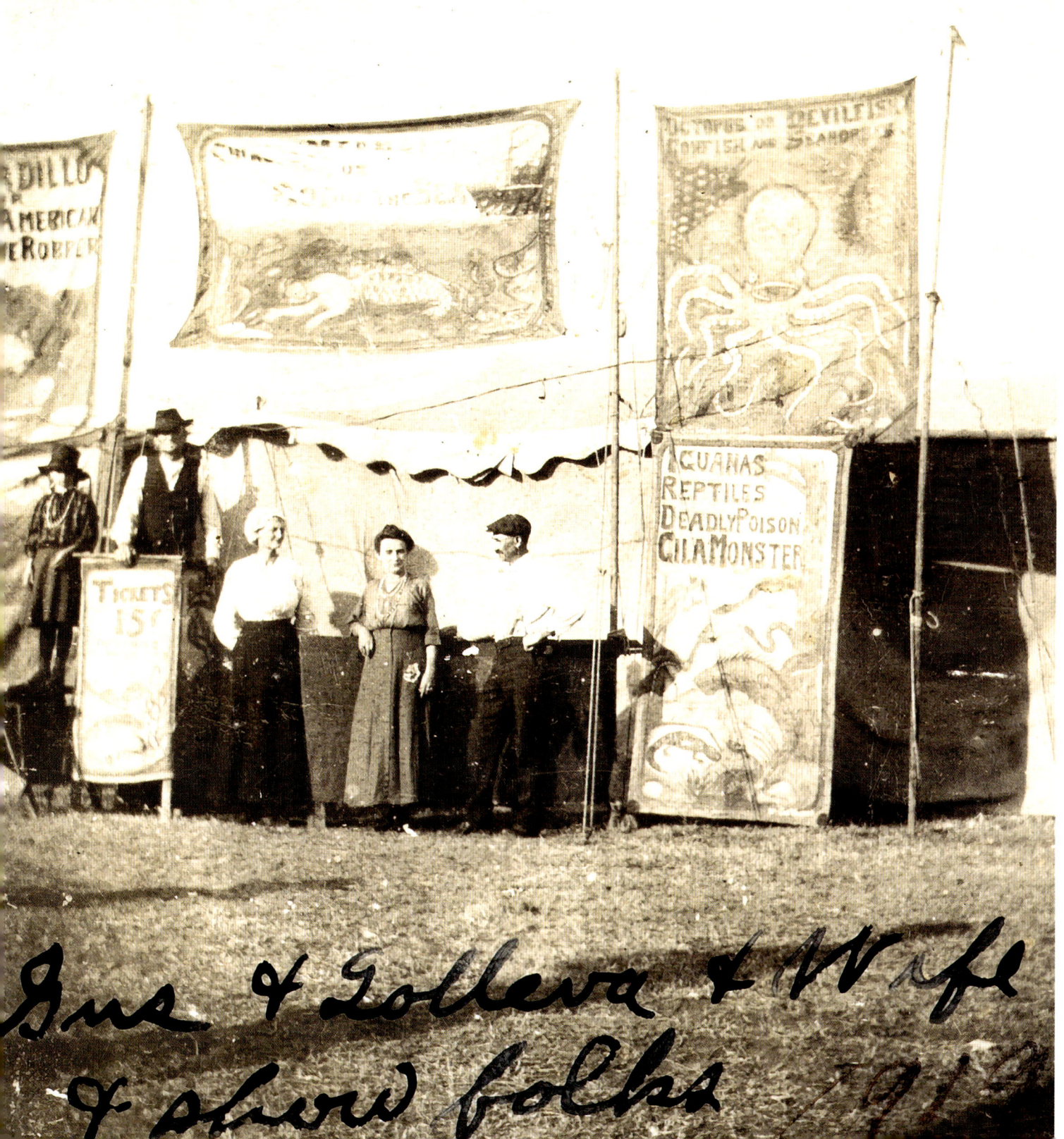

Lotteva, Maud, and Gus with show folks, 1919. *Photograph from Gus Wagner's scrapbook*

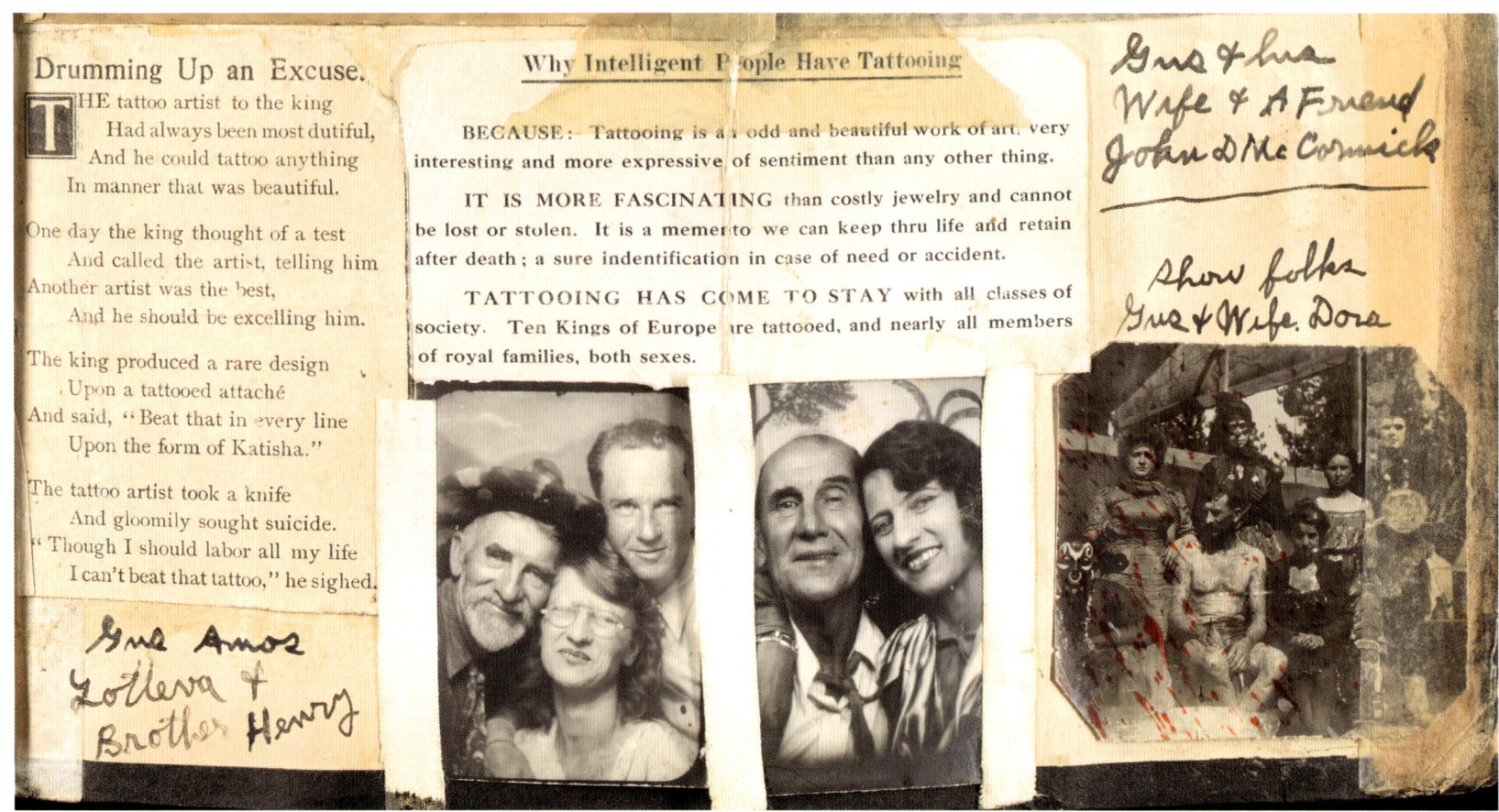

Drumming Up an Excuse.

THE tattoo artist to the king
    Had always been most dutiful,
    And he could tattoo anything
In manner that was beautiful.

One day the king thought of a test
    And called the artist, telling him
Another artist was the best,
    And he should be excelling him.

The king produced a rare design
    Upon a tattooed attaché
And said, "Beat that in every line
    Upon the form of Katisha."

The tattoo artist took a knife
    And gloomily sought suicide.
"Though I should labor all my life
    I can't beat that tattoo," he sighed.

Why Intelligent People Have Tattooing

BECAUSE: Tattooing is an odd and beautiful work of art, very interesting and more expressive of sentiment than any other thing.

IT IS MORE FASCINATING than costly jewelry and cannot be lost or stolen. It is a memento we can keep thru life and retain after death; a sure indentification in case of need or accident.

TATTOOING HAS COME TO STAY with all classes of society. Ten Kings of Europe are tattooed, and nearly all members of royal families, both sexes.

Gus Amos Lotteva & Brother Henry

Gus & his Wife & A Friend John D. McCormick

show folks Gus & Wife. Dora

Detail from Gus Wagner's scrapbook

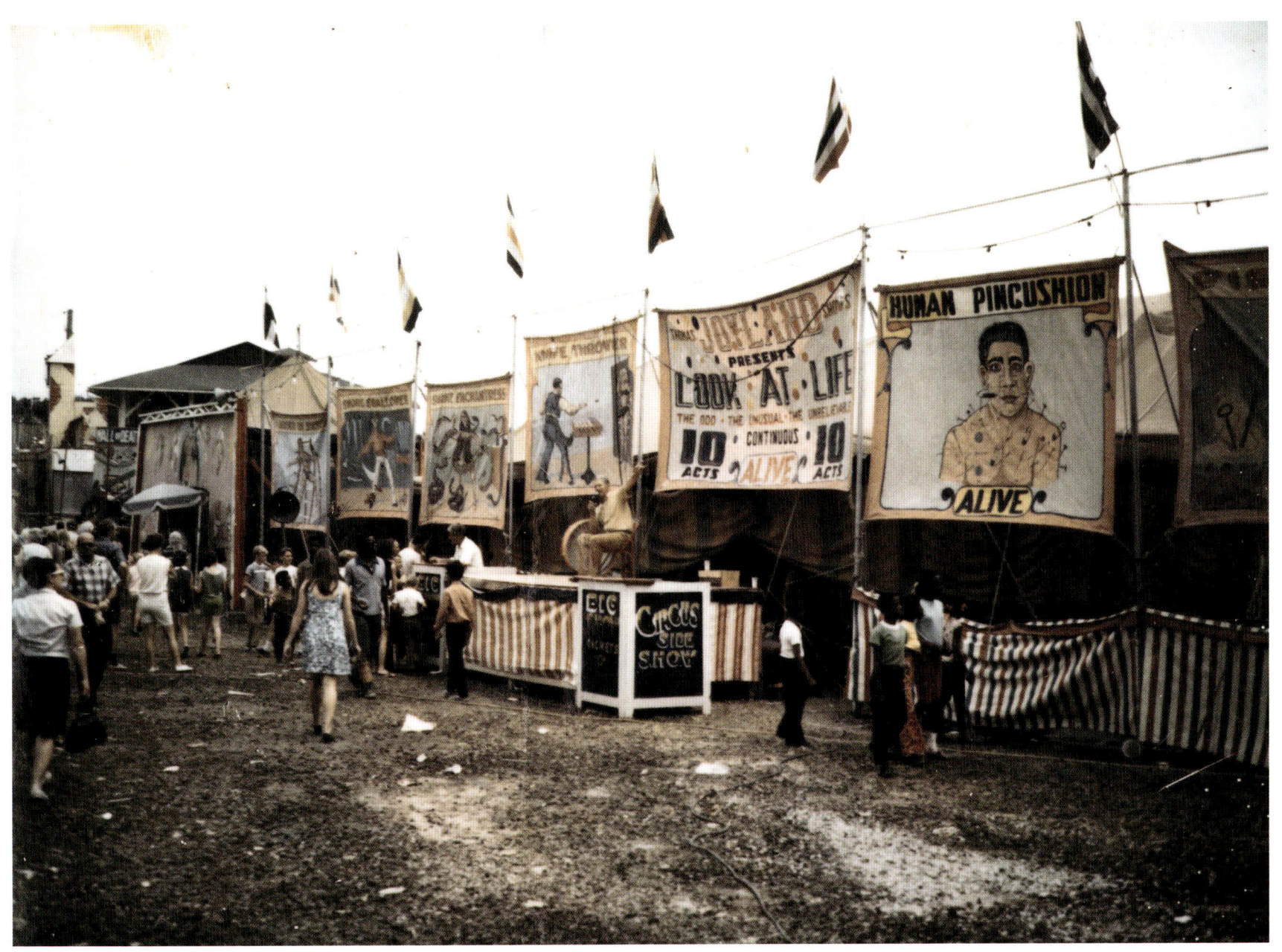

Sideshow, ca. 1960s

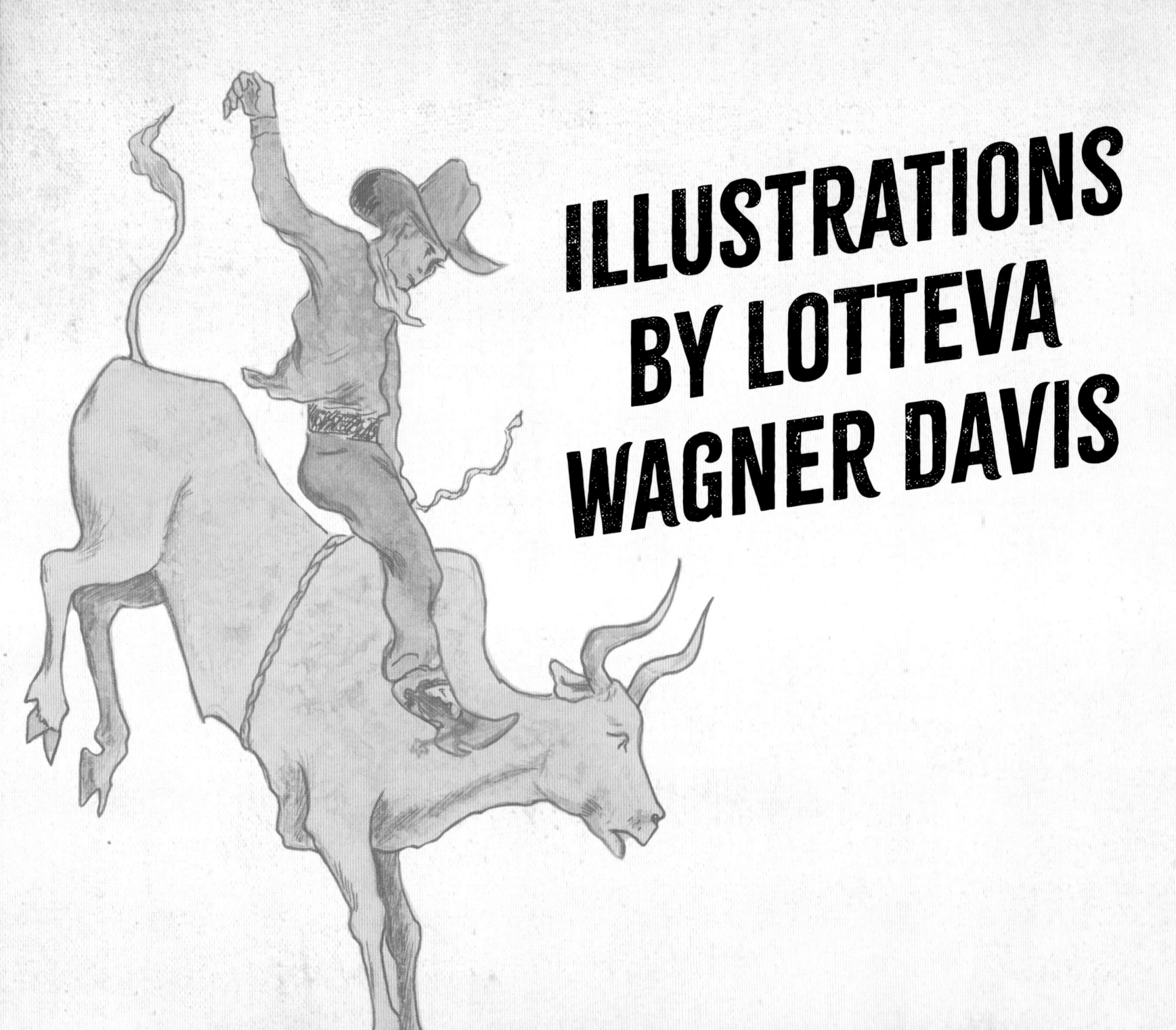

ILLUSTRATIONS BY LOTTEVA WAGNER DAVIS

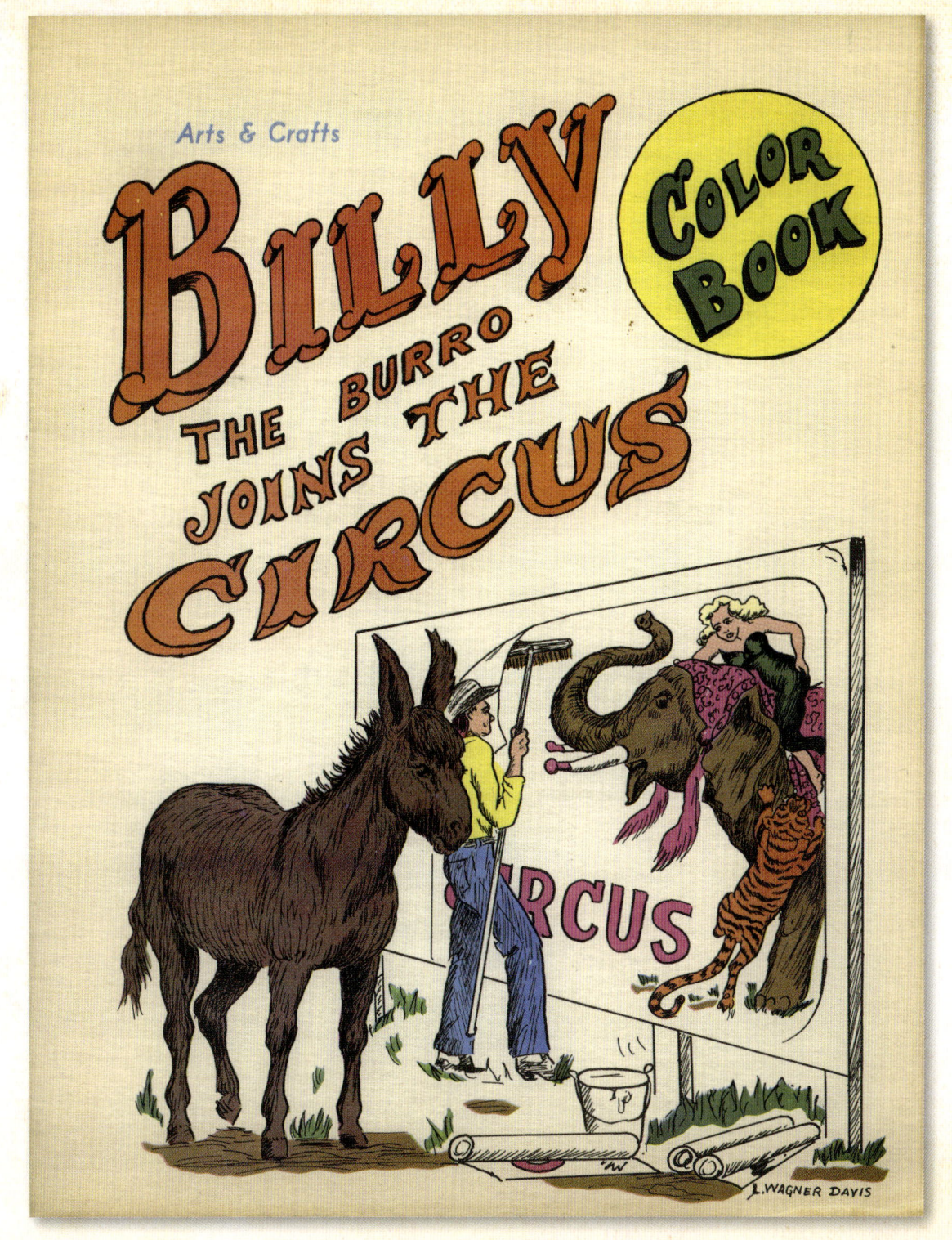

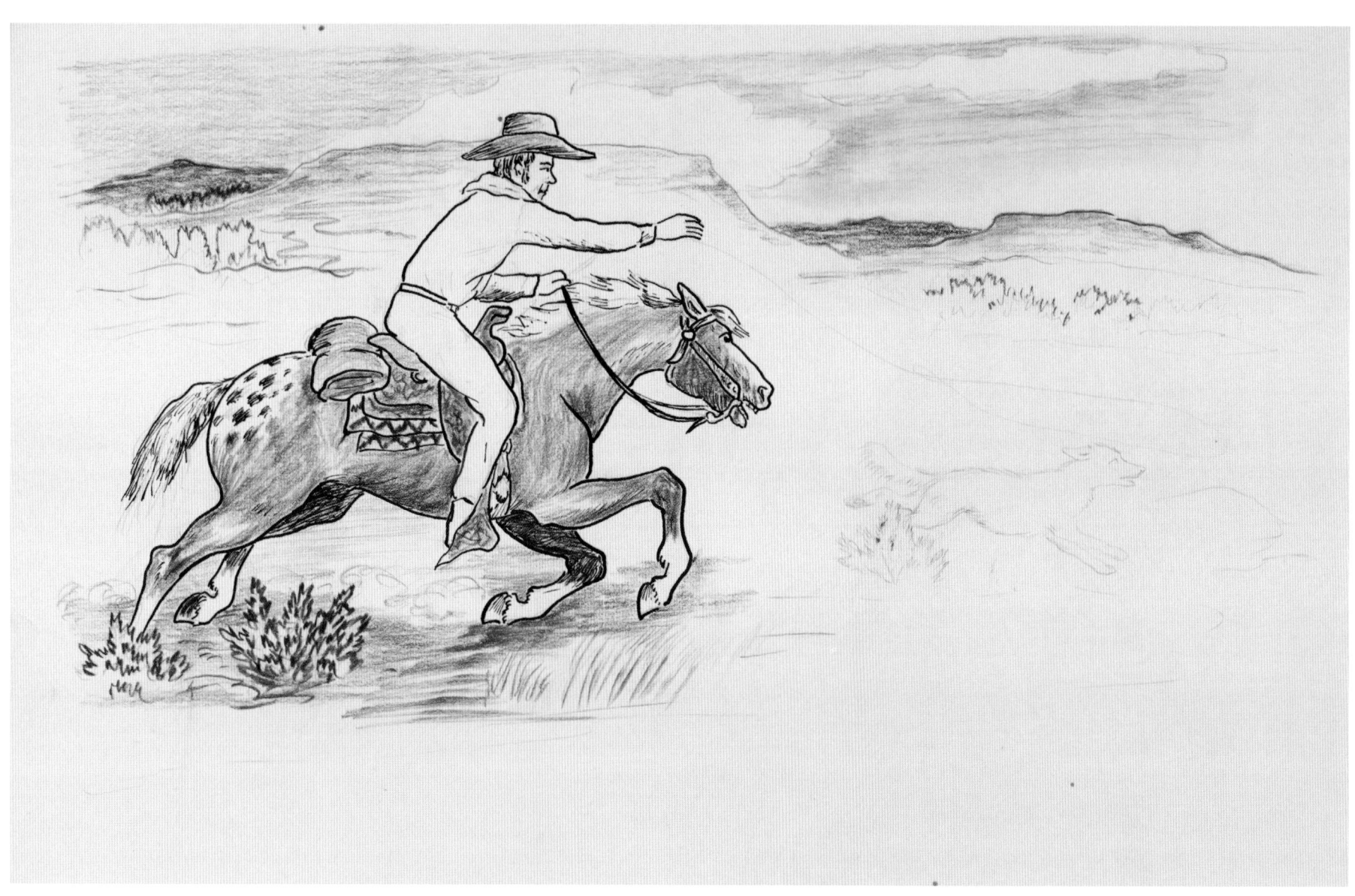

Illustrations by Lotteva Wagner Davis

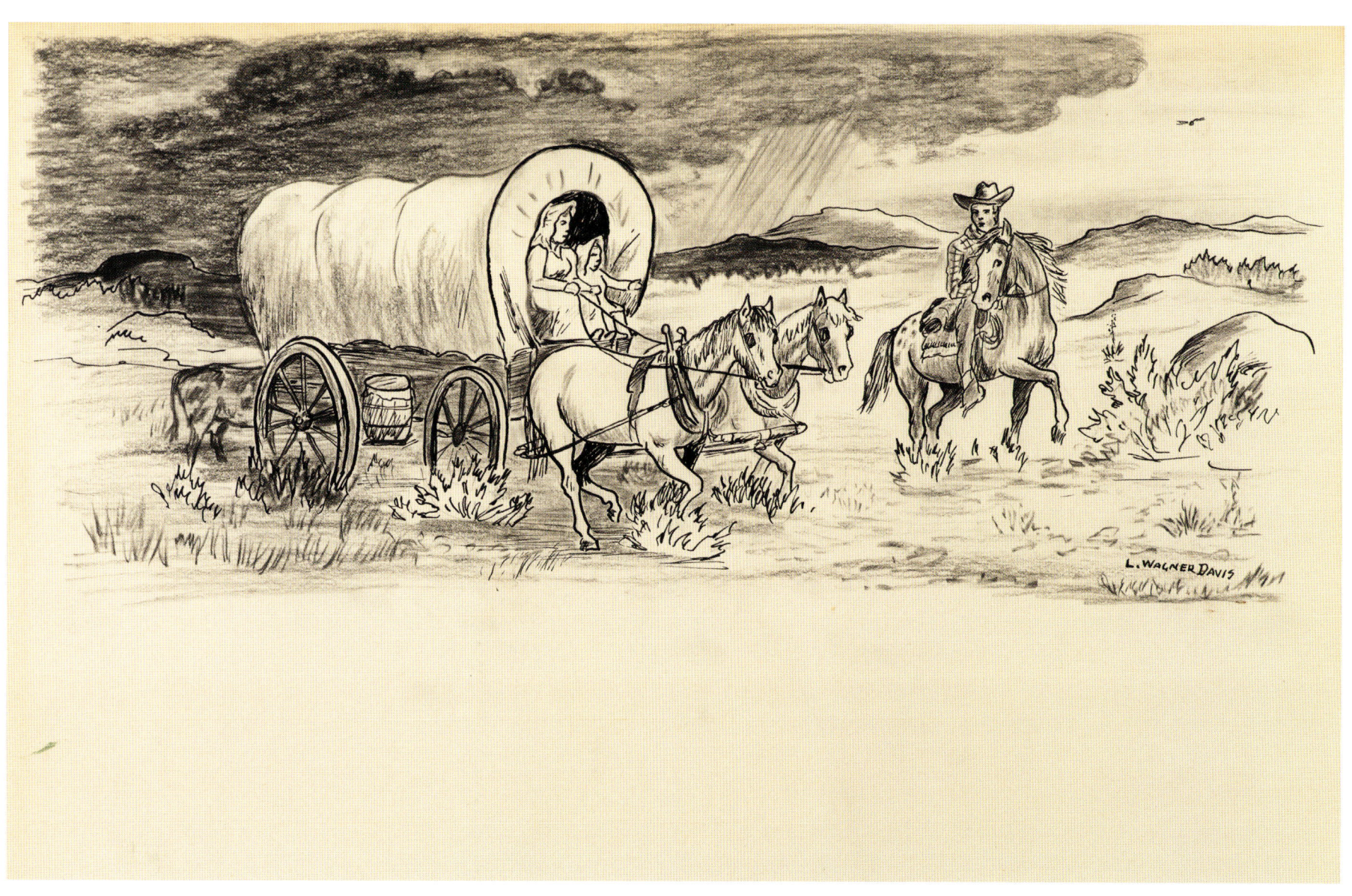

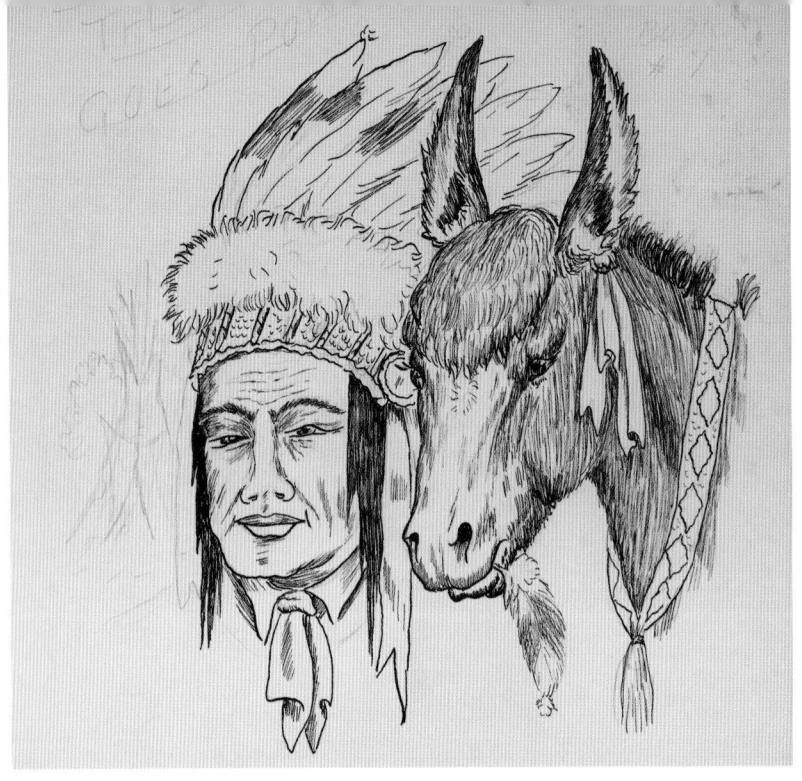

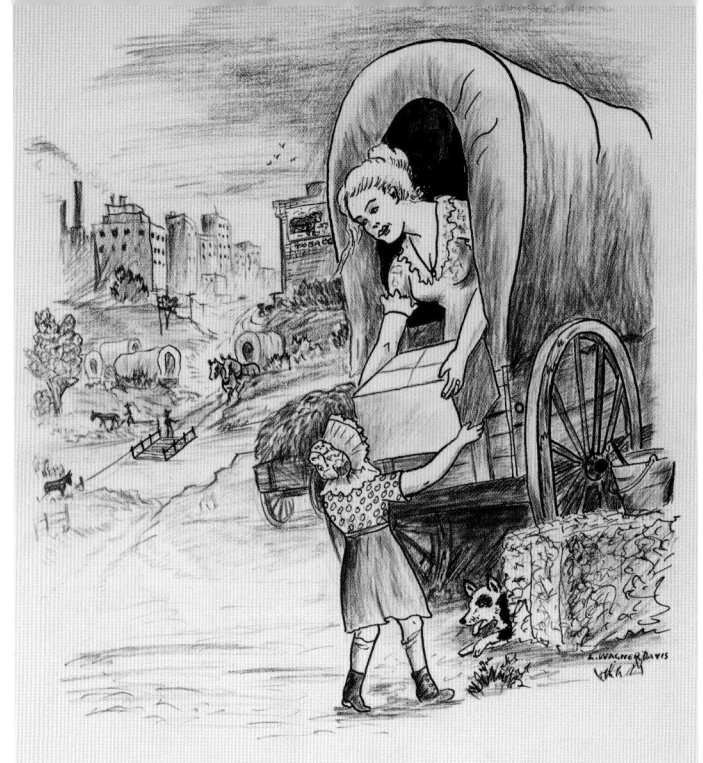

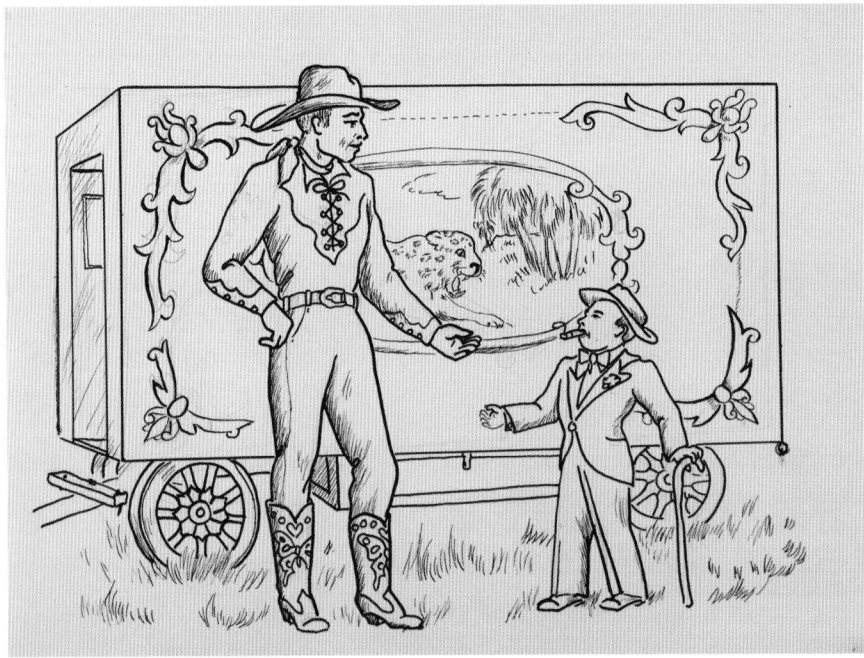

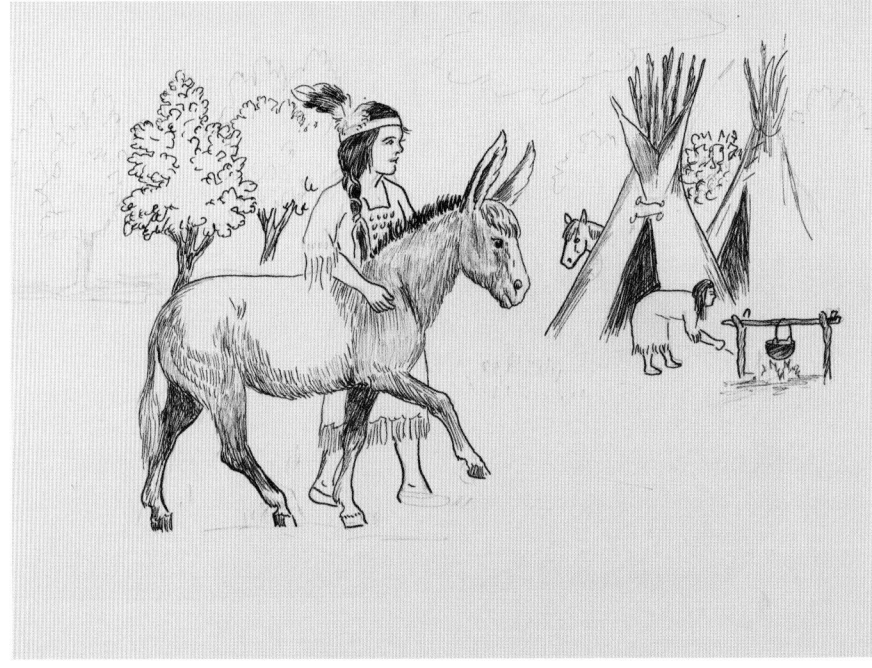

Illustrations by Lotteva Wagner Davis

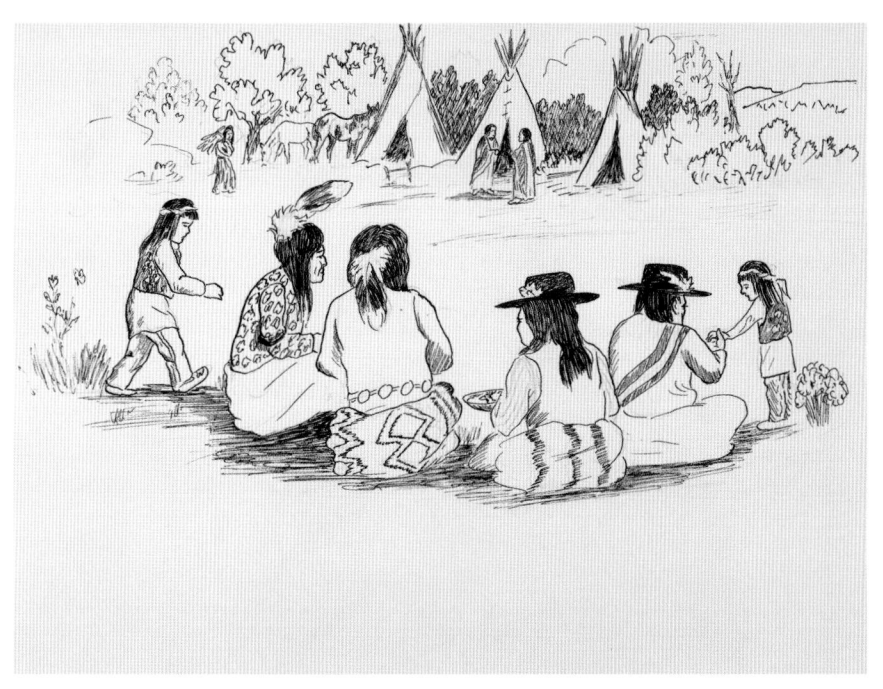

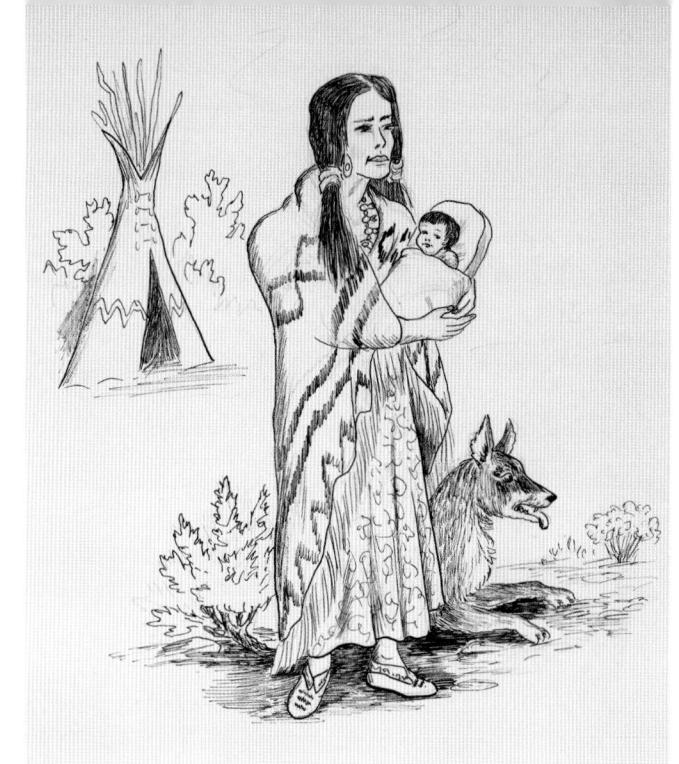

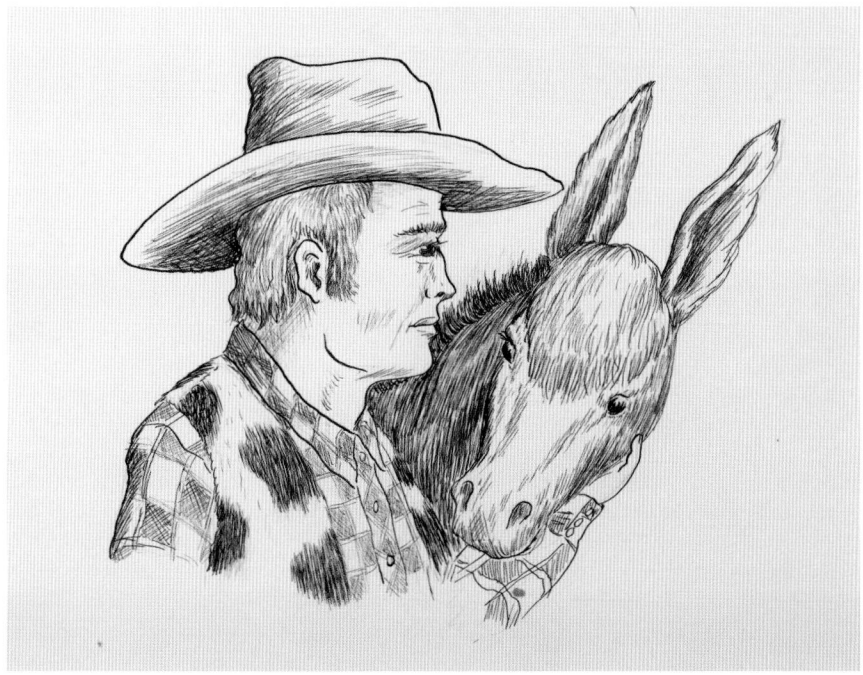

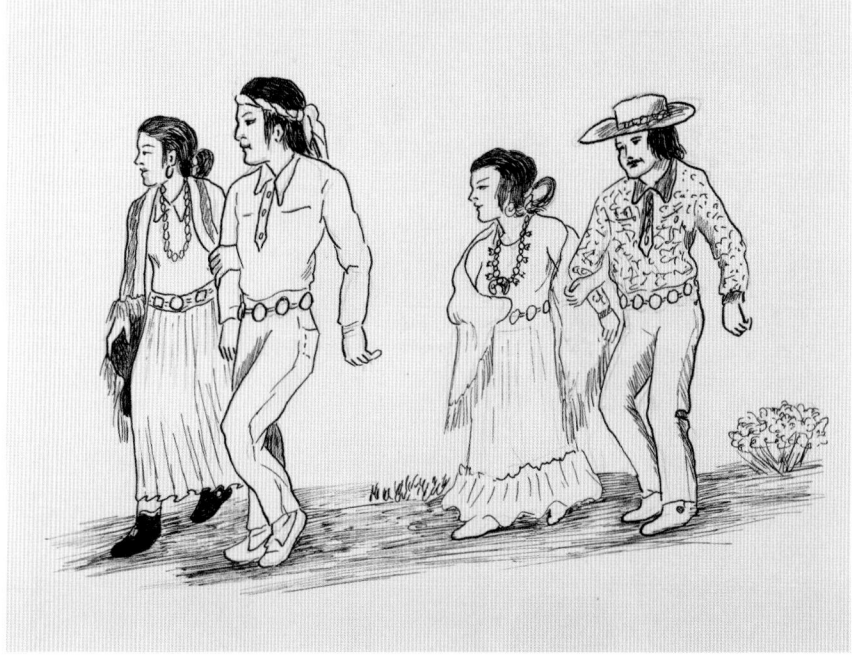

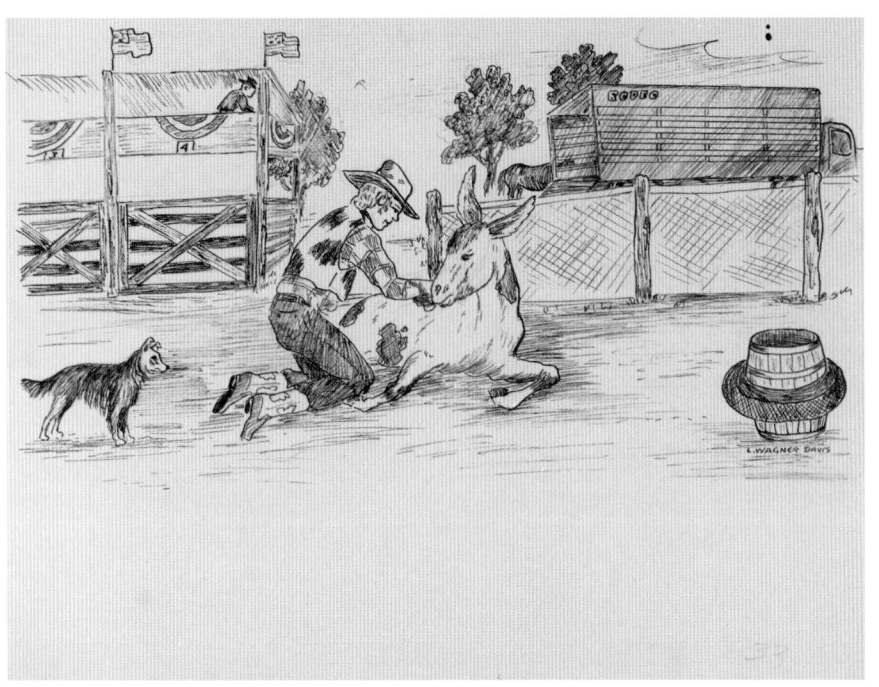
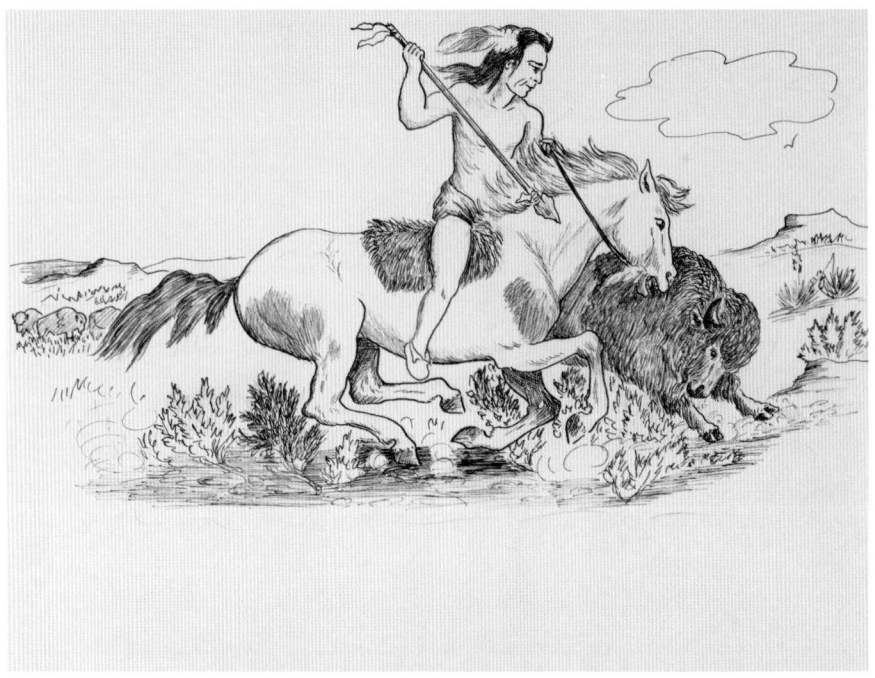
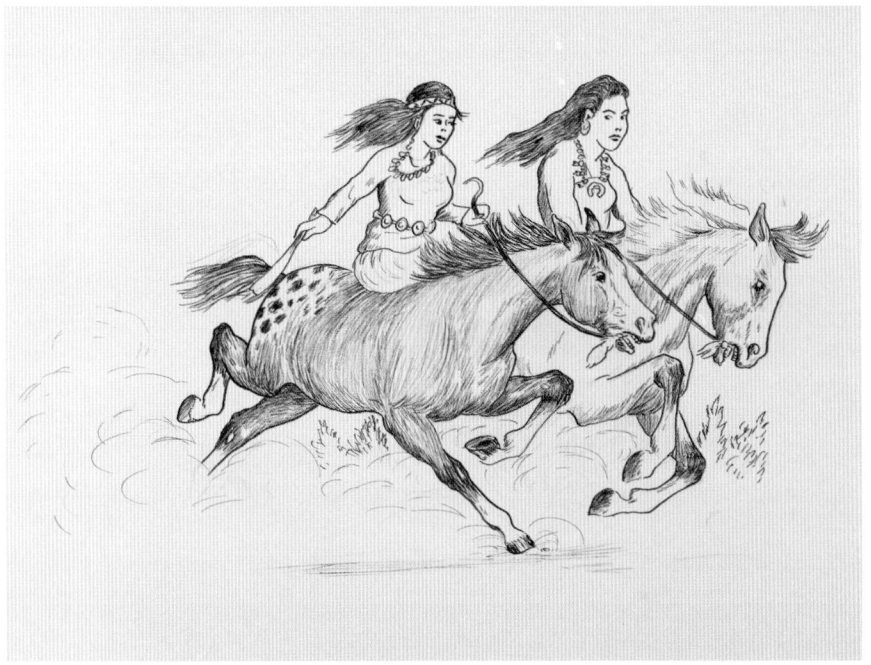
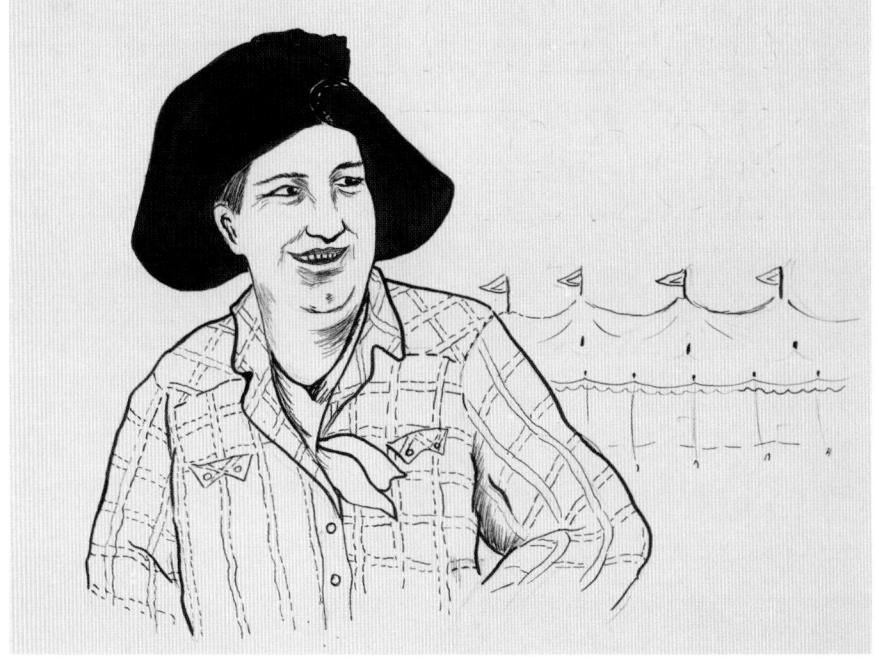

Illustrations by Lotteva Wagner Davis

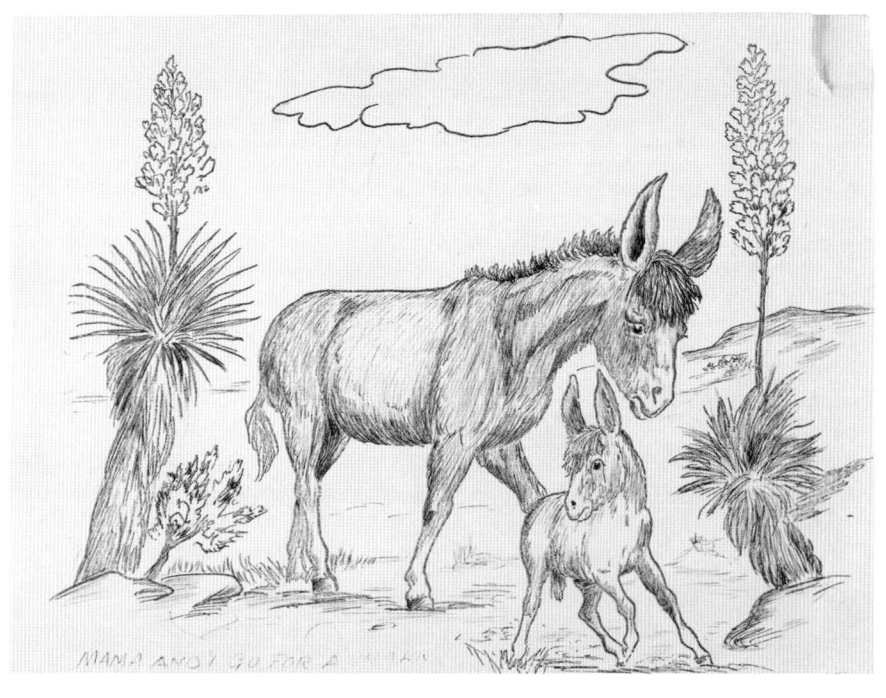

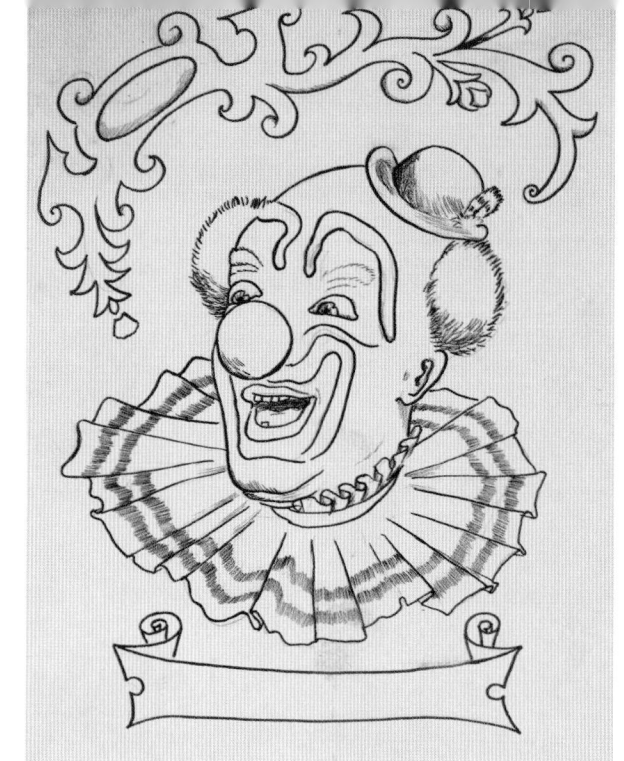

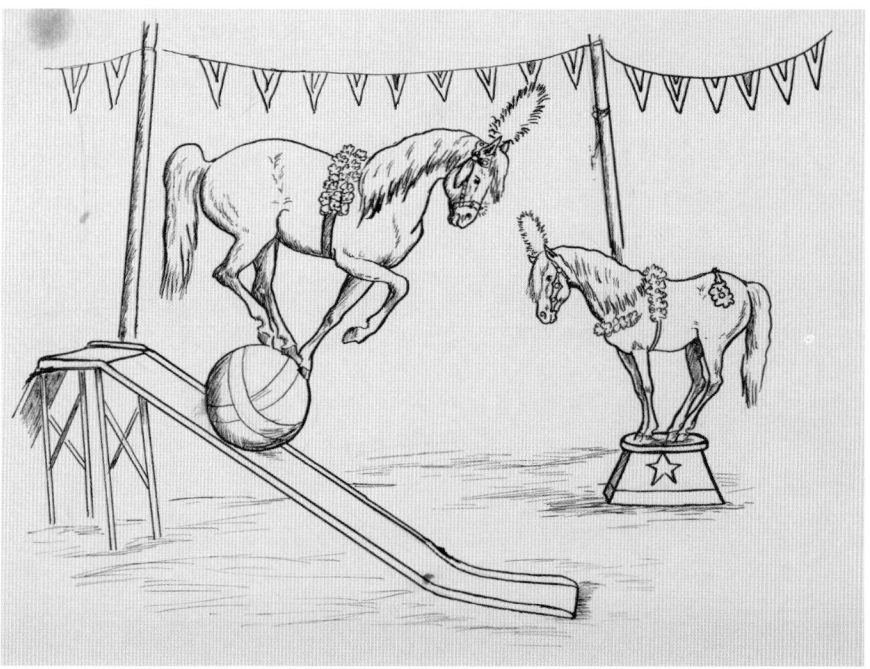

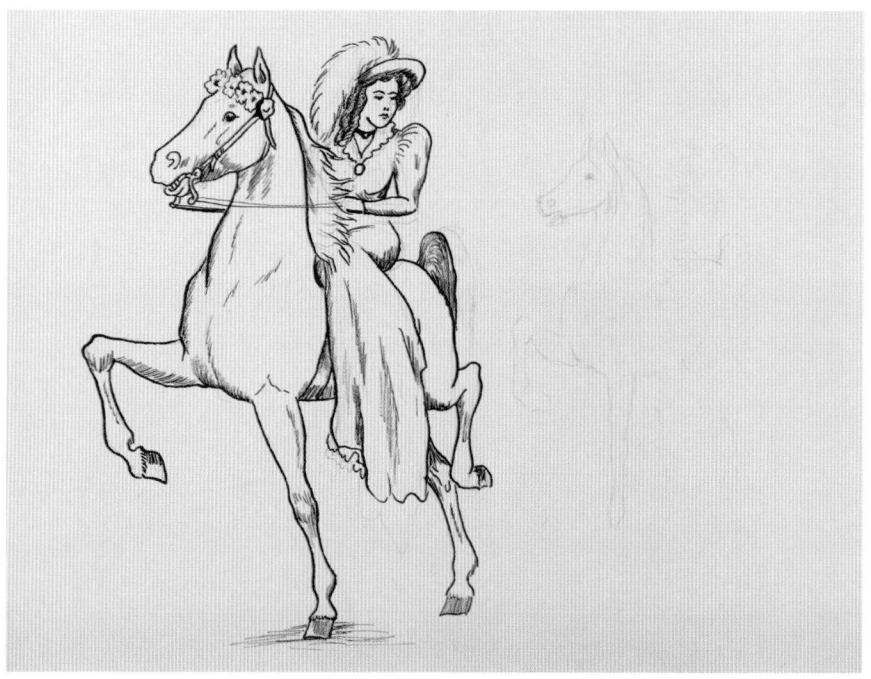

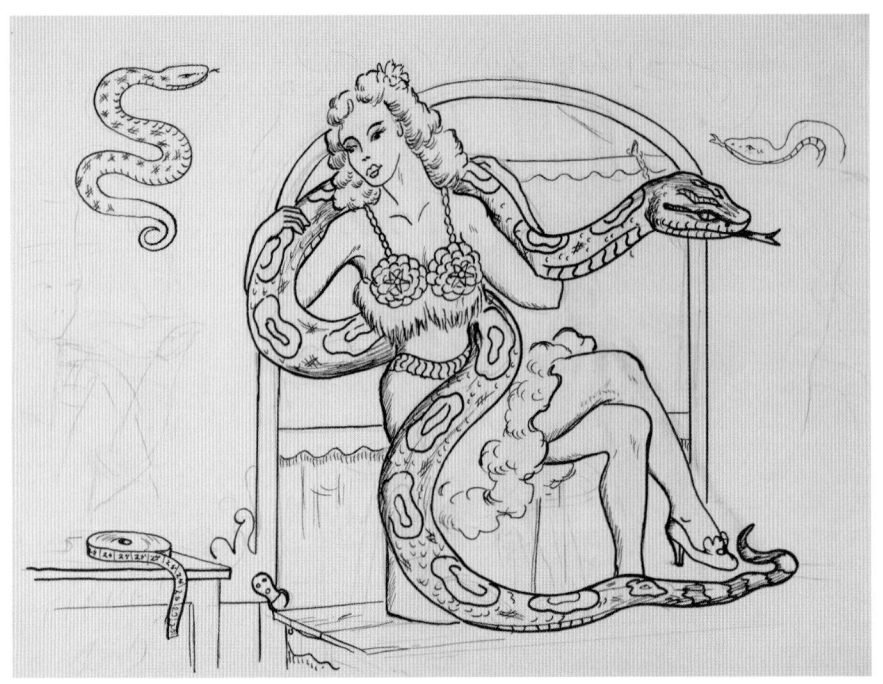

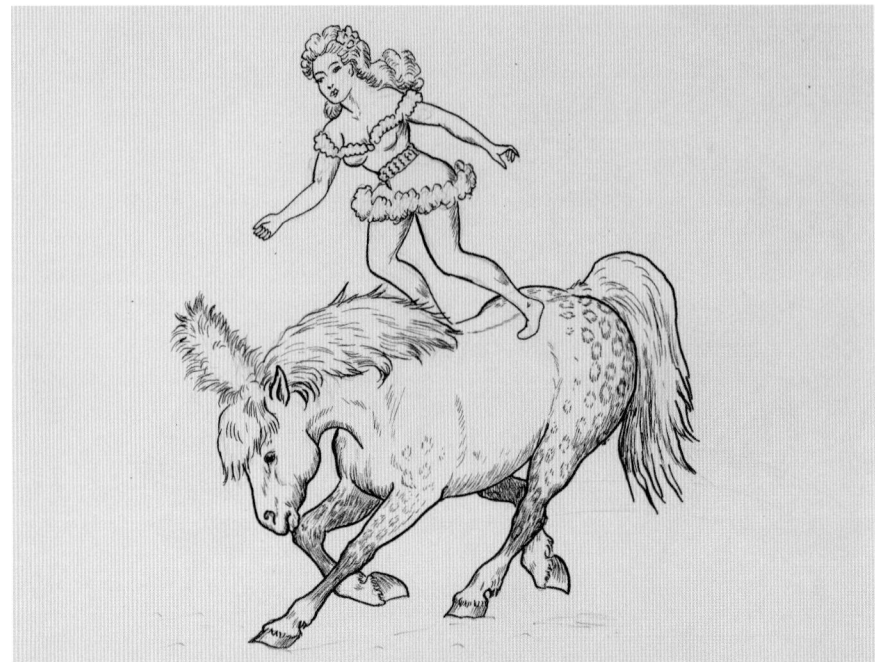

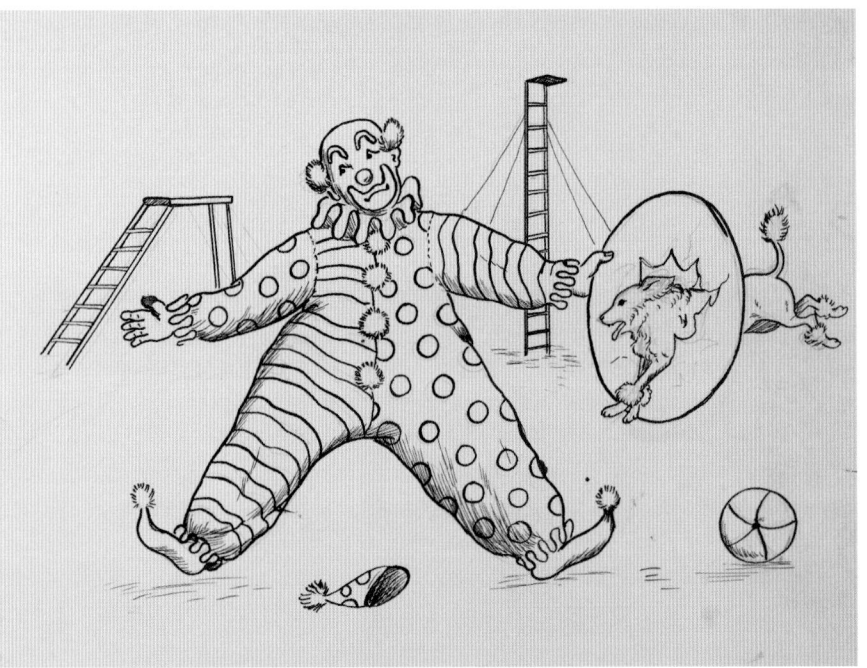

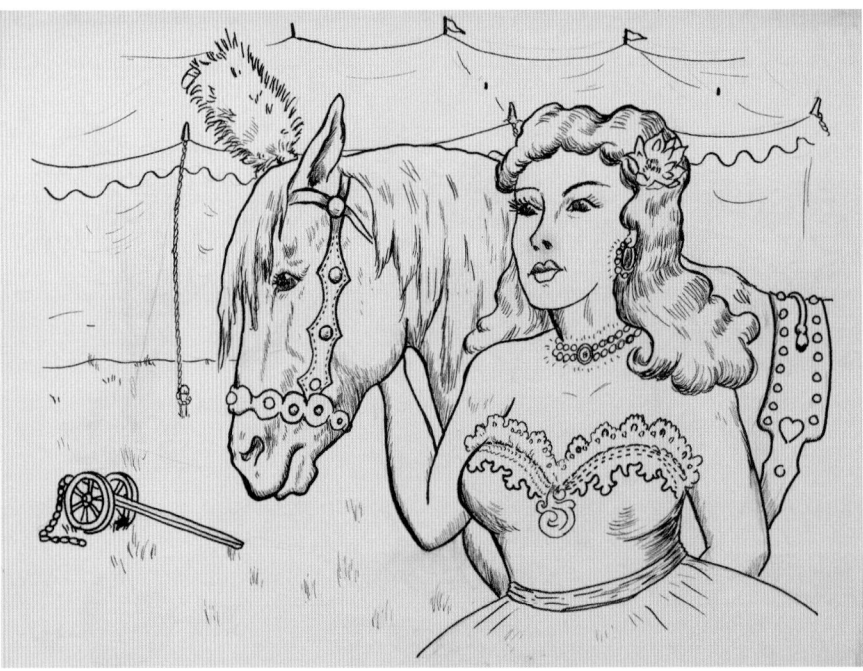

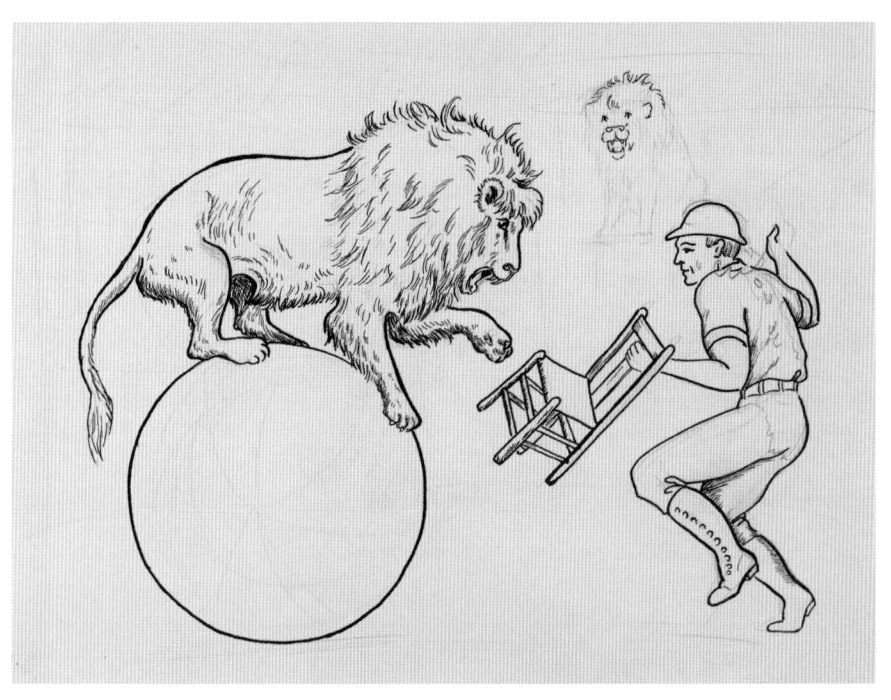

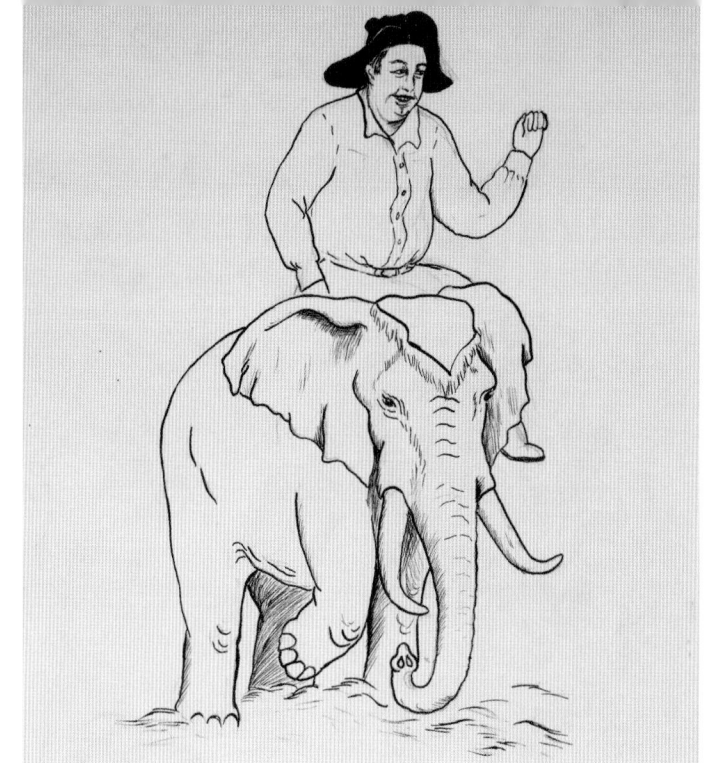

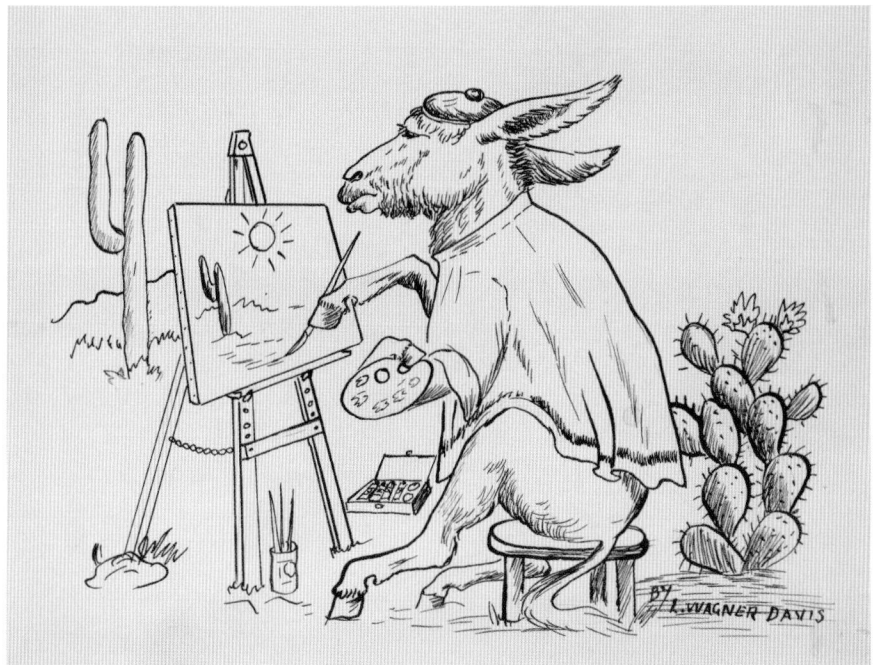

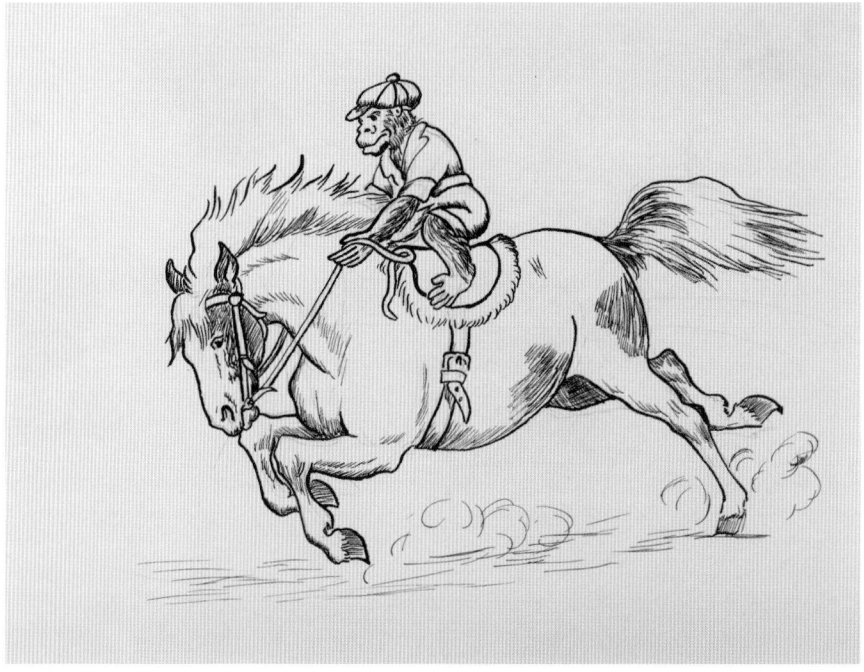

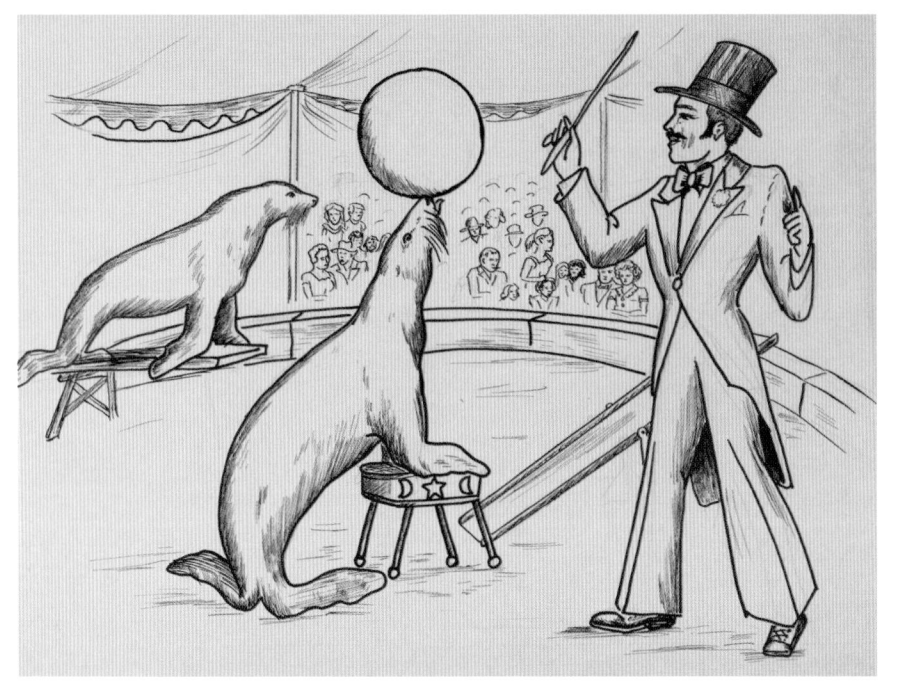

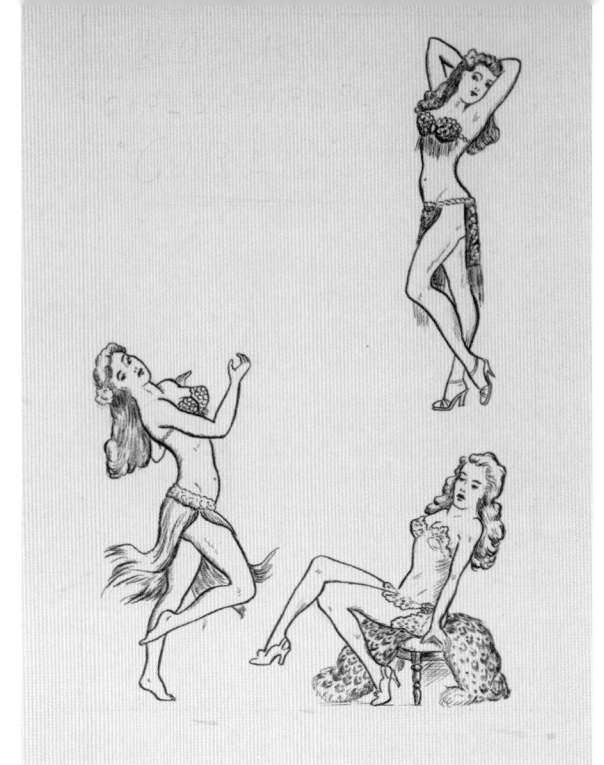

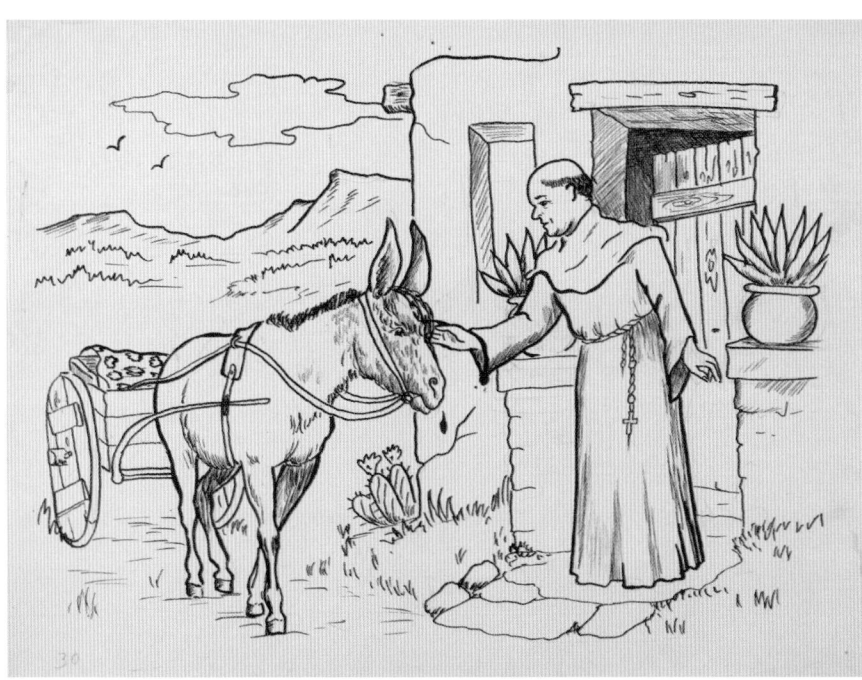

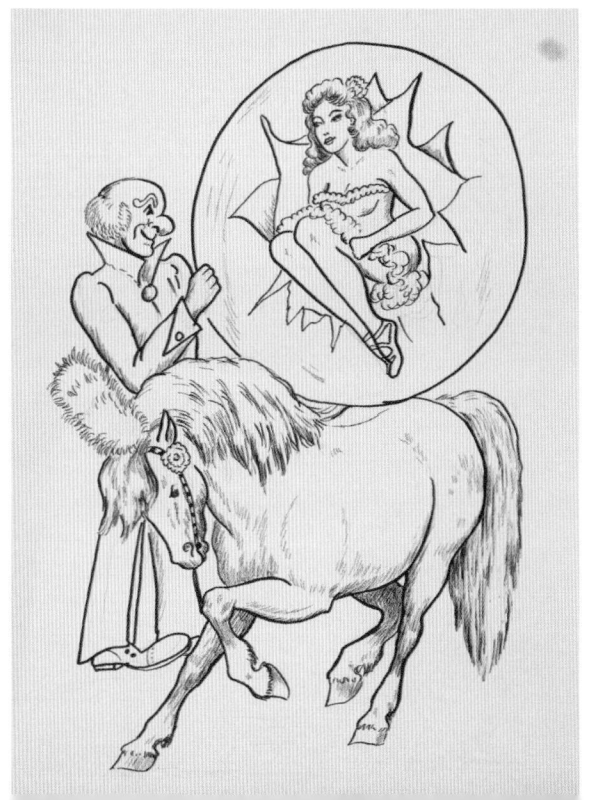

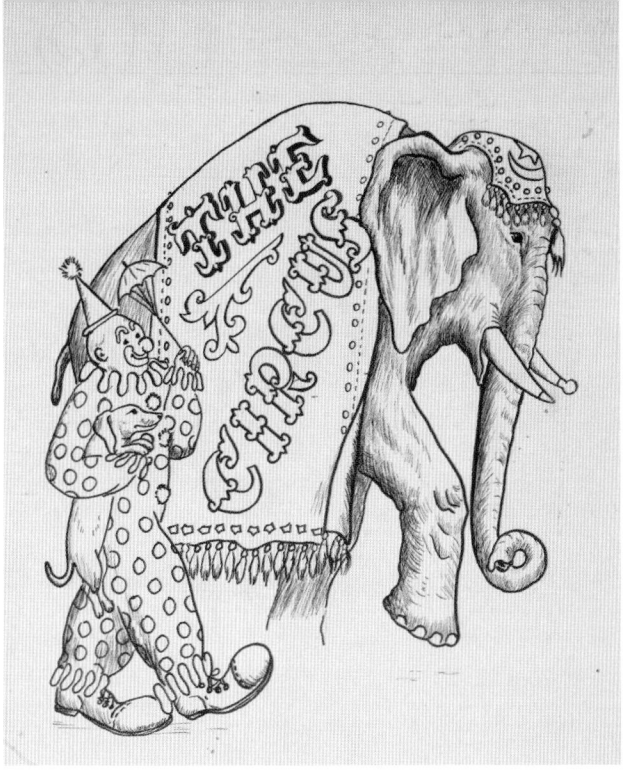

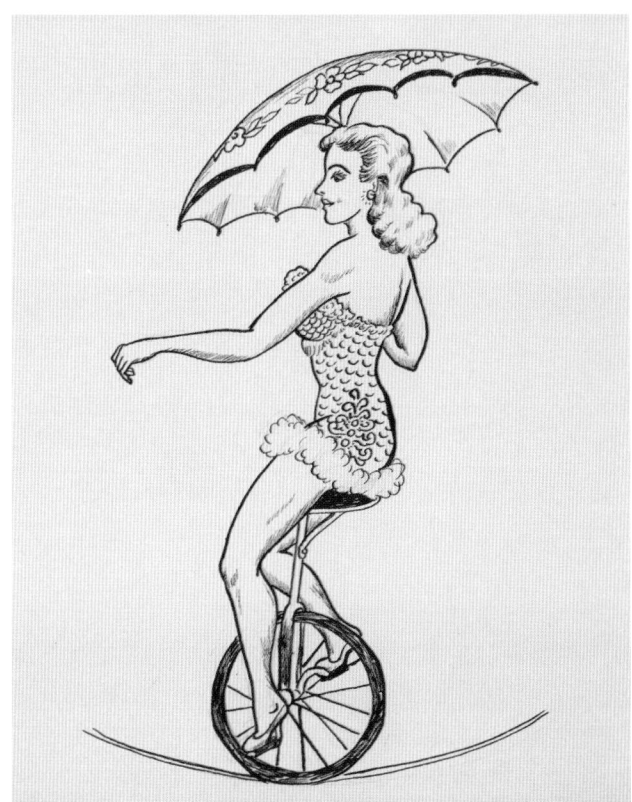

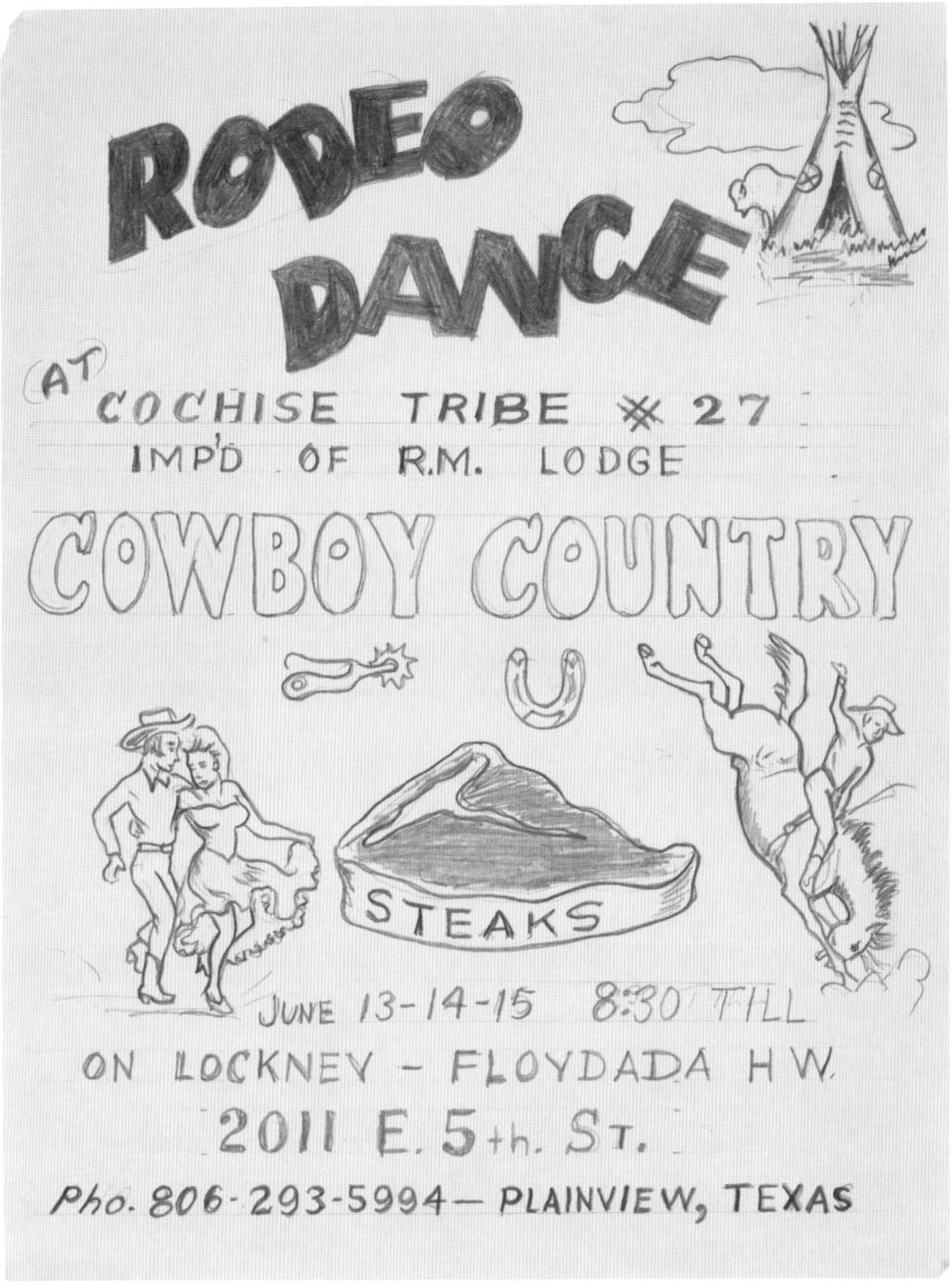

Rodeo Dance flyer illustration

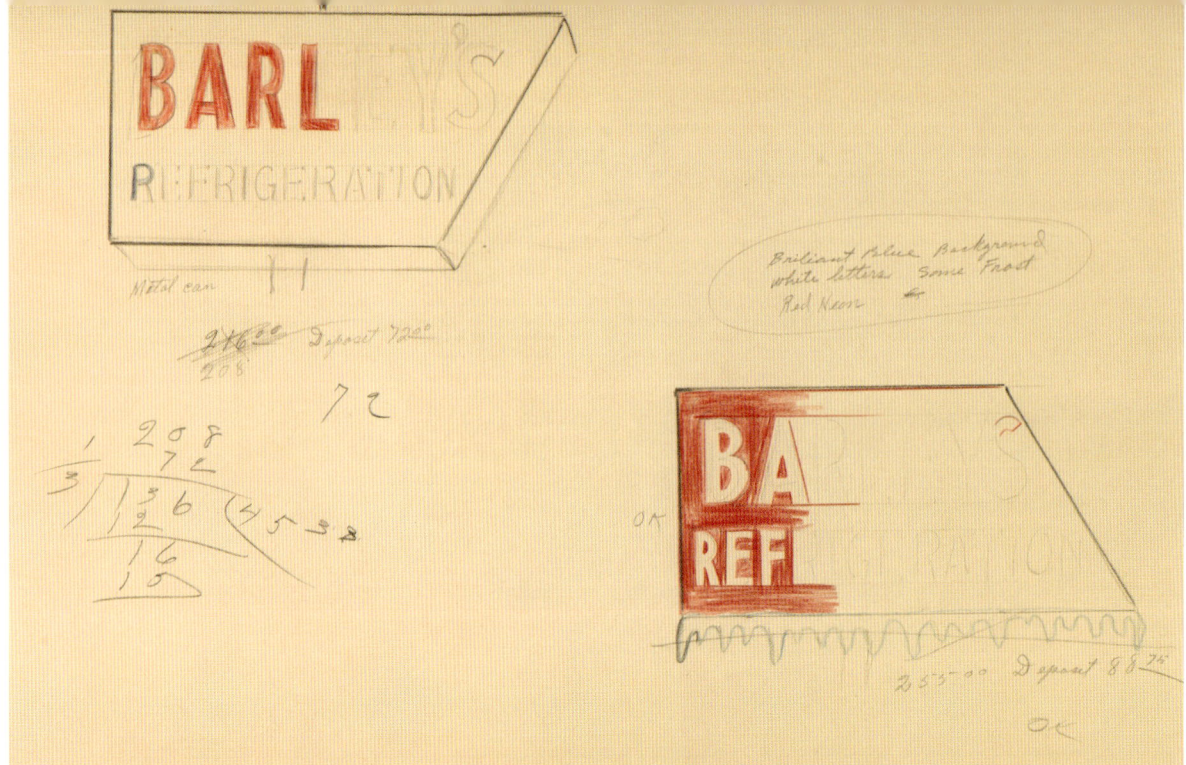

Sign design sketches

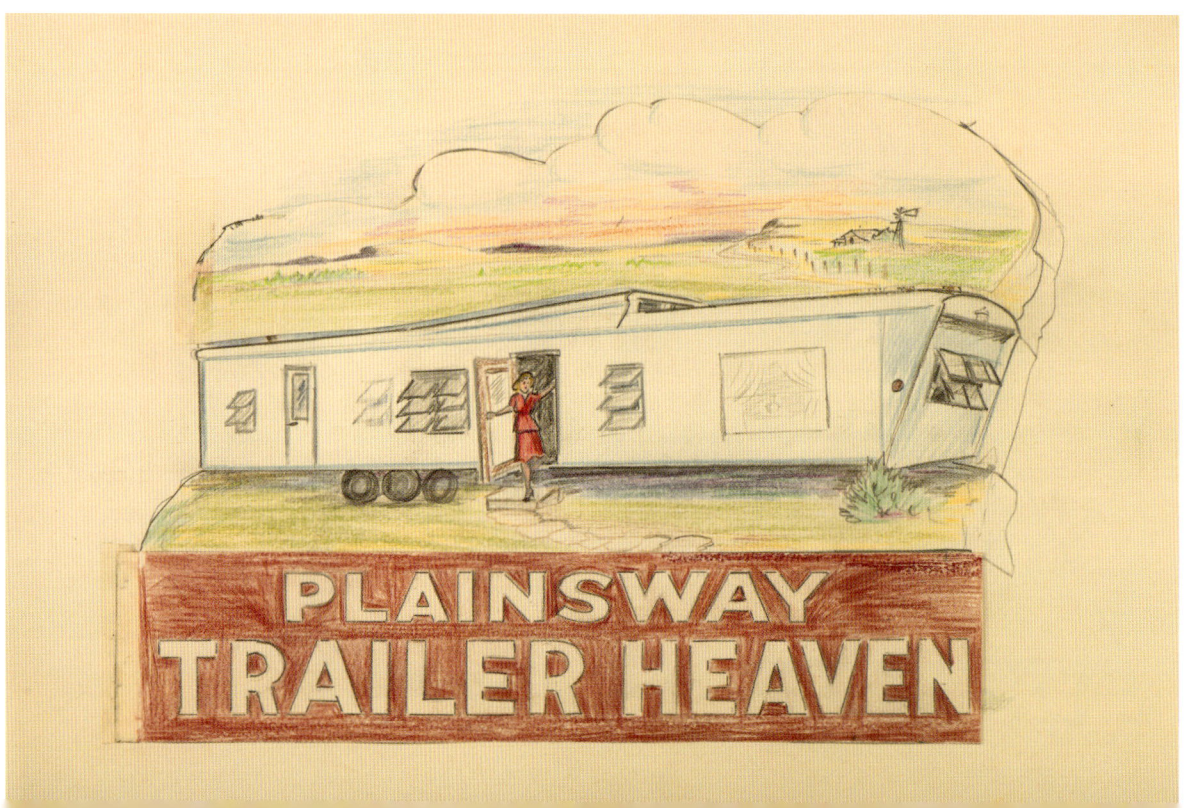

Illustrations by Lotteva Wagner Davis

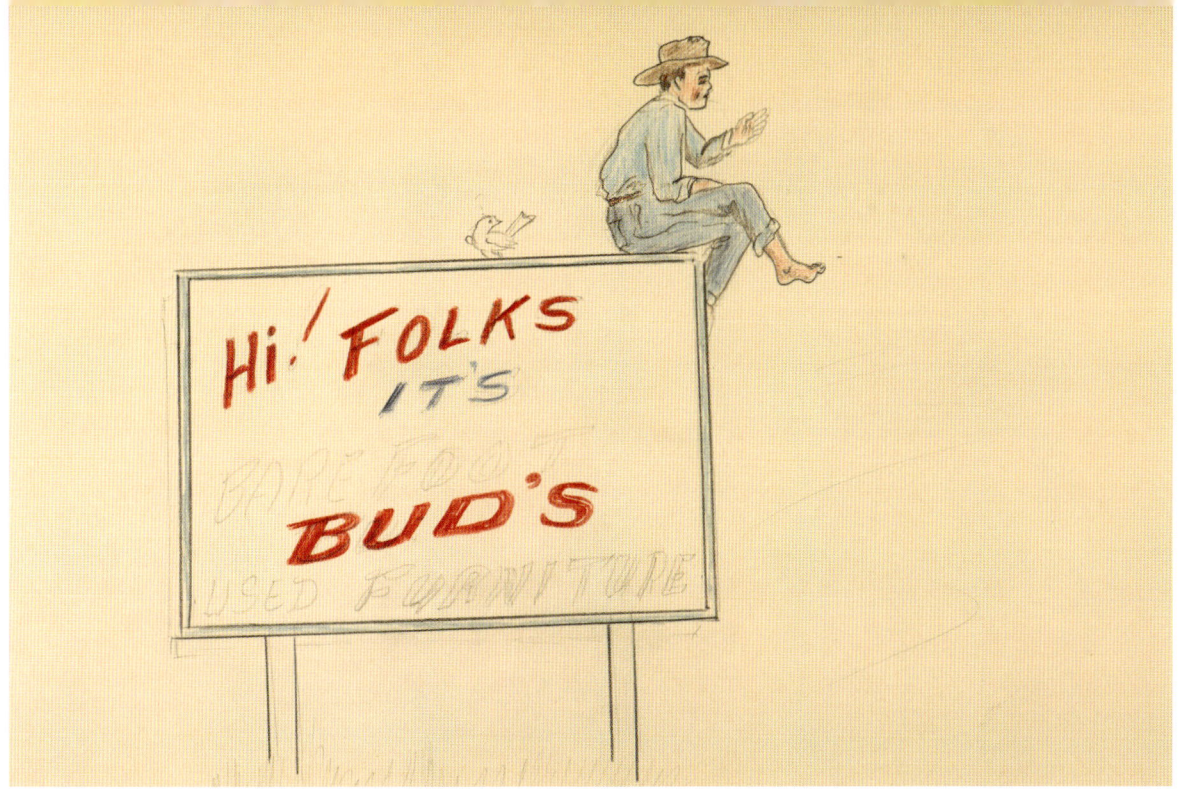

Sign design sketches

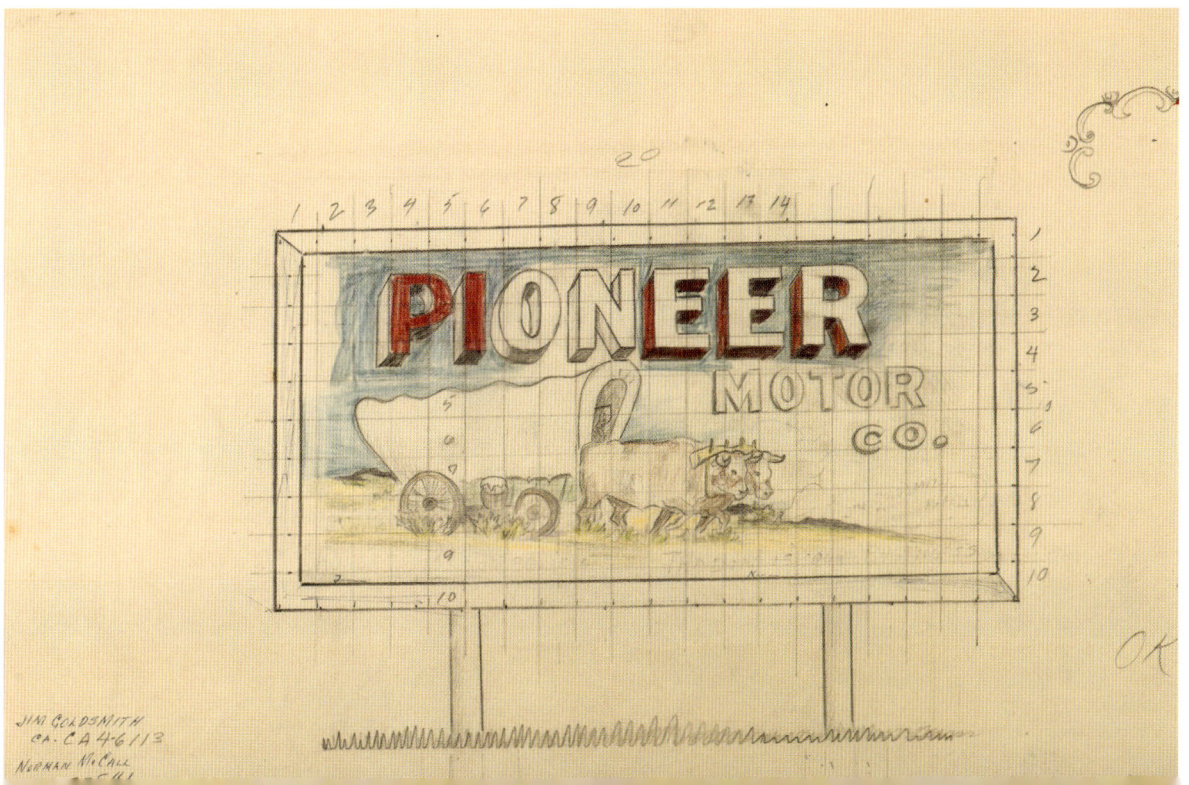

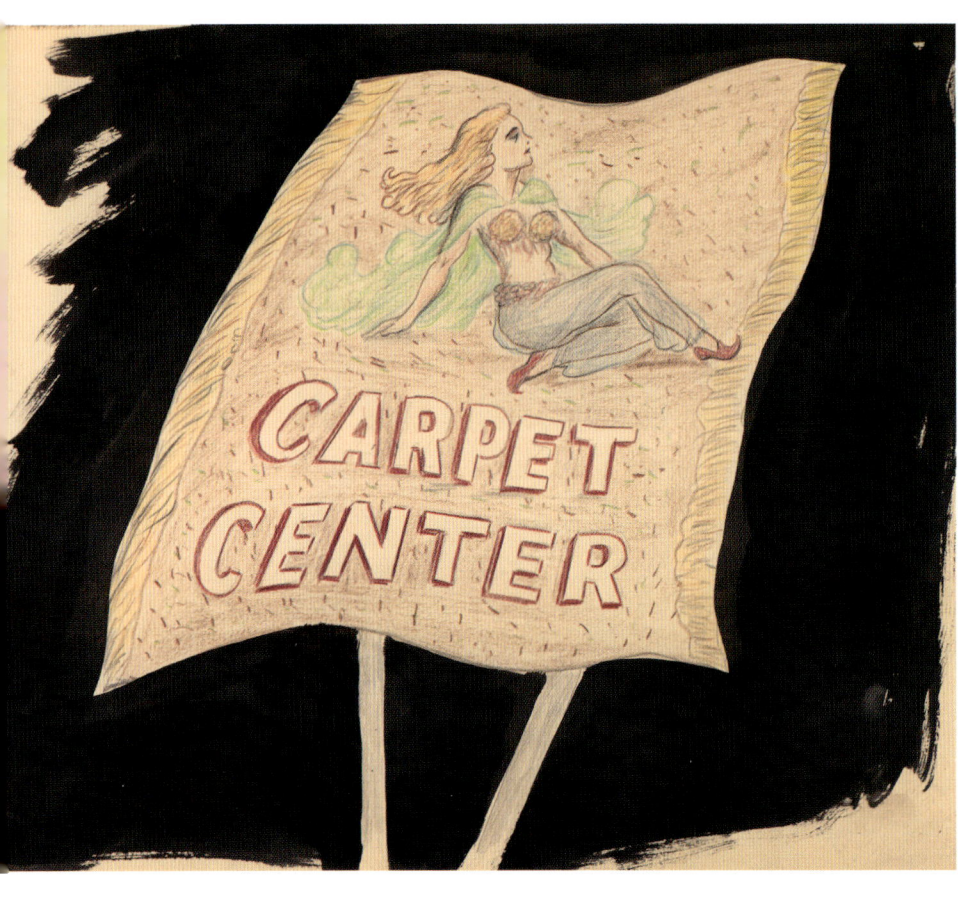

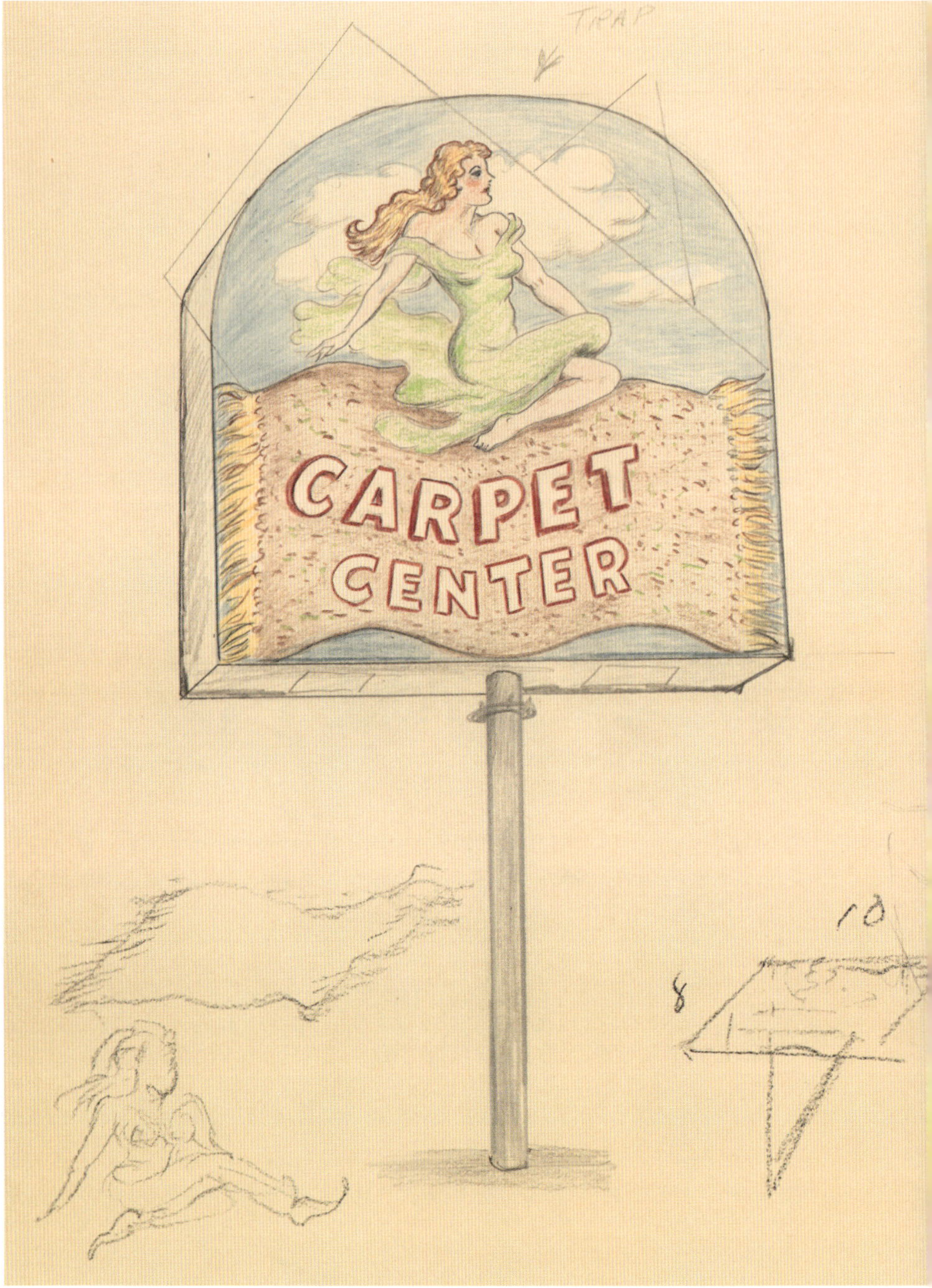

Sign design sketches

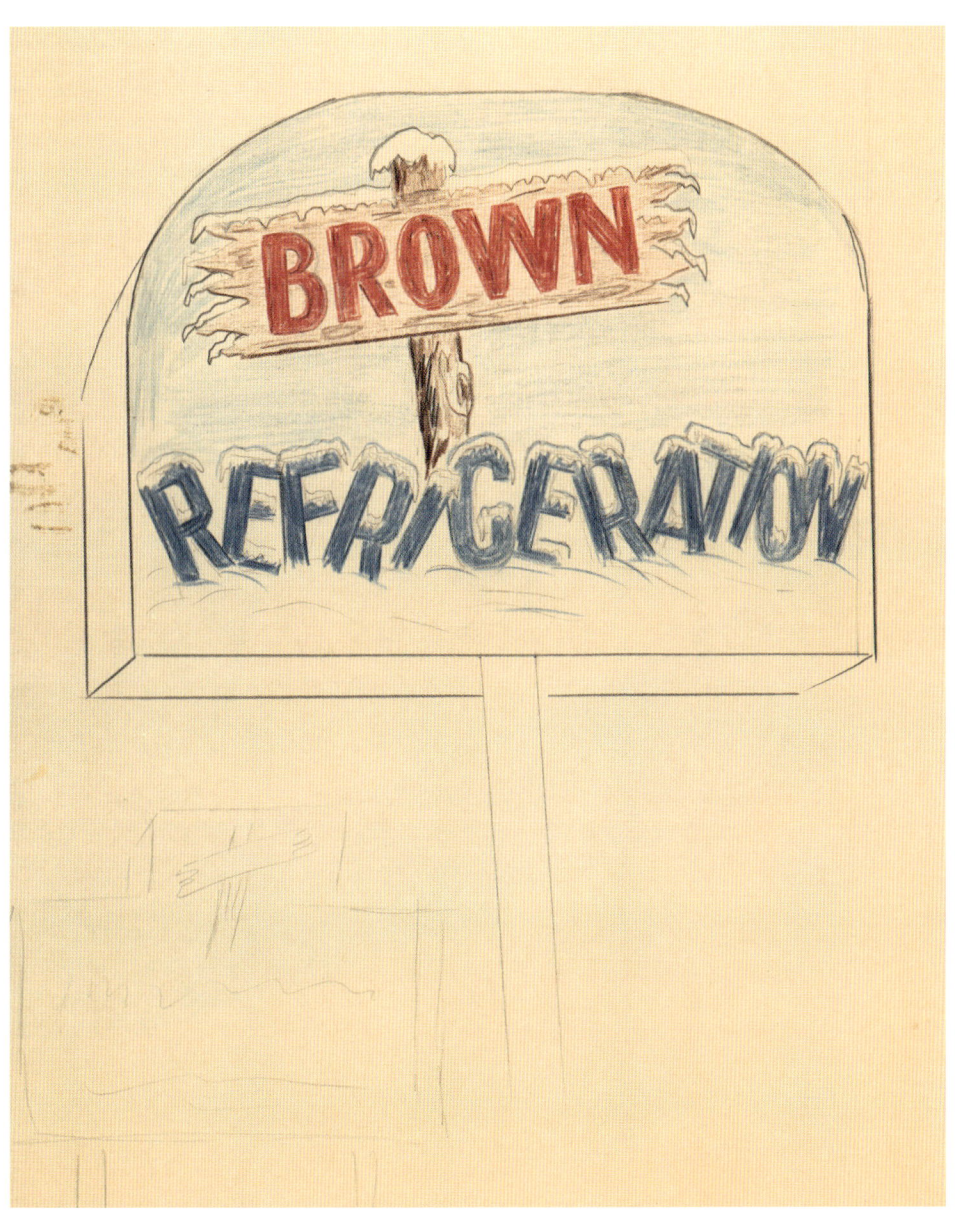

Sign design sketches

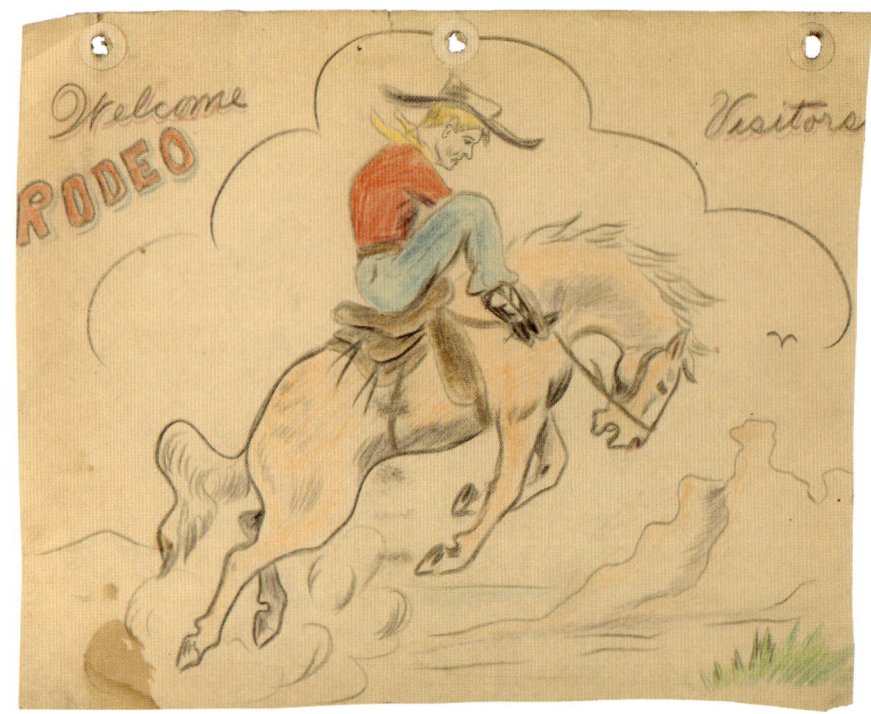

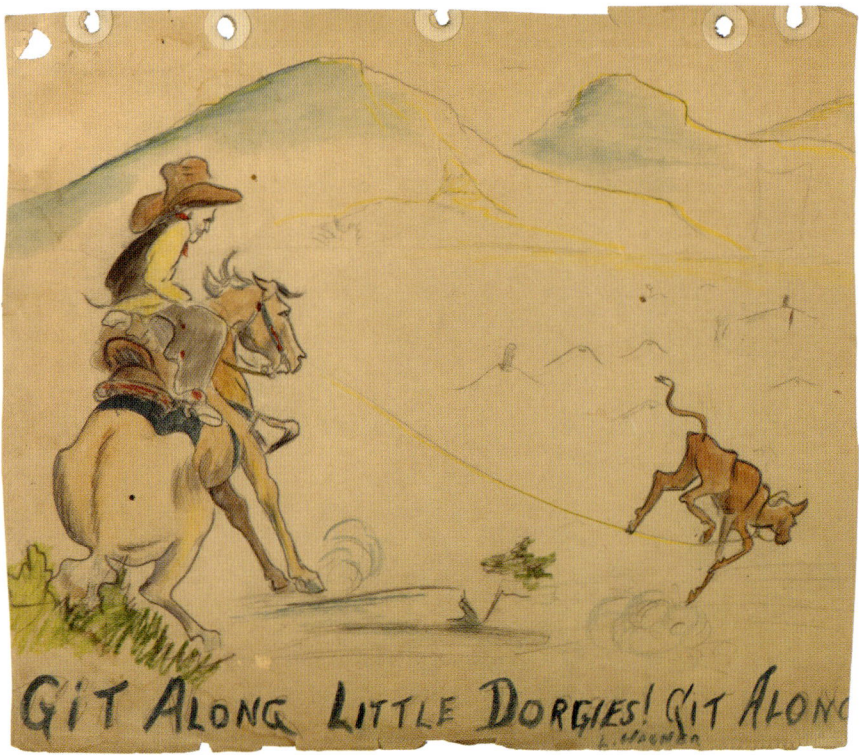

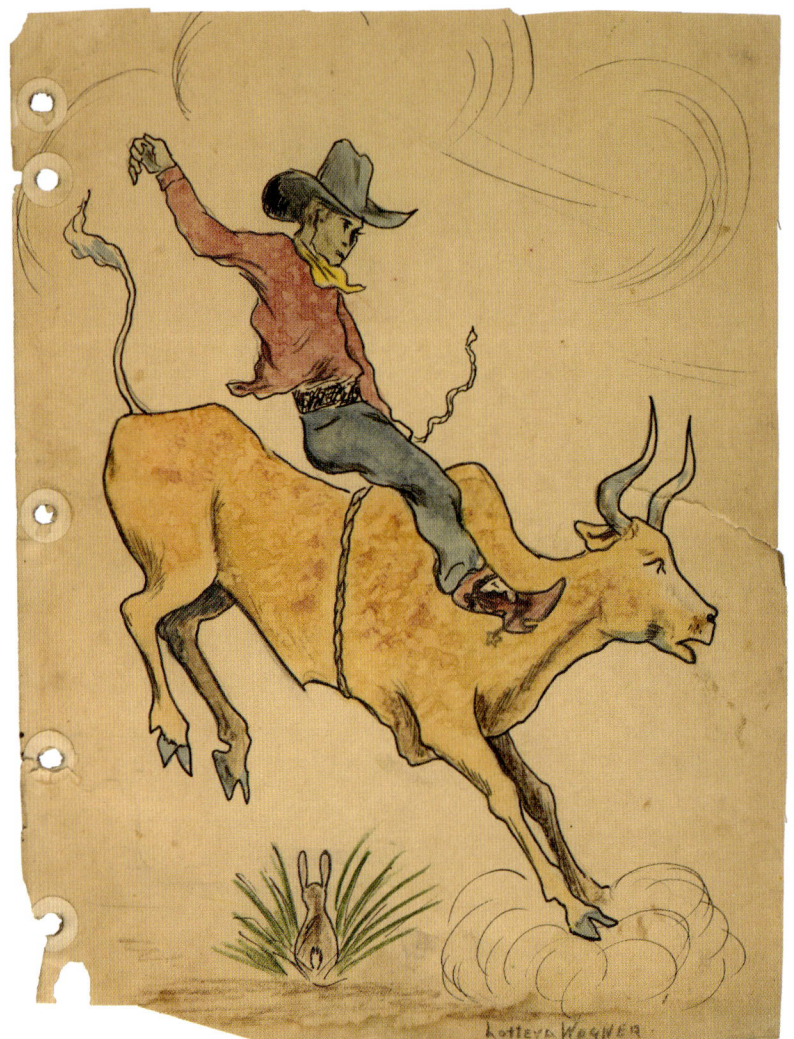

94

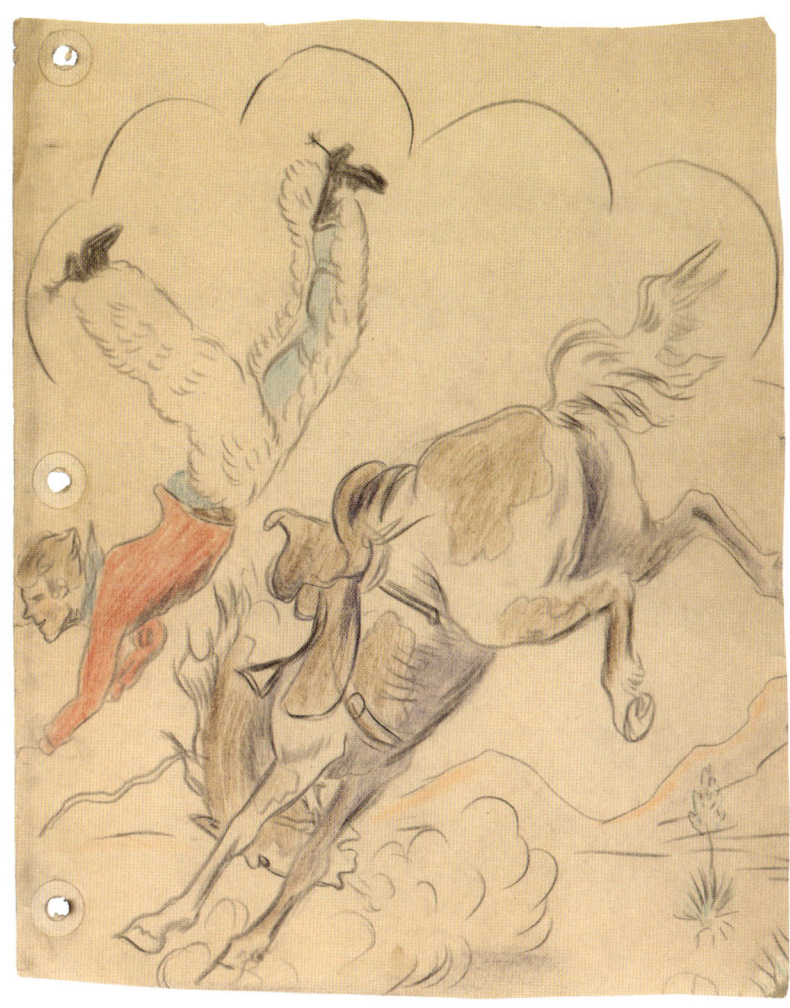

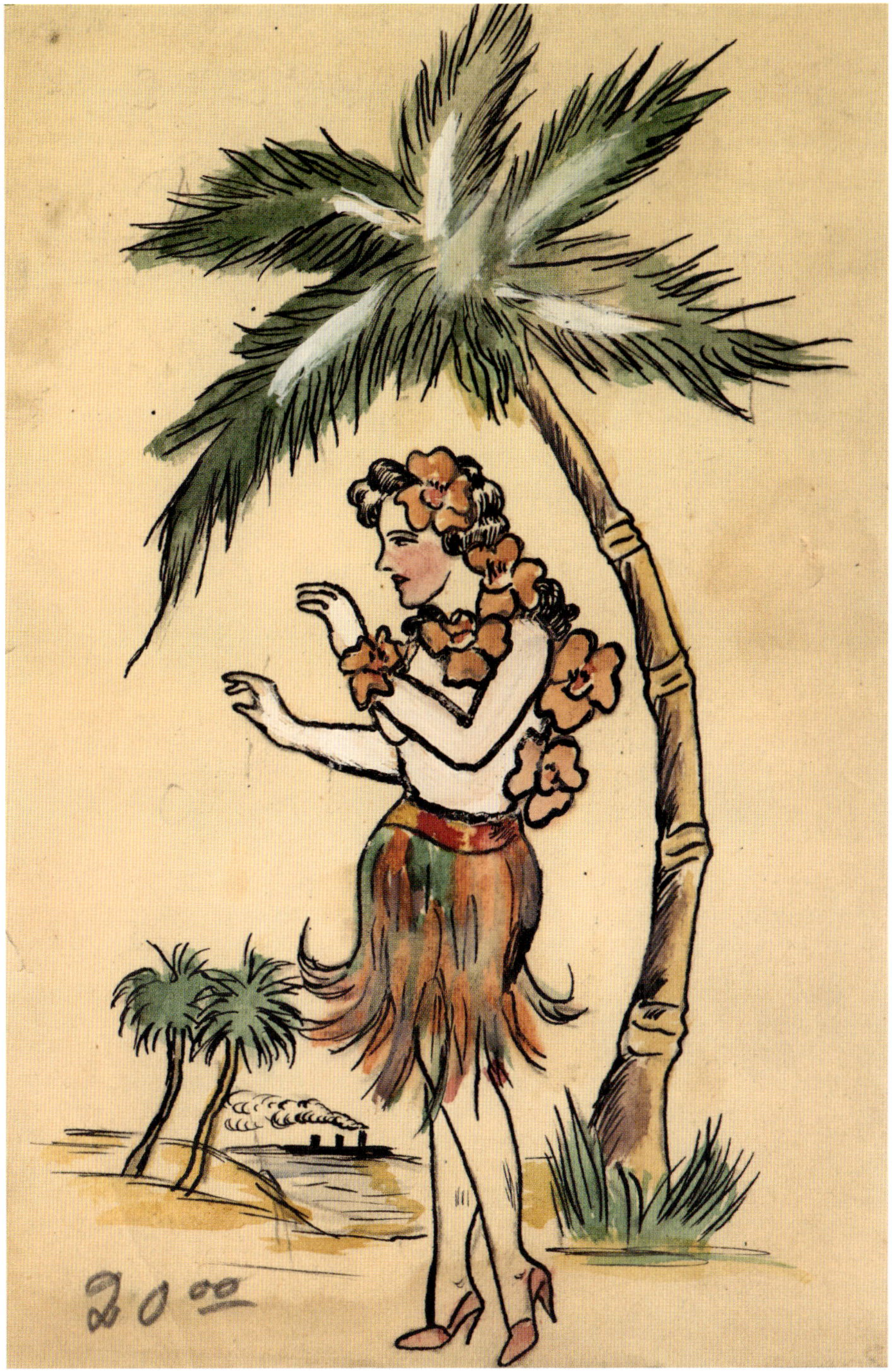

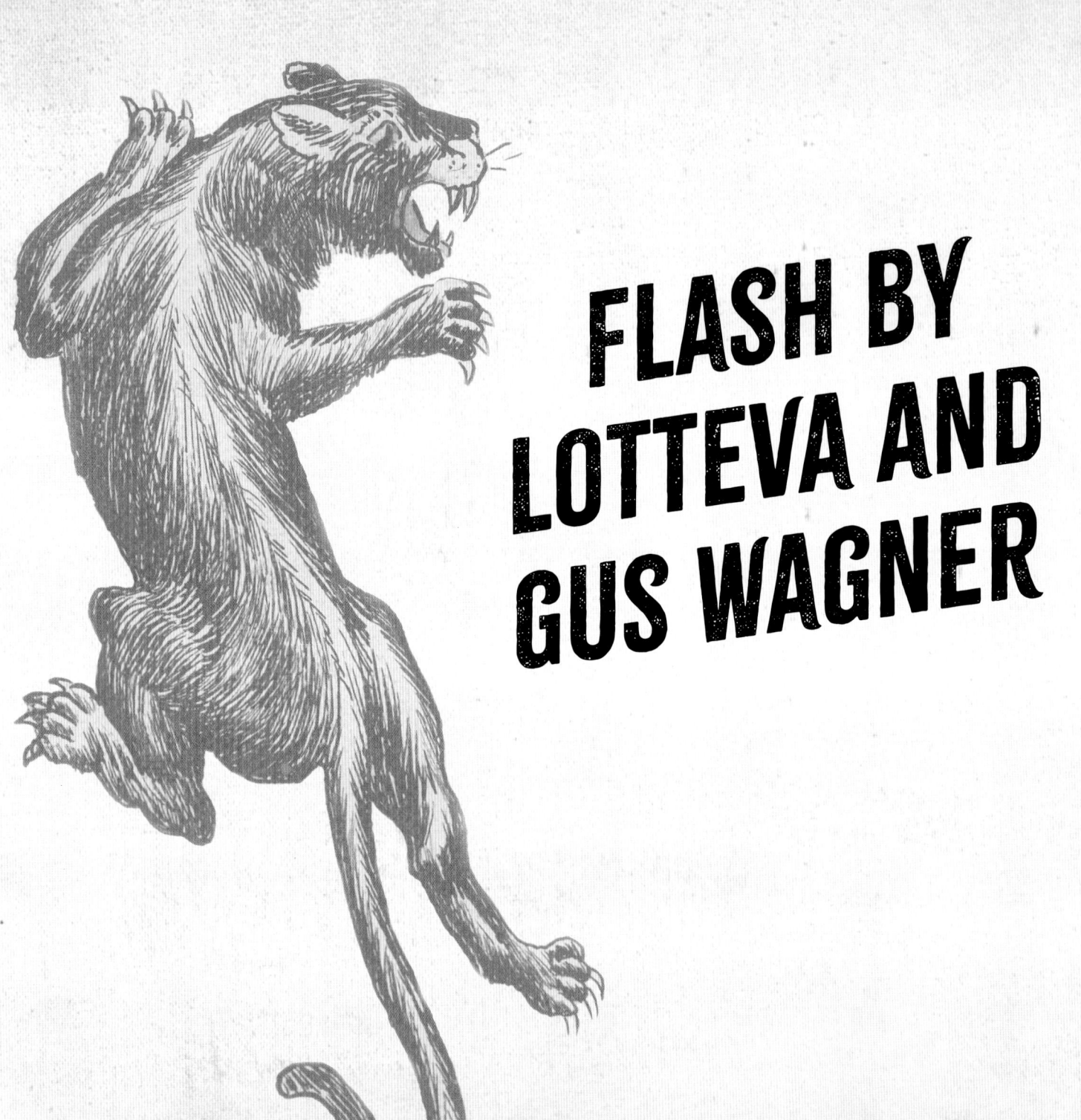

FLASH BY LOTTEVA AND GUS WAGNER

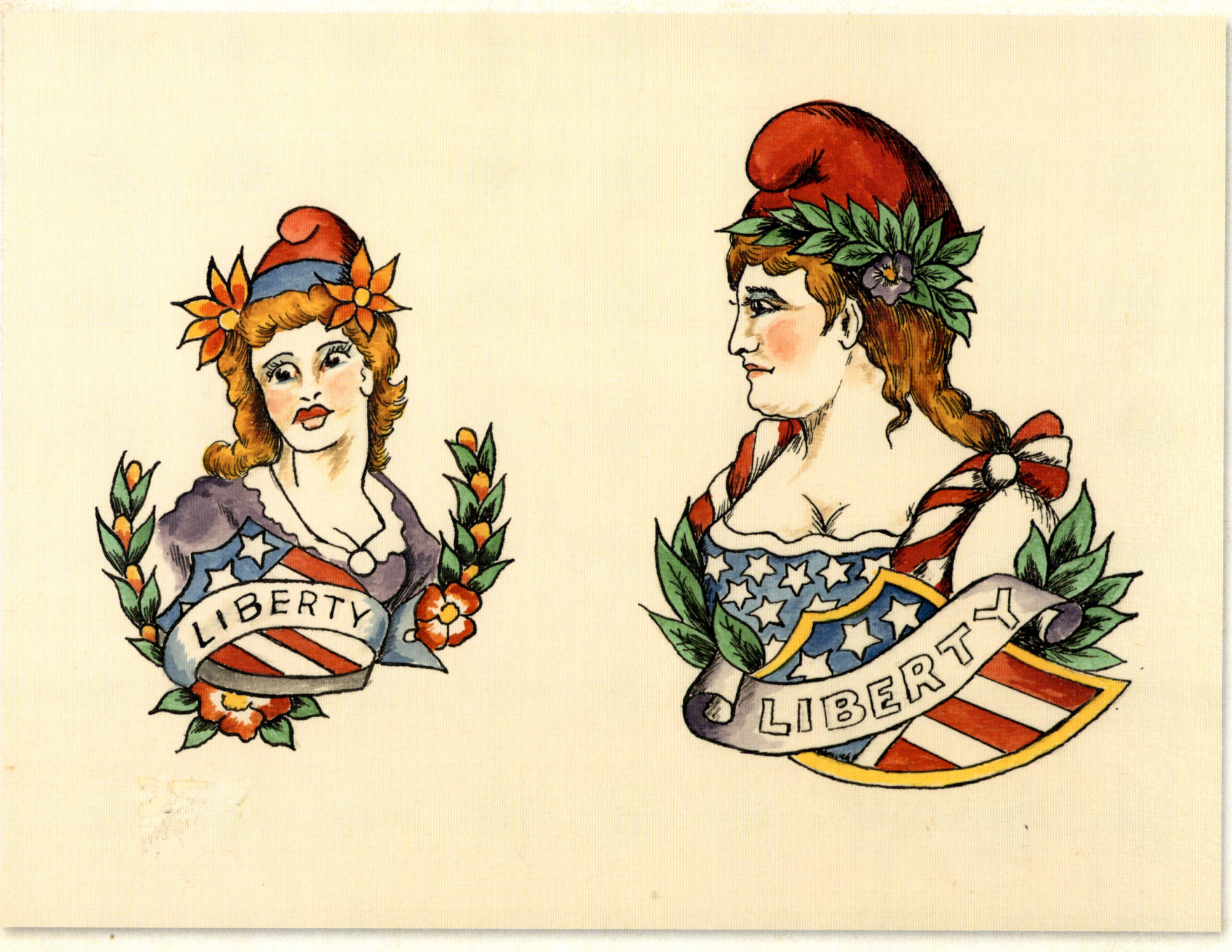

Lotteva Wagner Davis flash

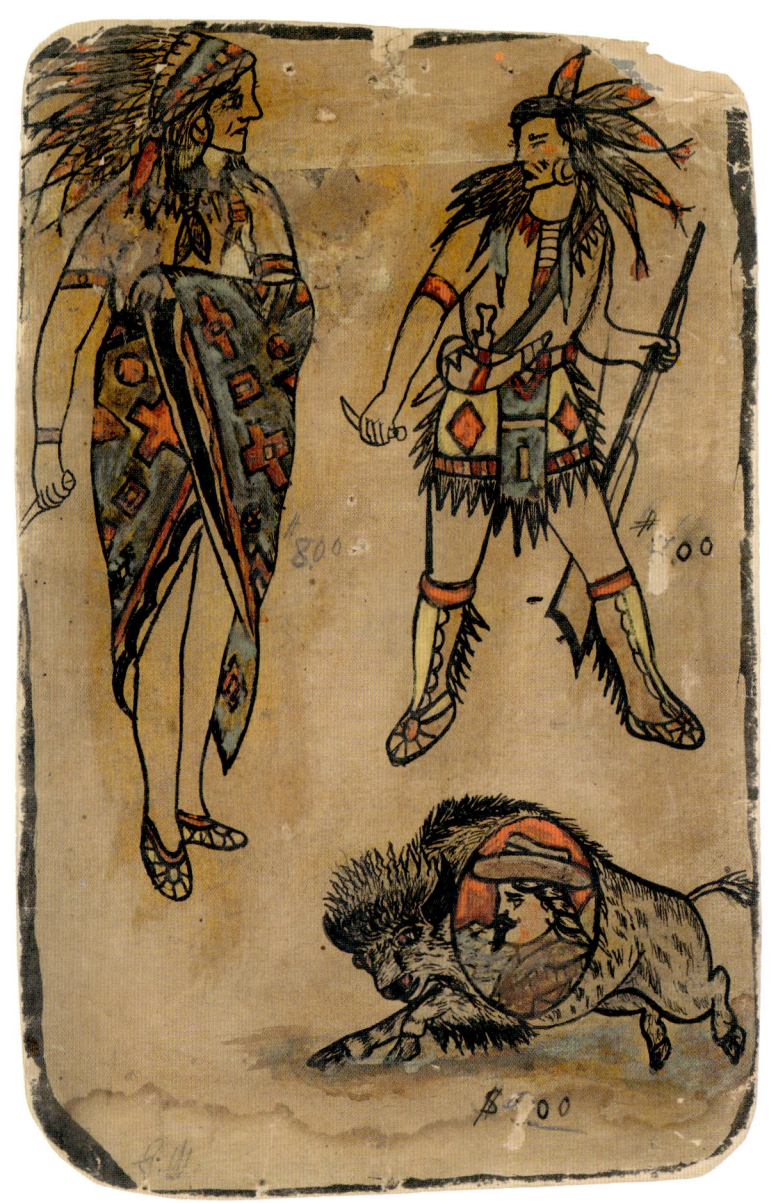

Gus Wagner flash

Lotteva Wagner Davis flash

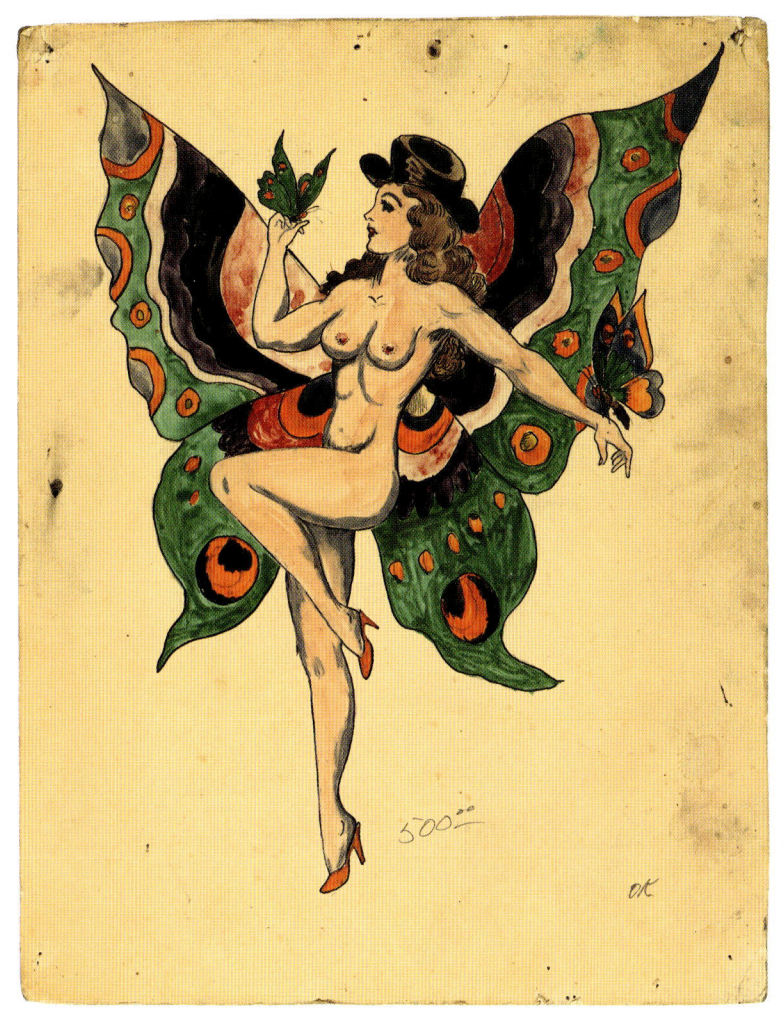

Gus Wagner flash

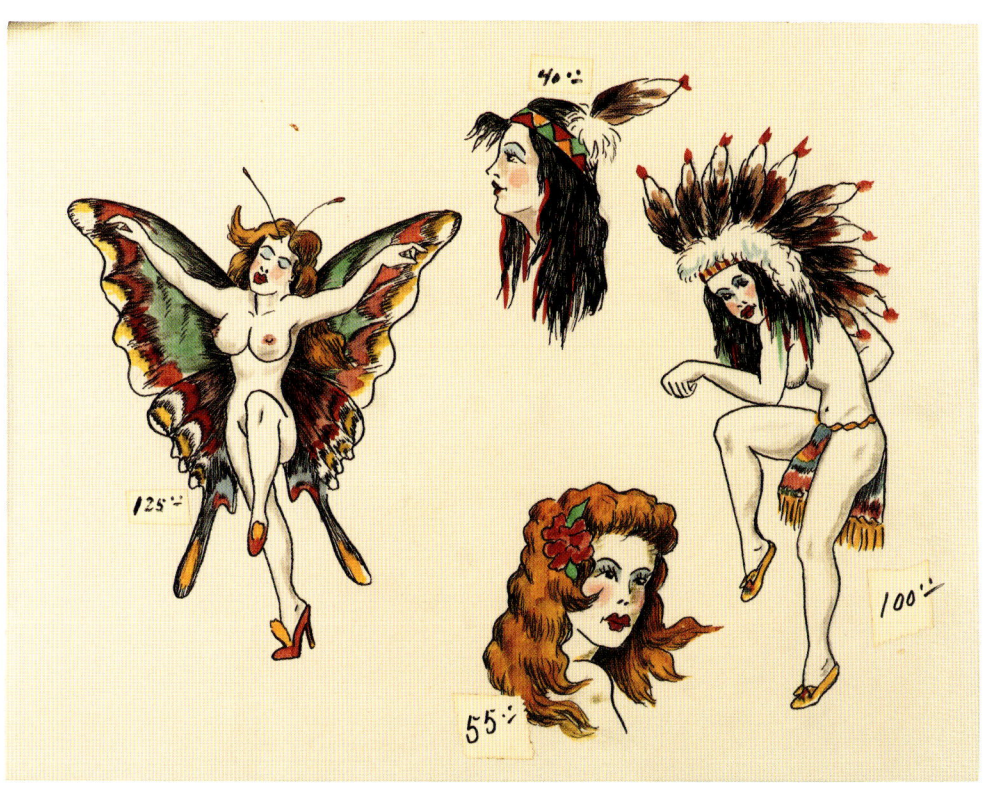

Lotteva Wagner Davis flash

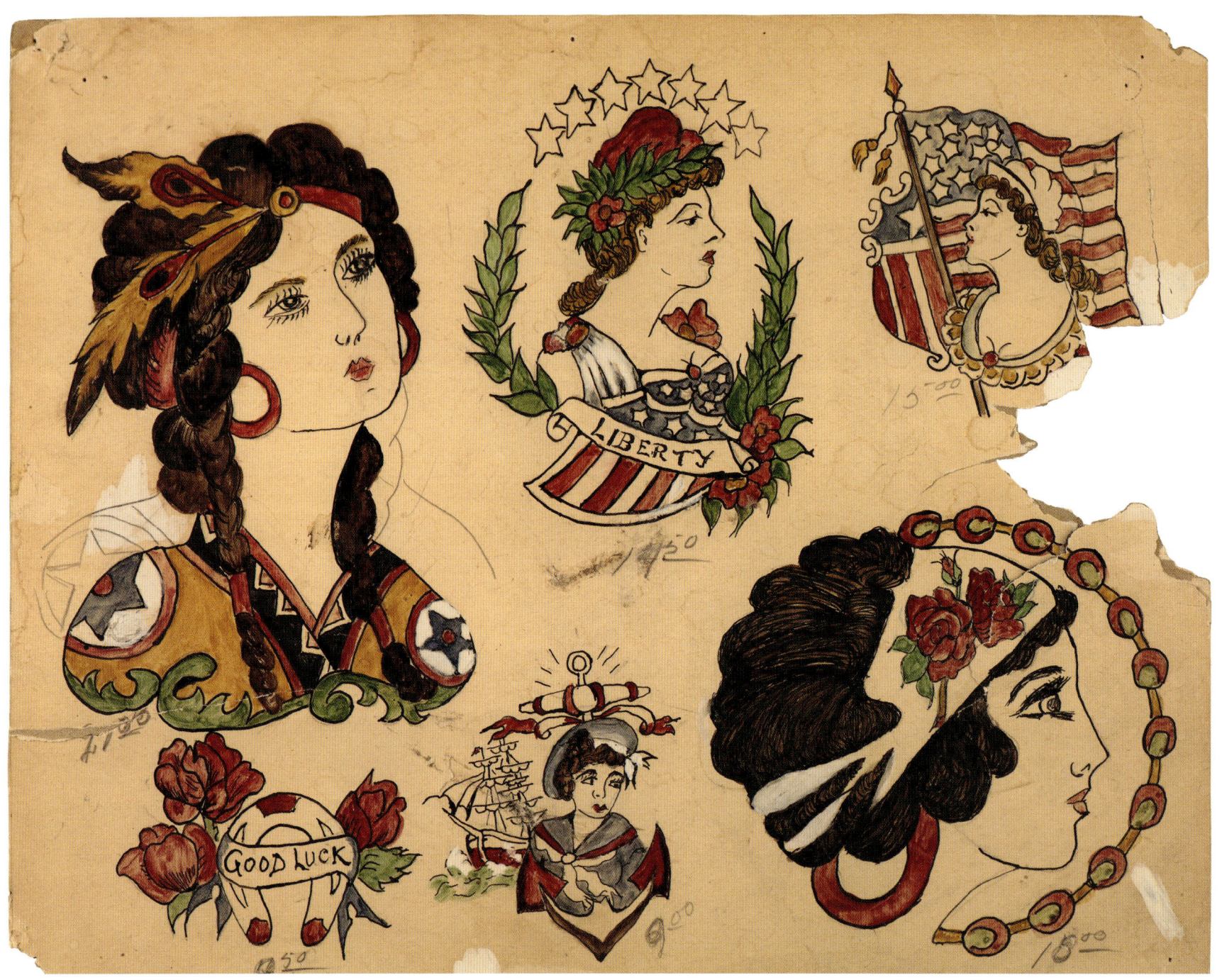

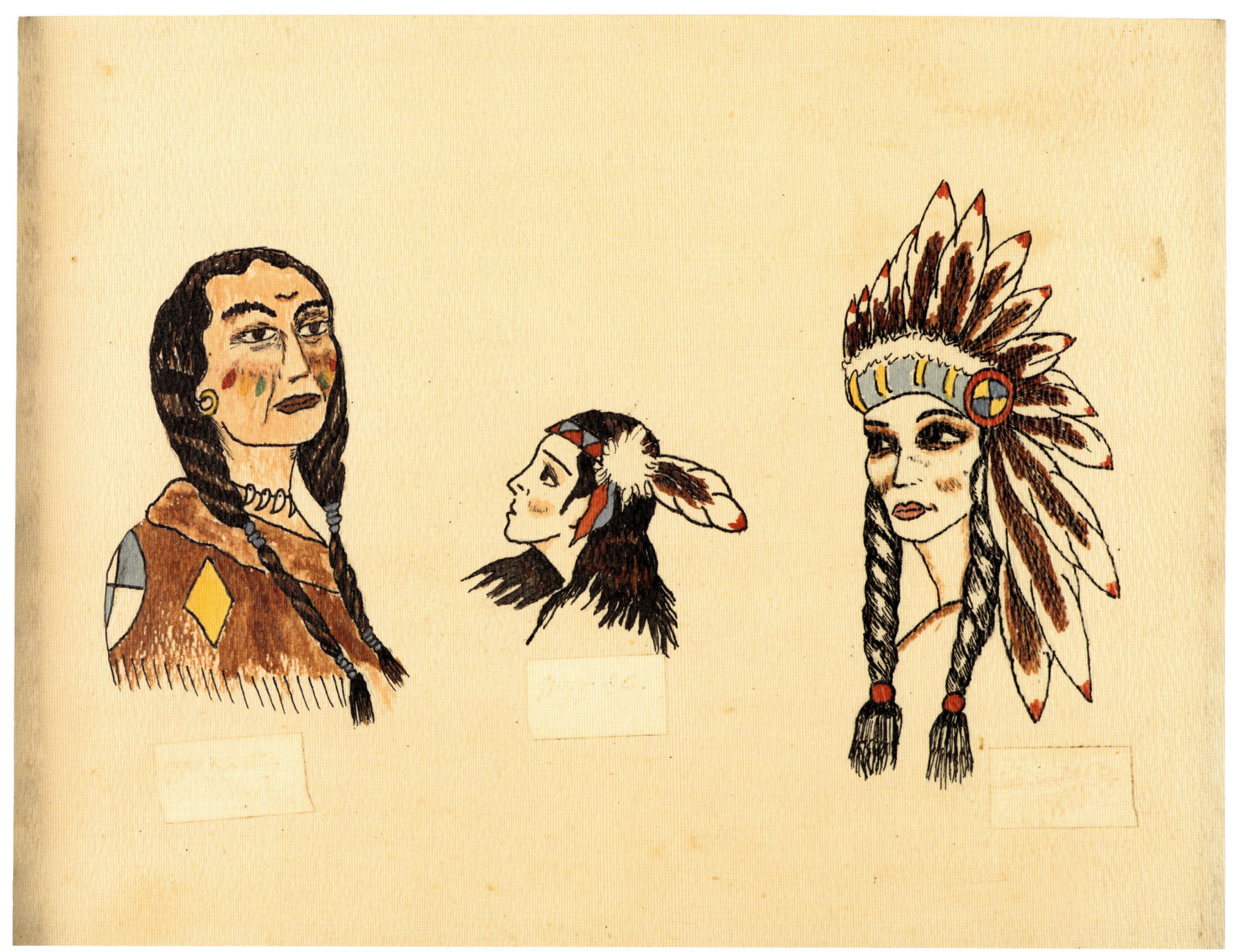

Lotteva Wagner Davis flash

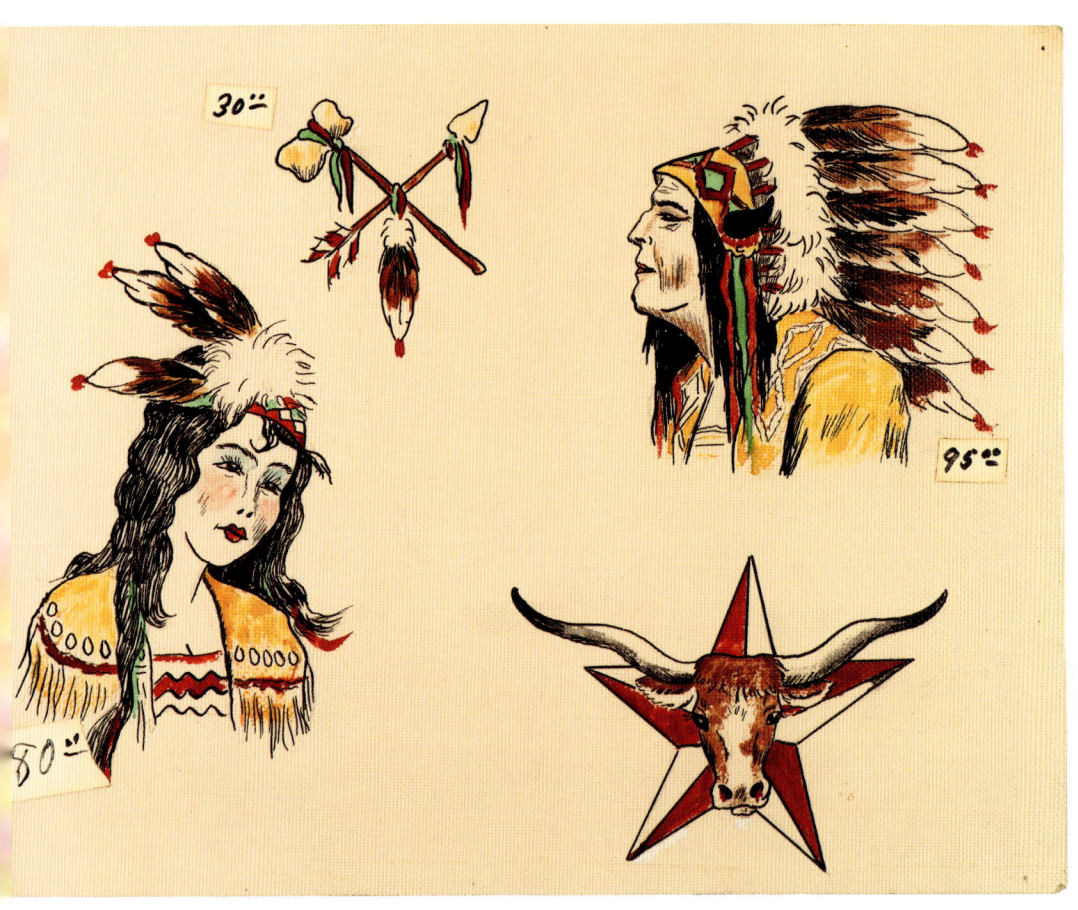

Lotteva Wagner Davis flash

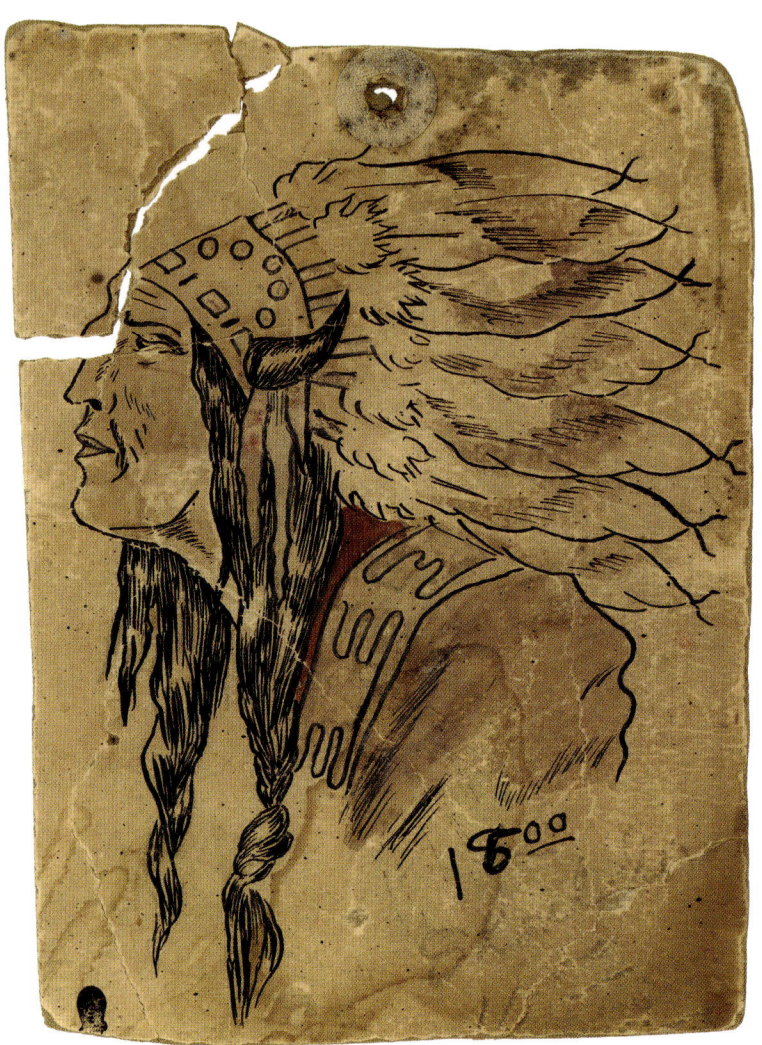

Gus Wagner flash

Flash by Lotteva and Gus Wagner

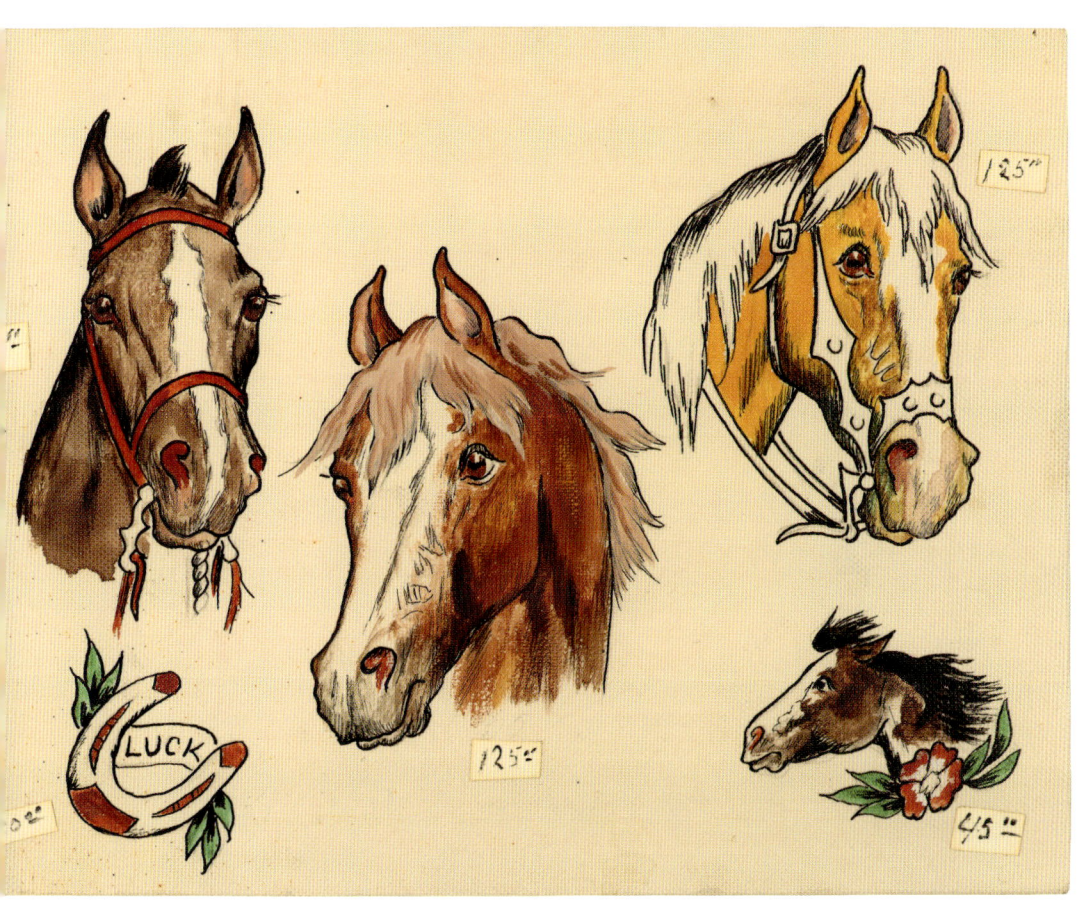

Lotteva Wagner Davis flash

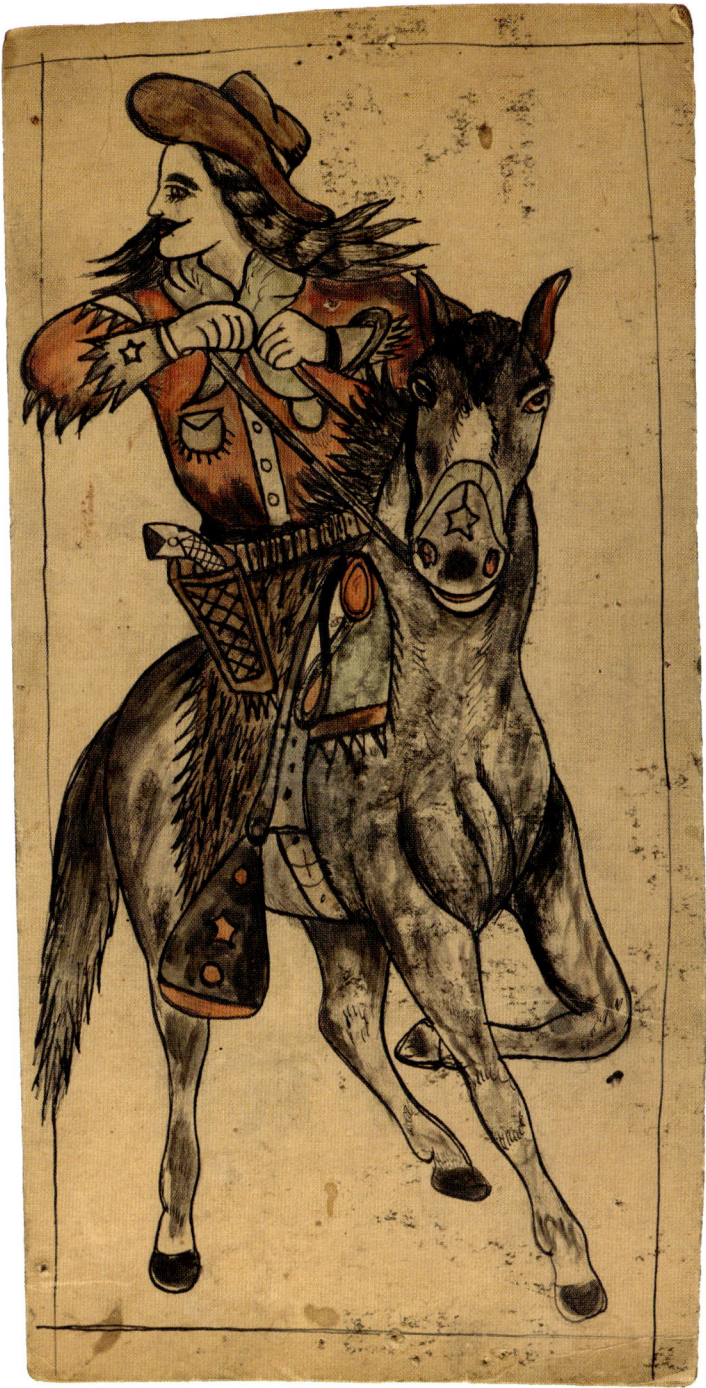

Gus Wagner flash

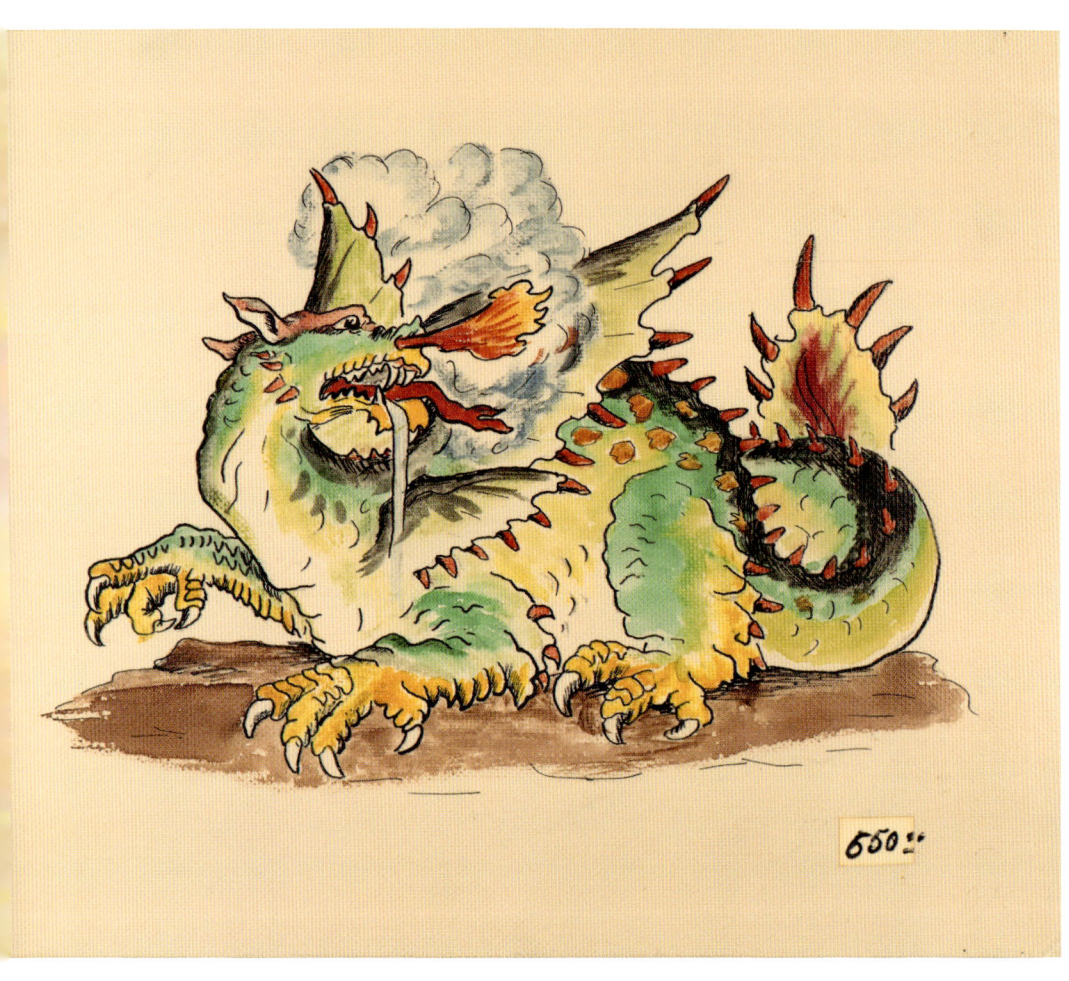

Lotteva Wagner Davis flash

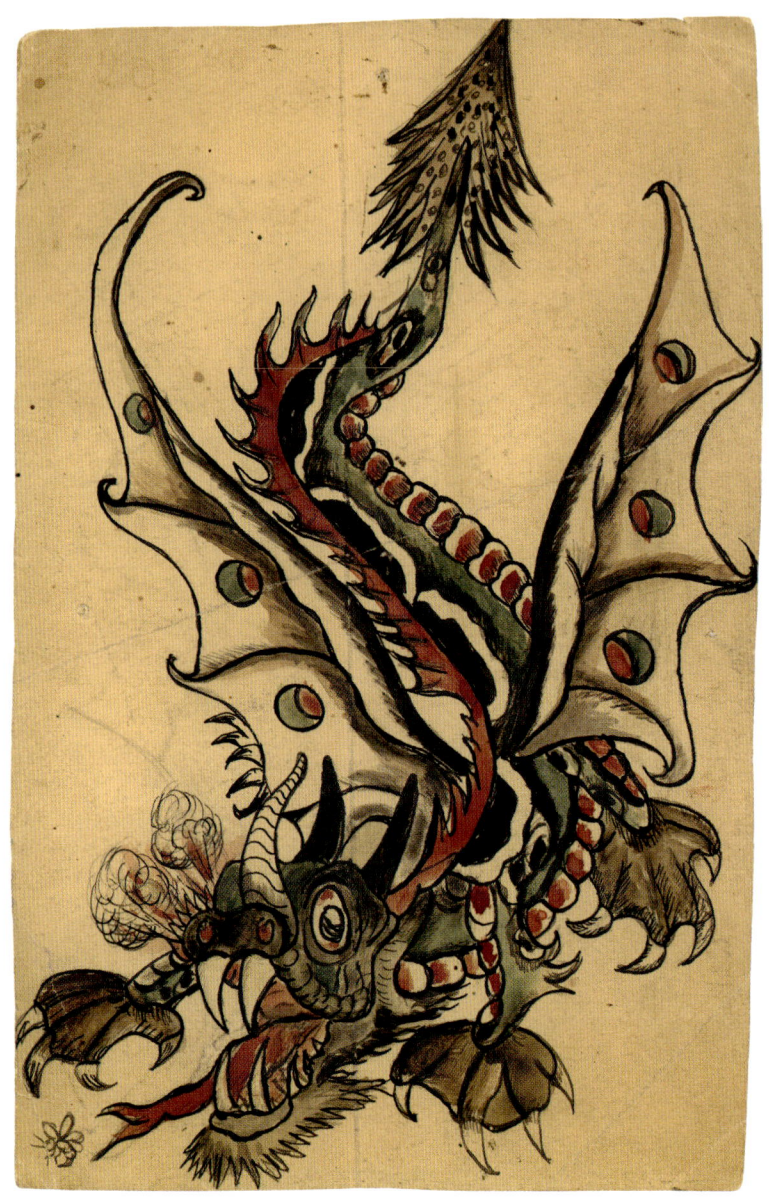

Gus Wagner flash

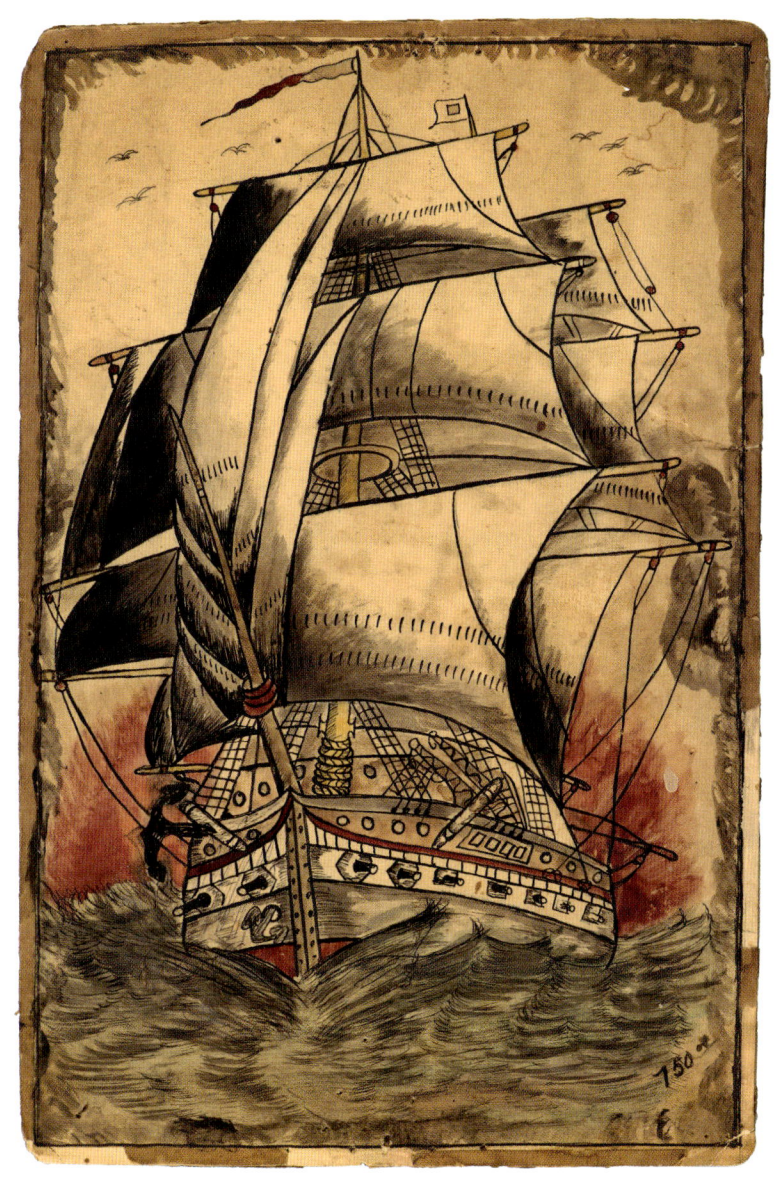

Gus Wagner flash

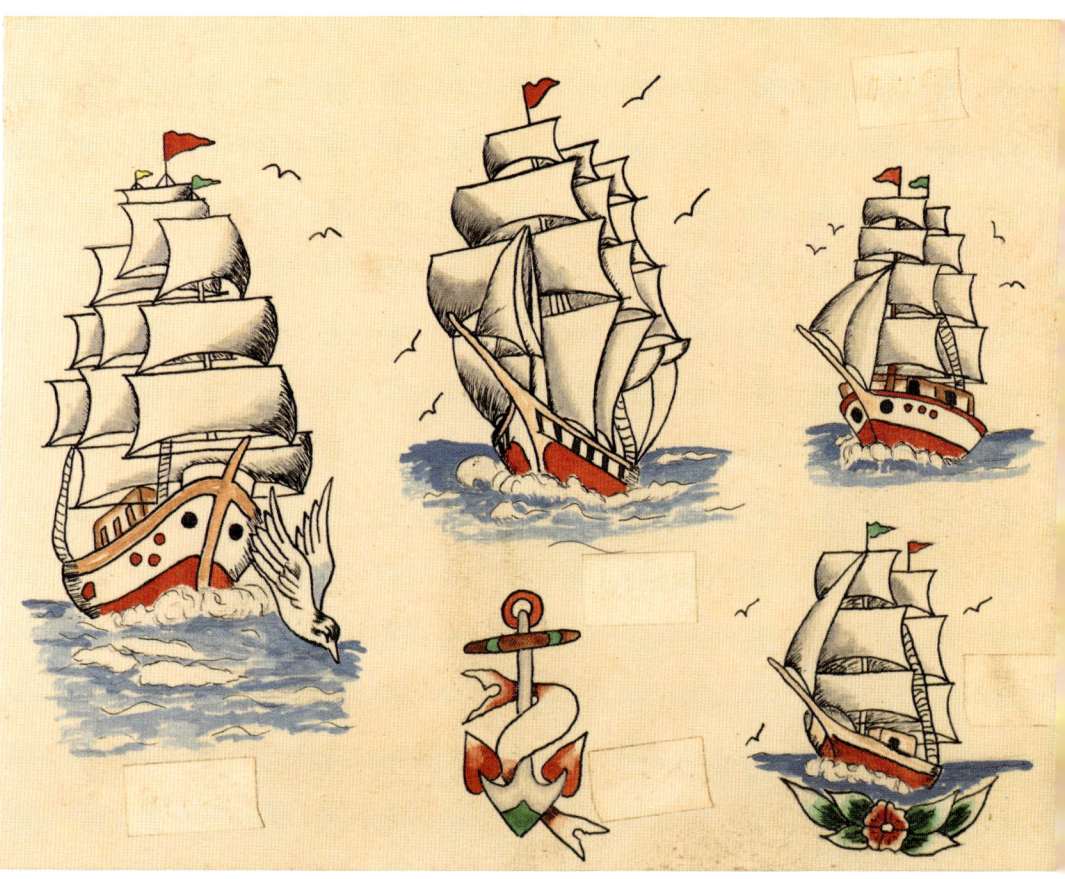

Lotteva Wagner Davis flash

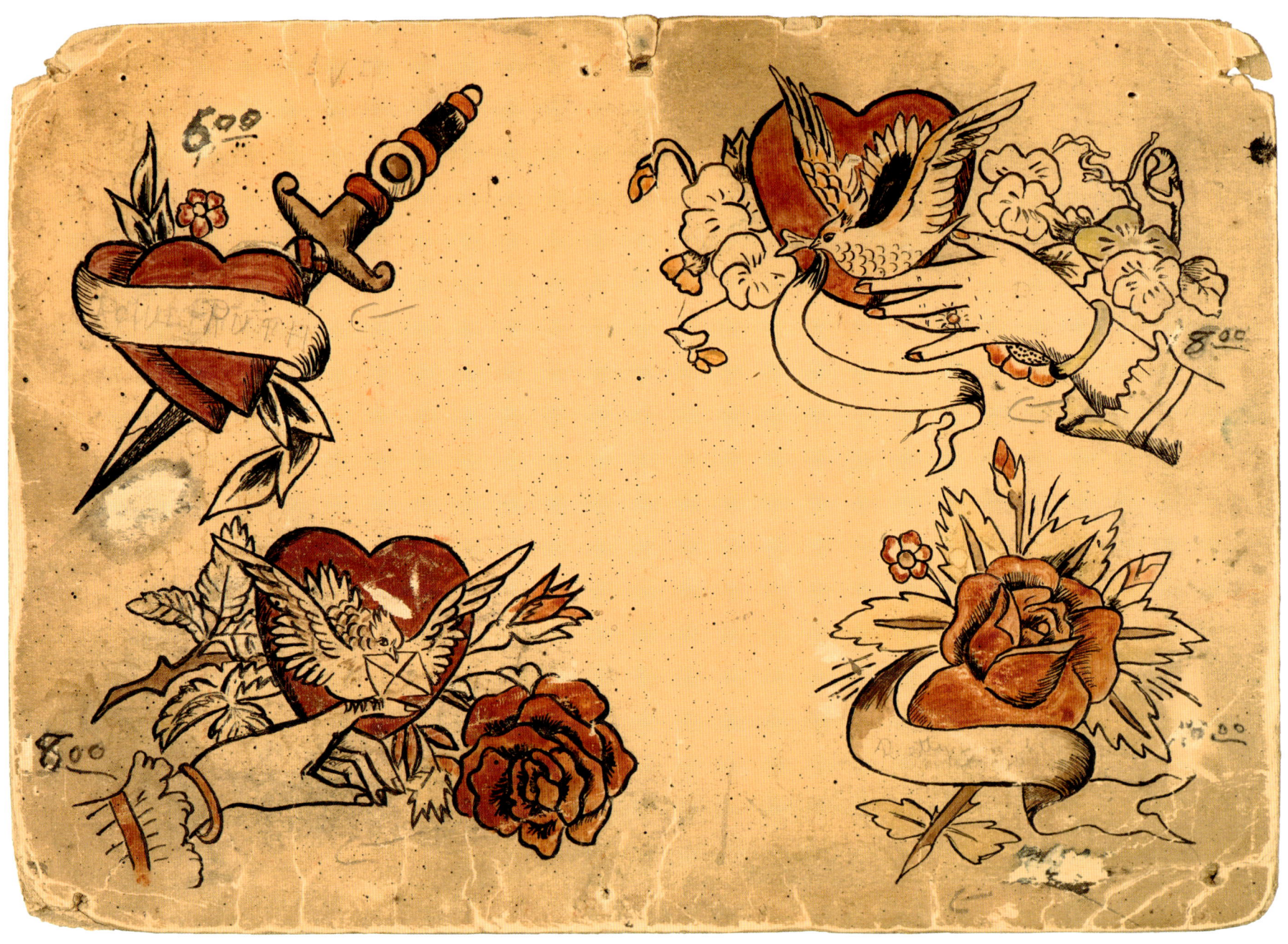

Flash by Lotteva and Gus Wagner

Gus Wagner flash

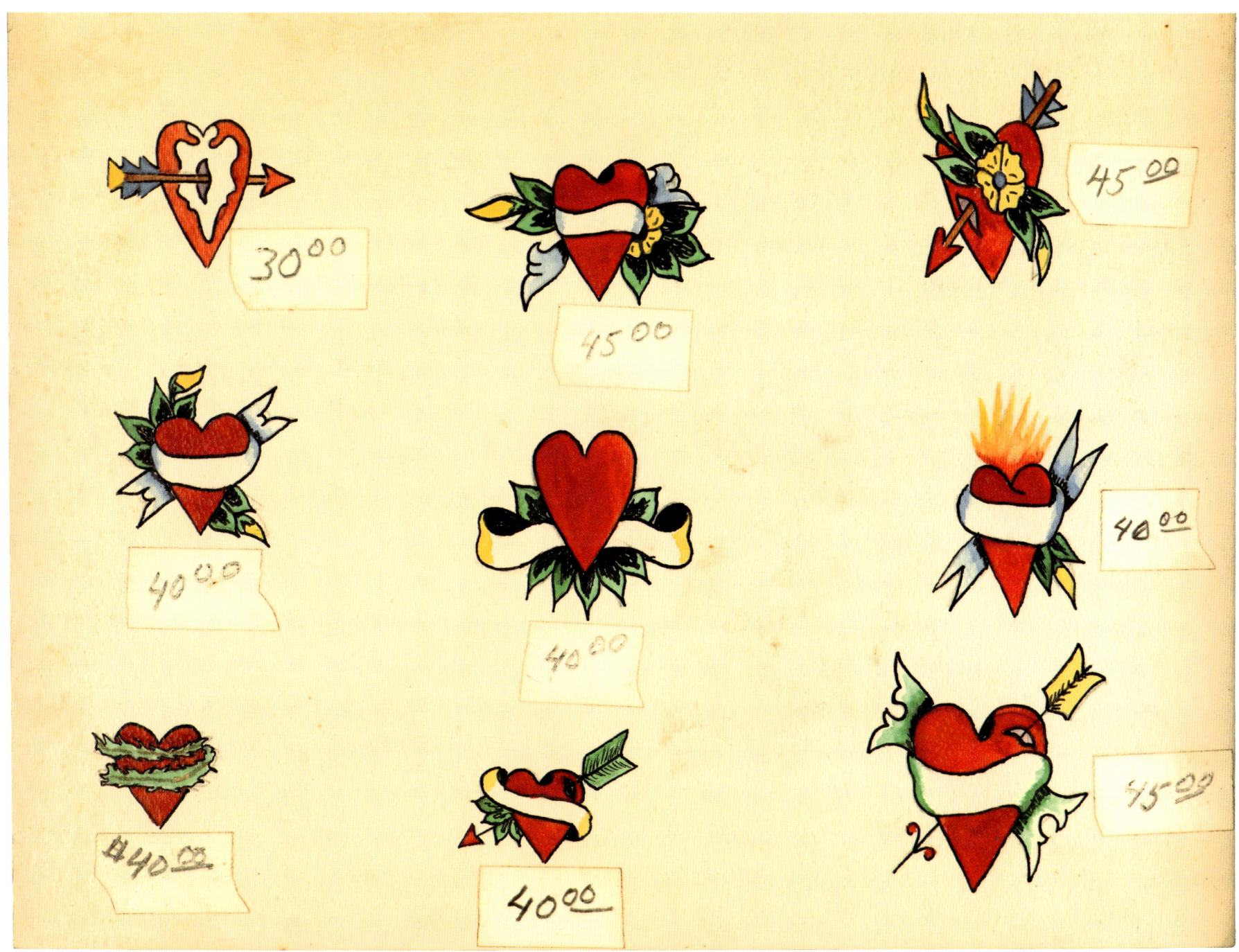

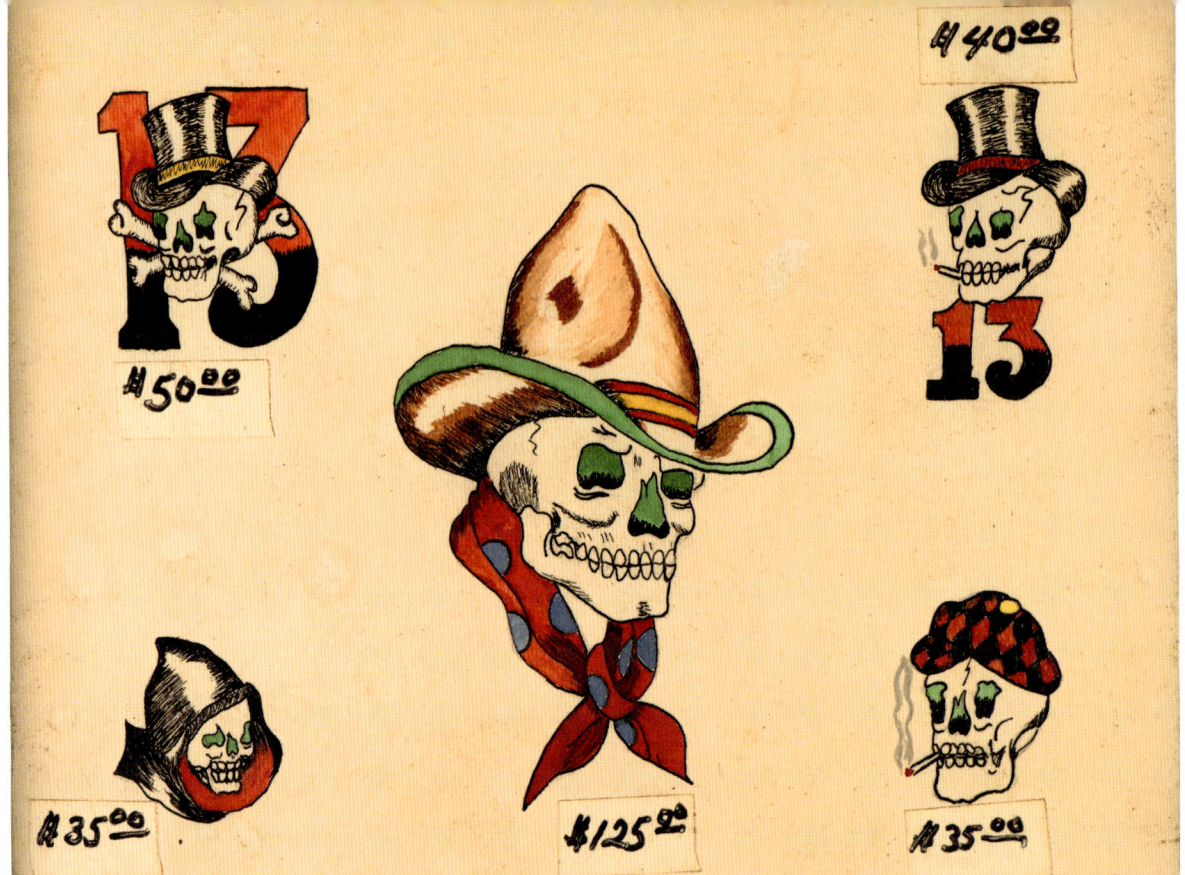

Lotteva Wagner Davis flash

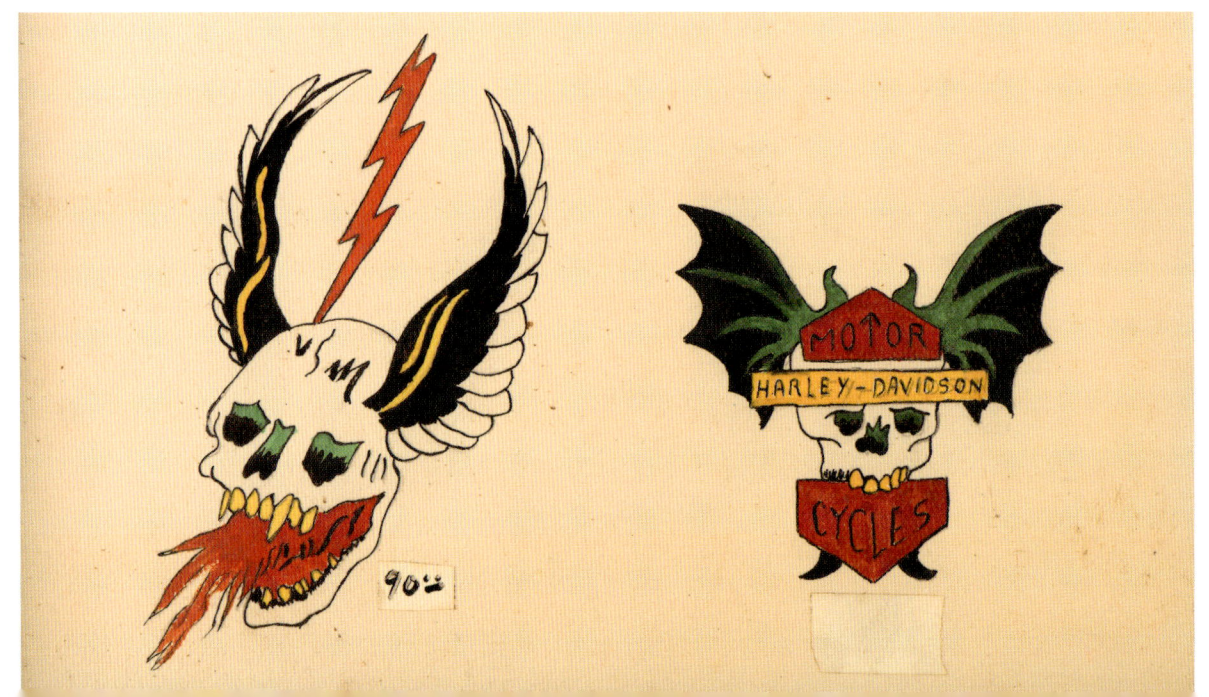

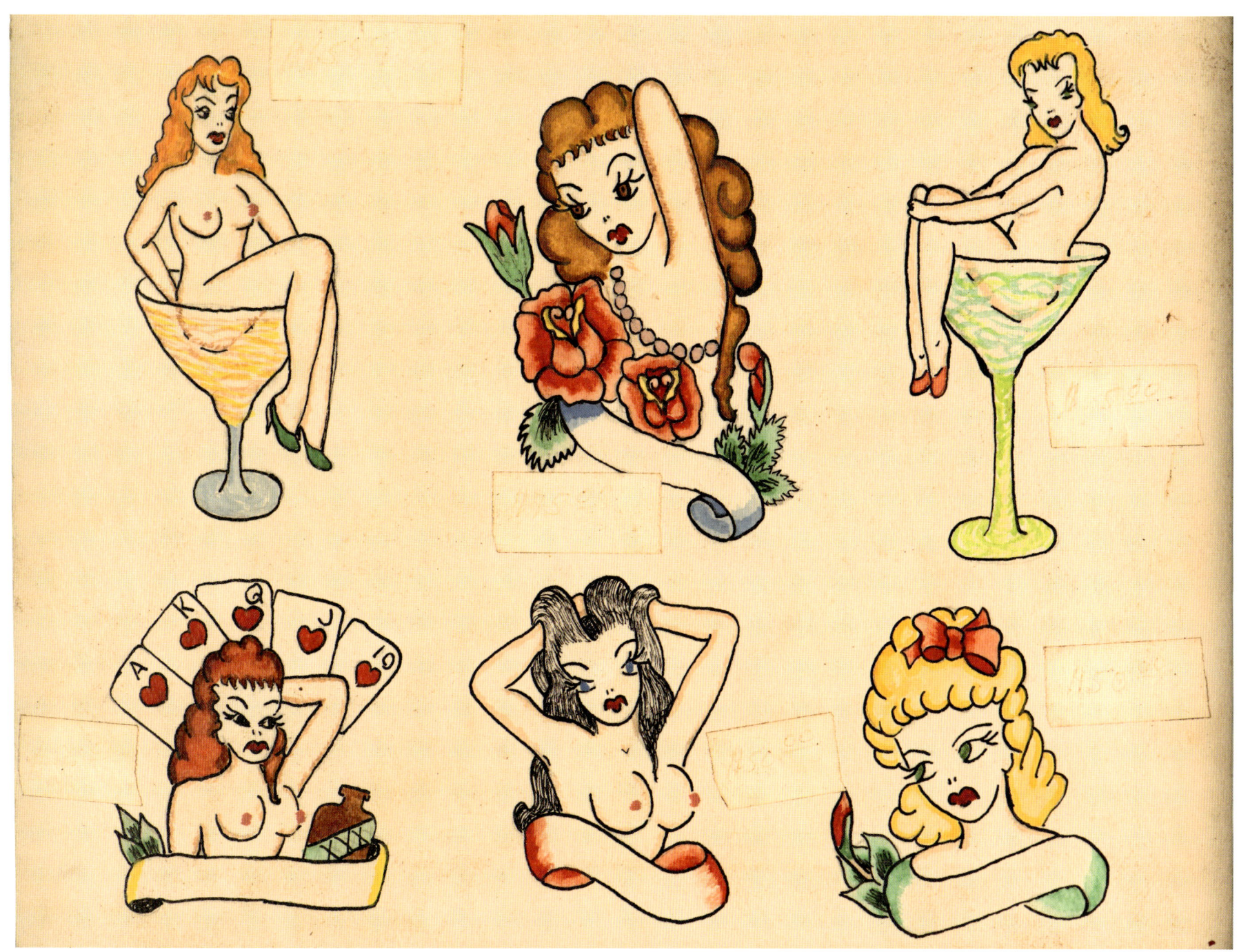

Lotteva Wagner Davis flash

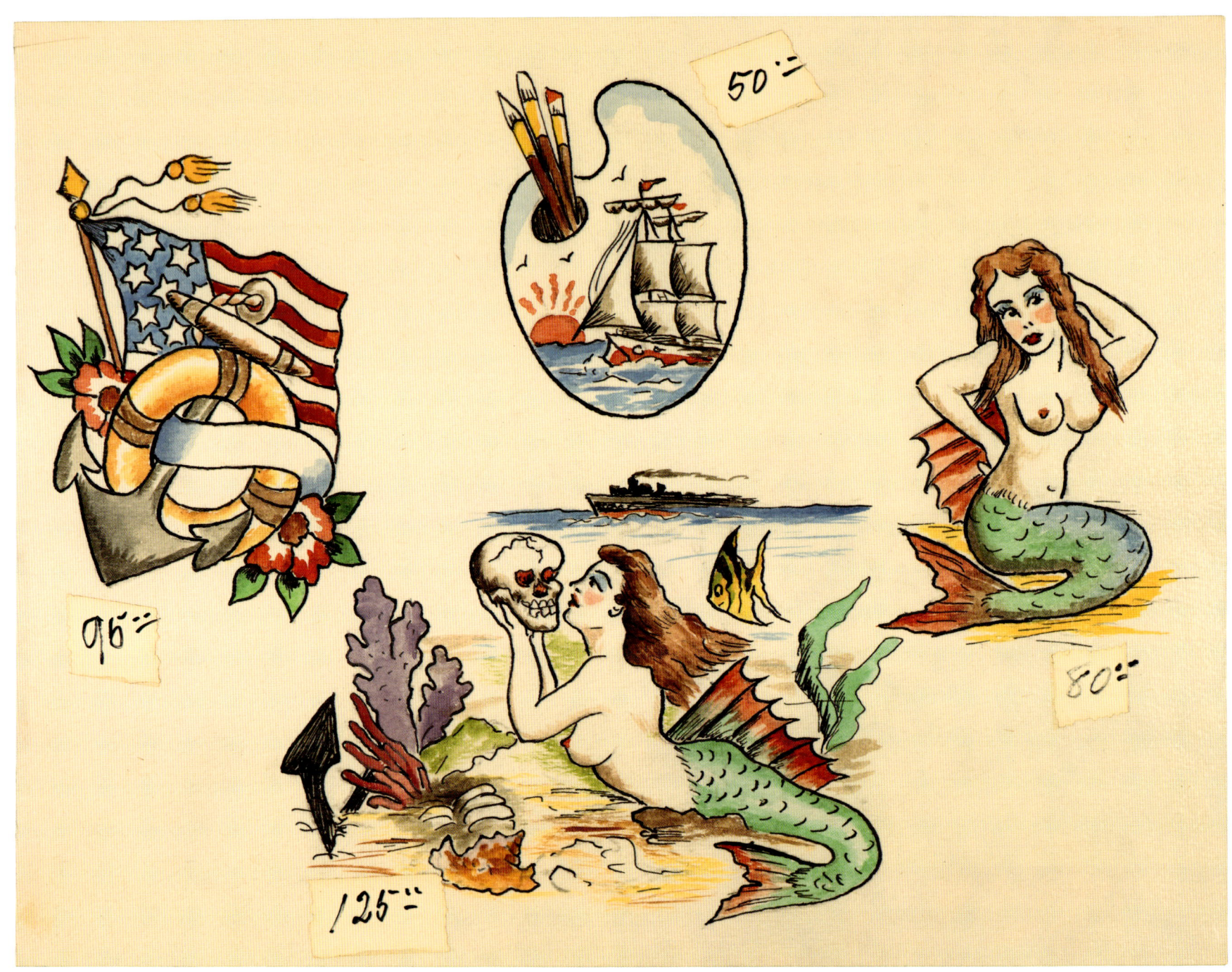

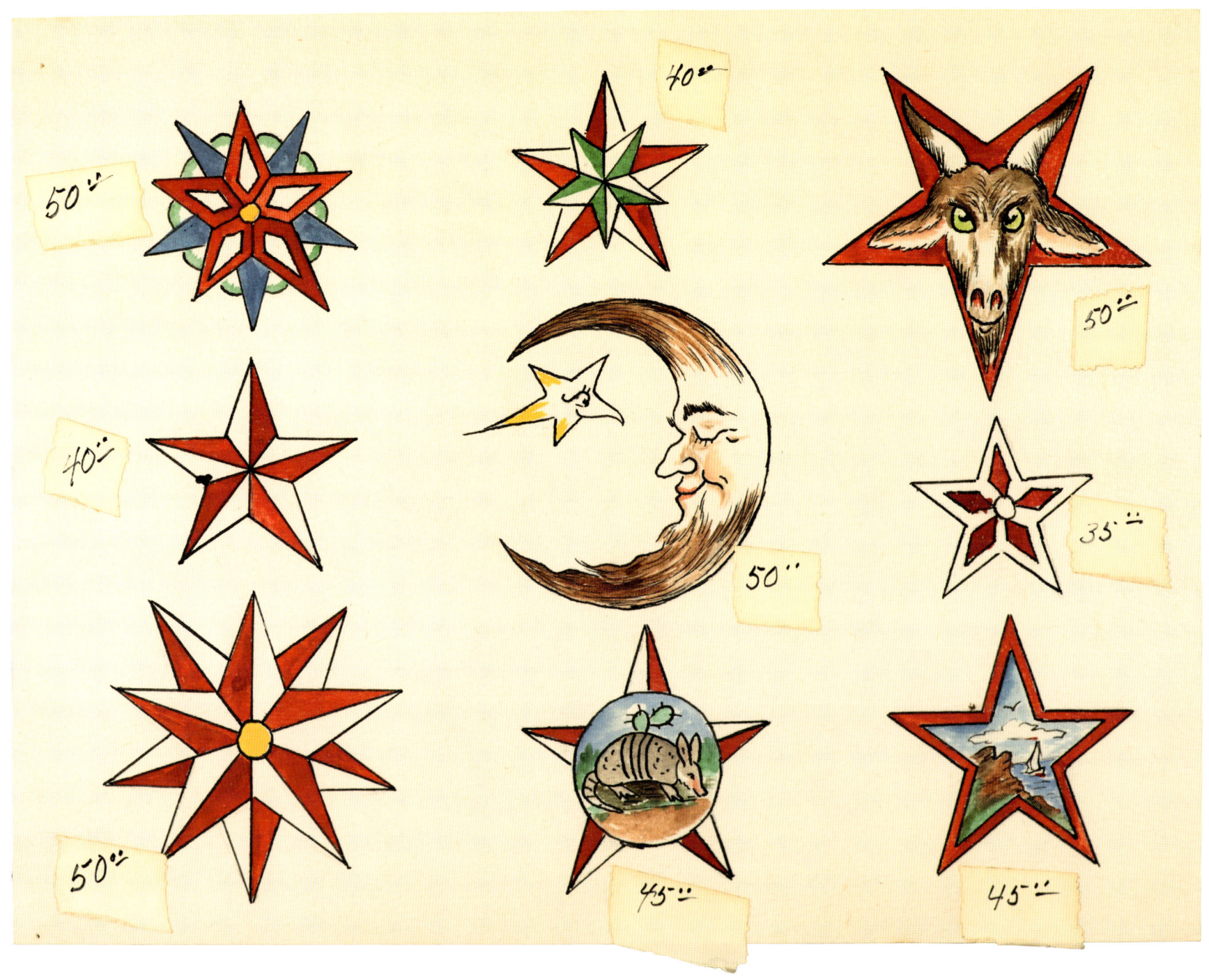

Lotteva Wagner Davis flash

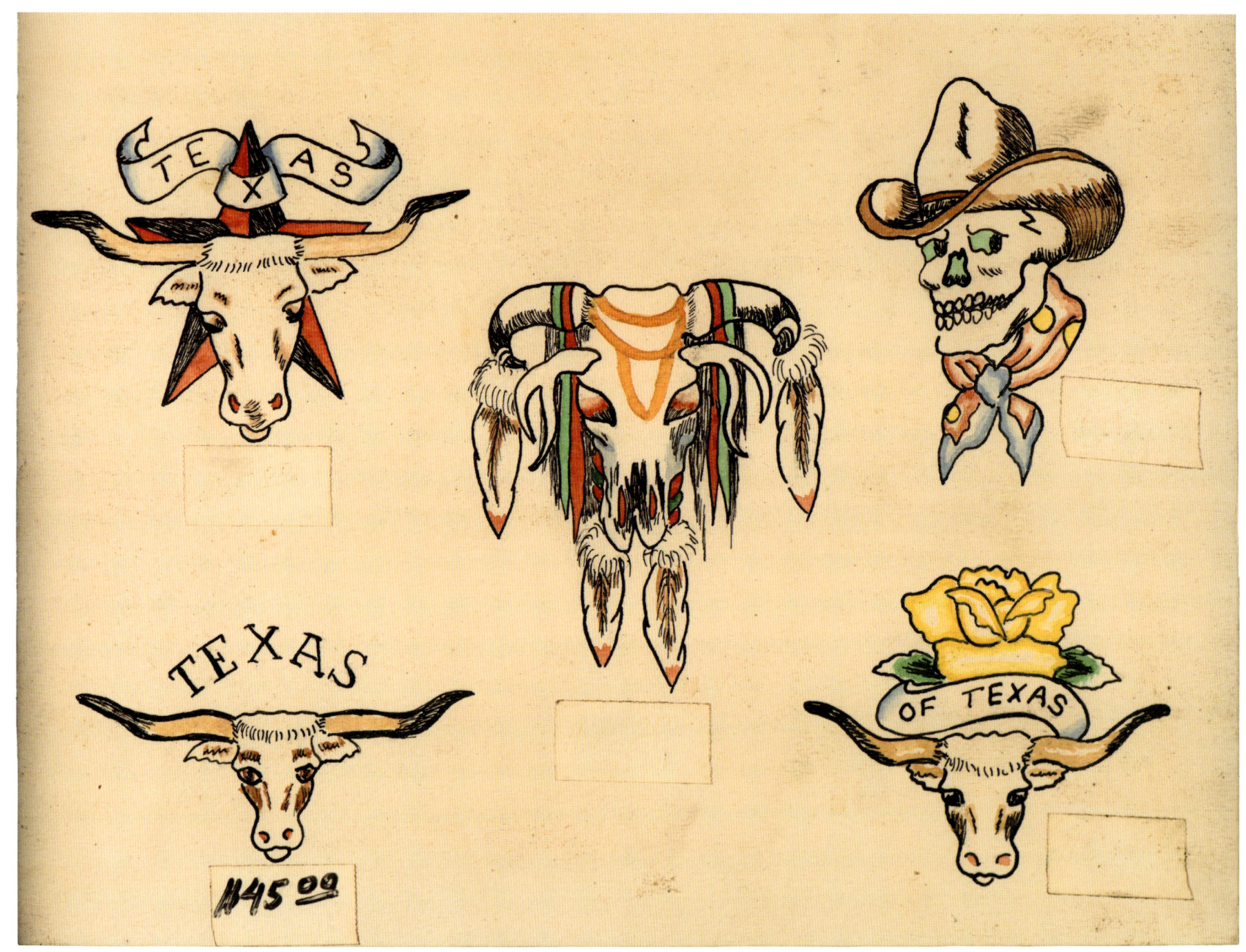

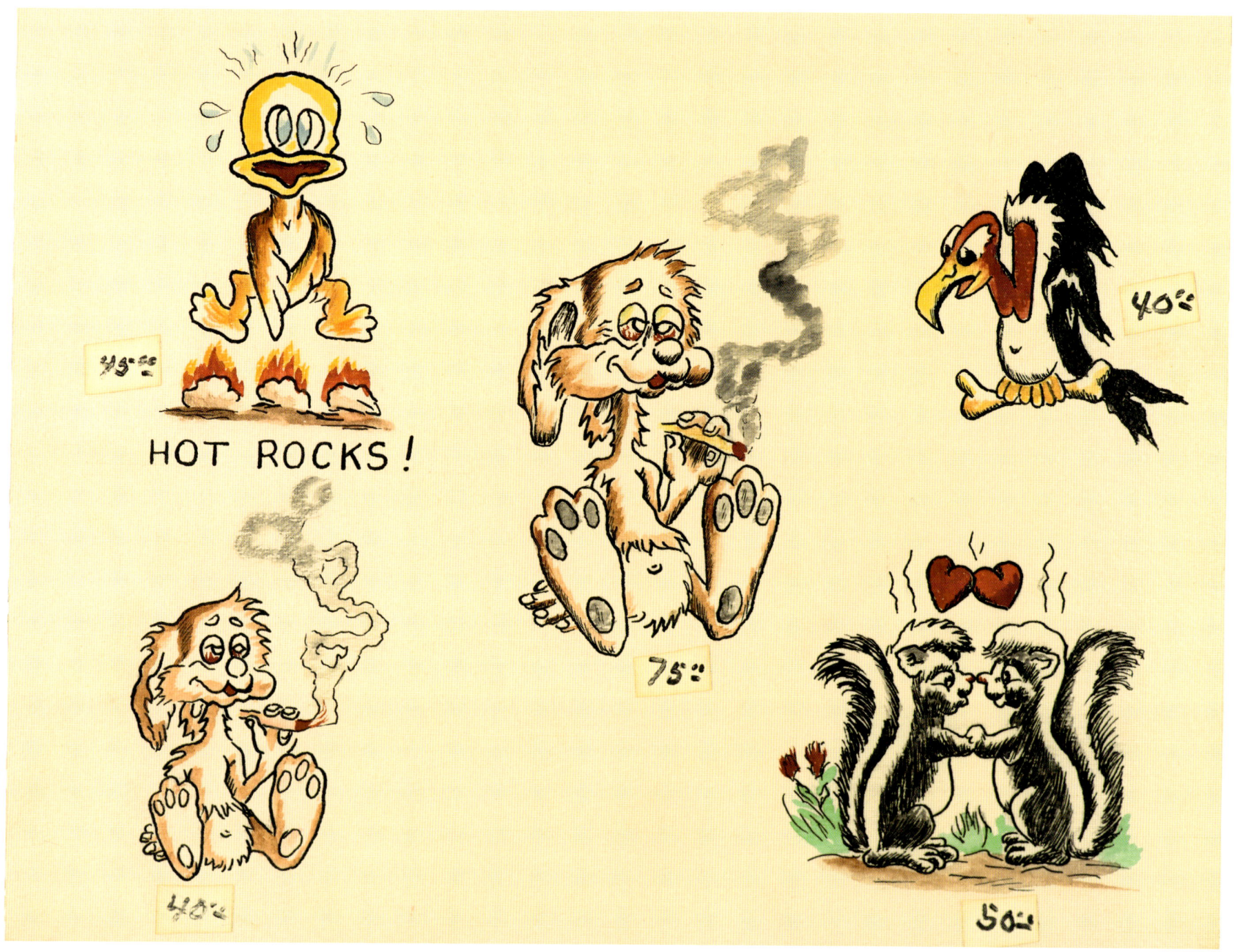

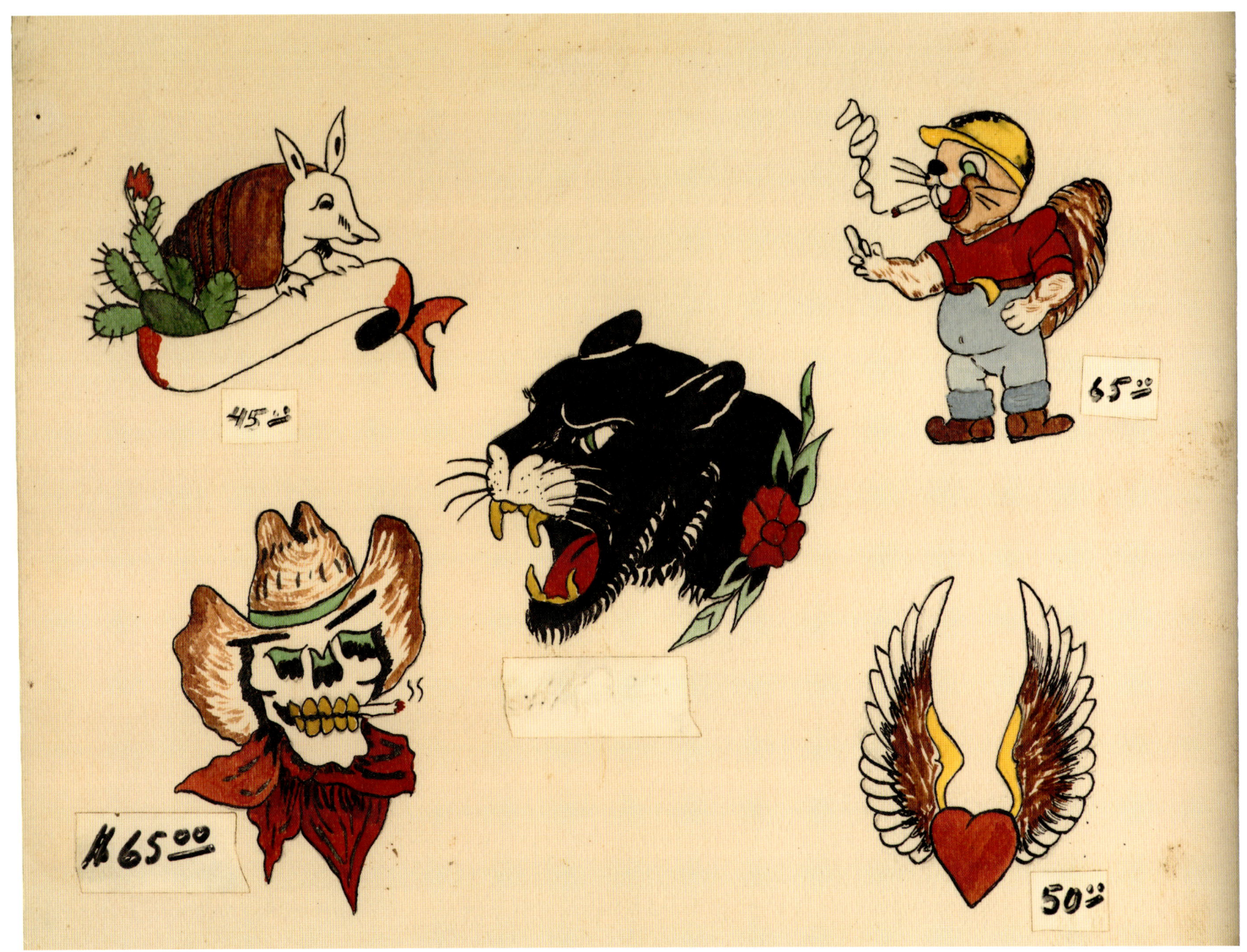

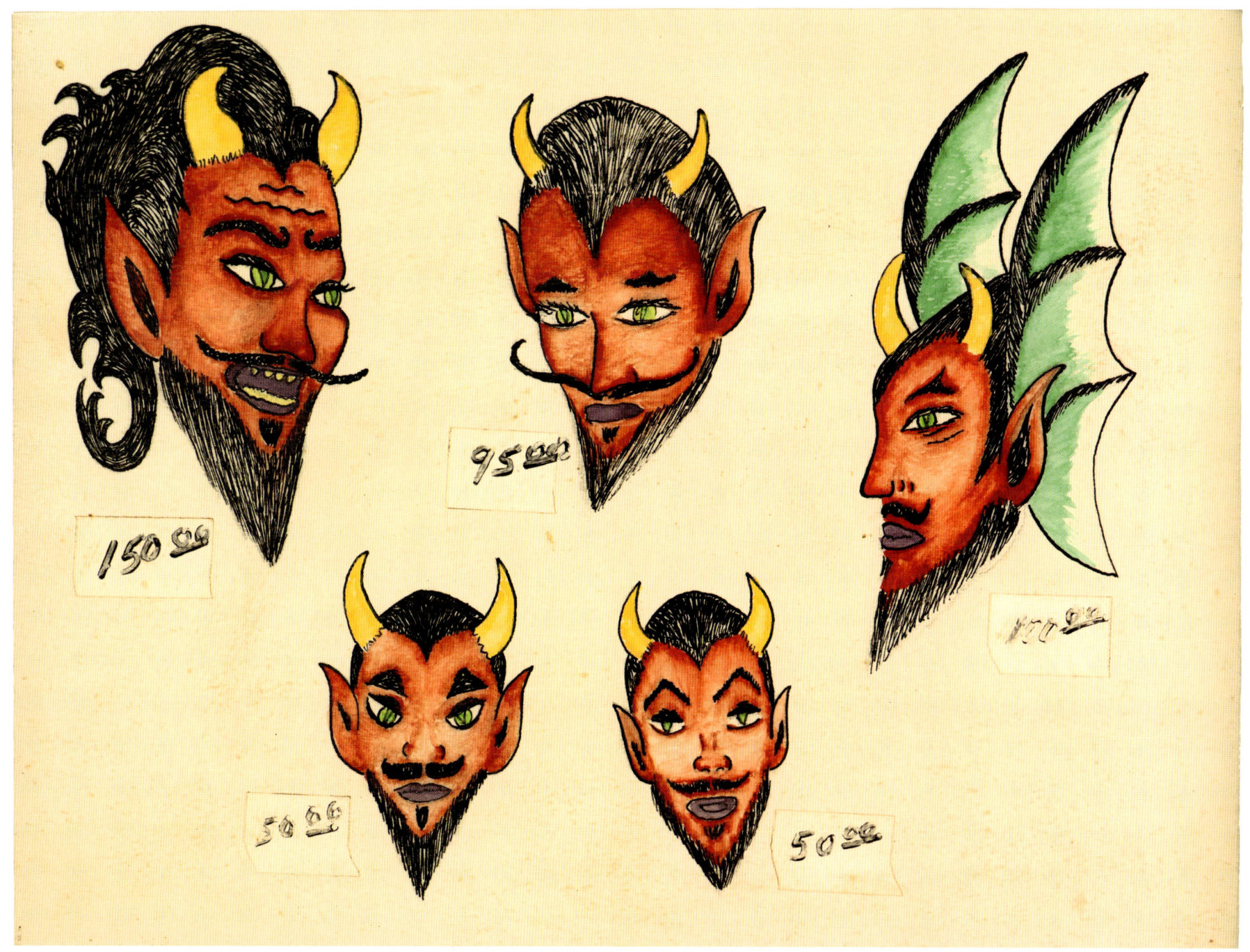

Lotteva Wagner Davis flash

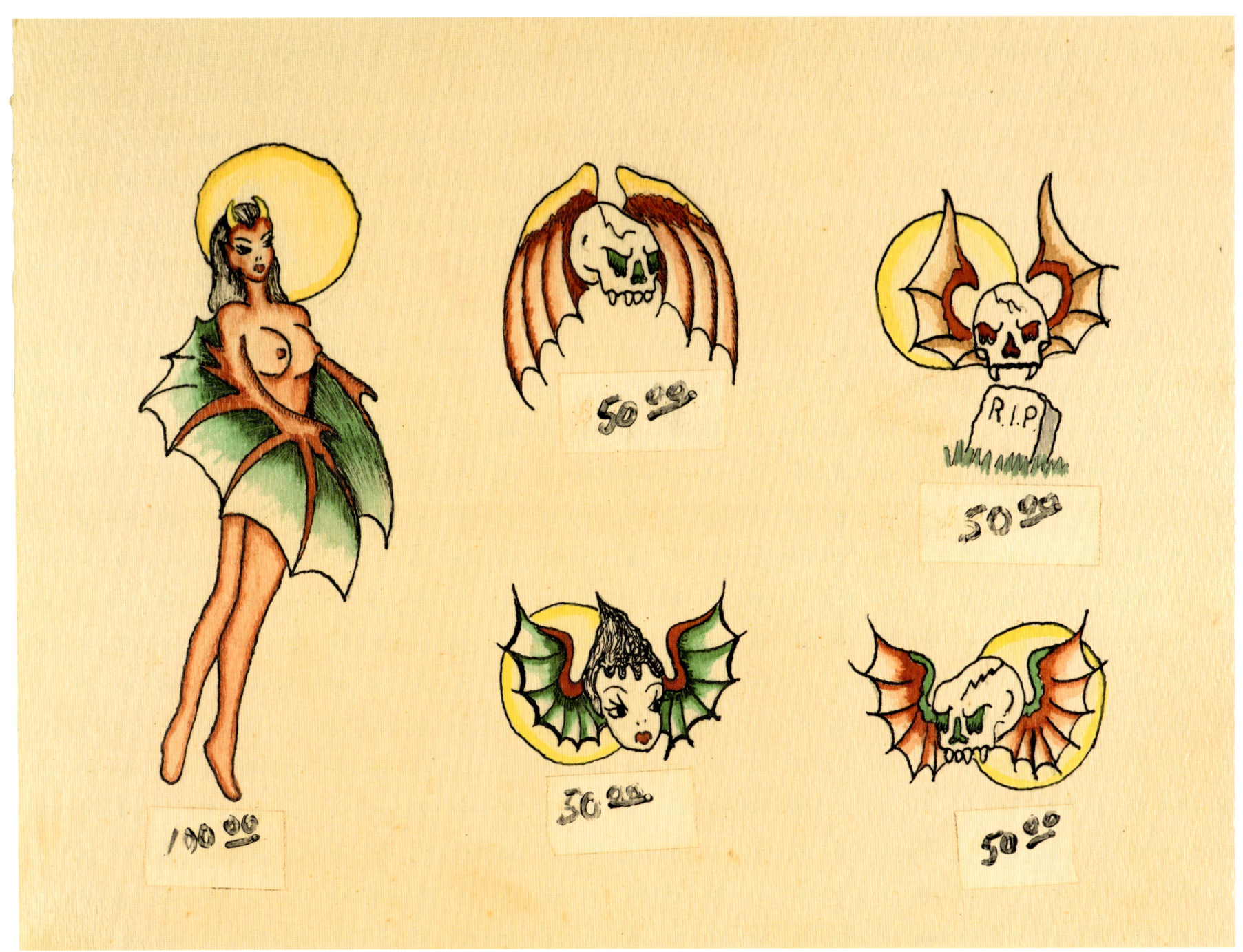

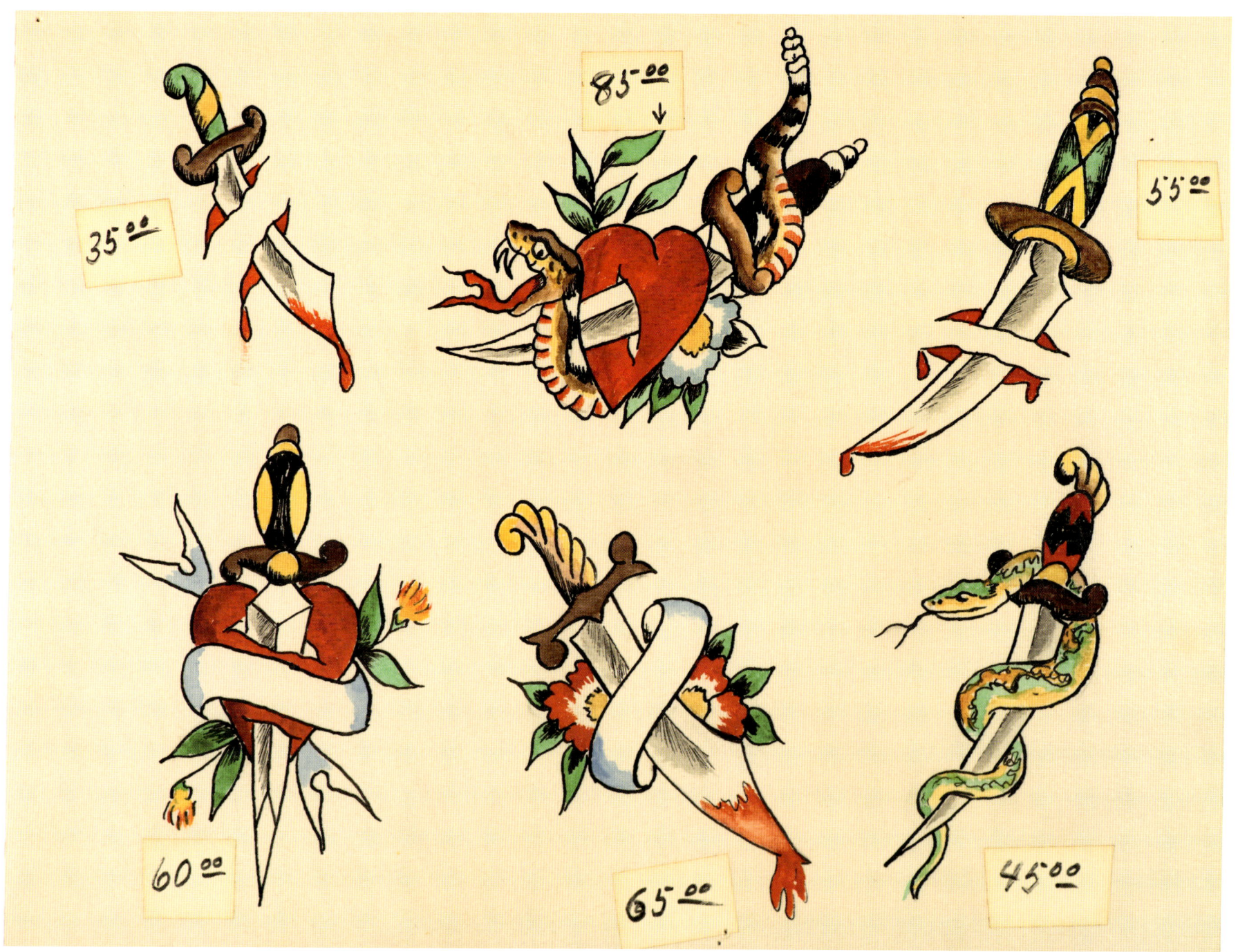

Lotteva Wagner Davis flash

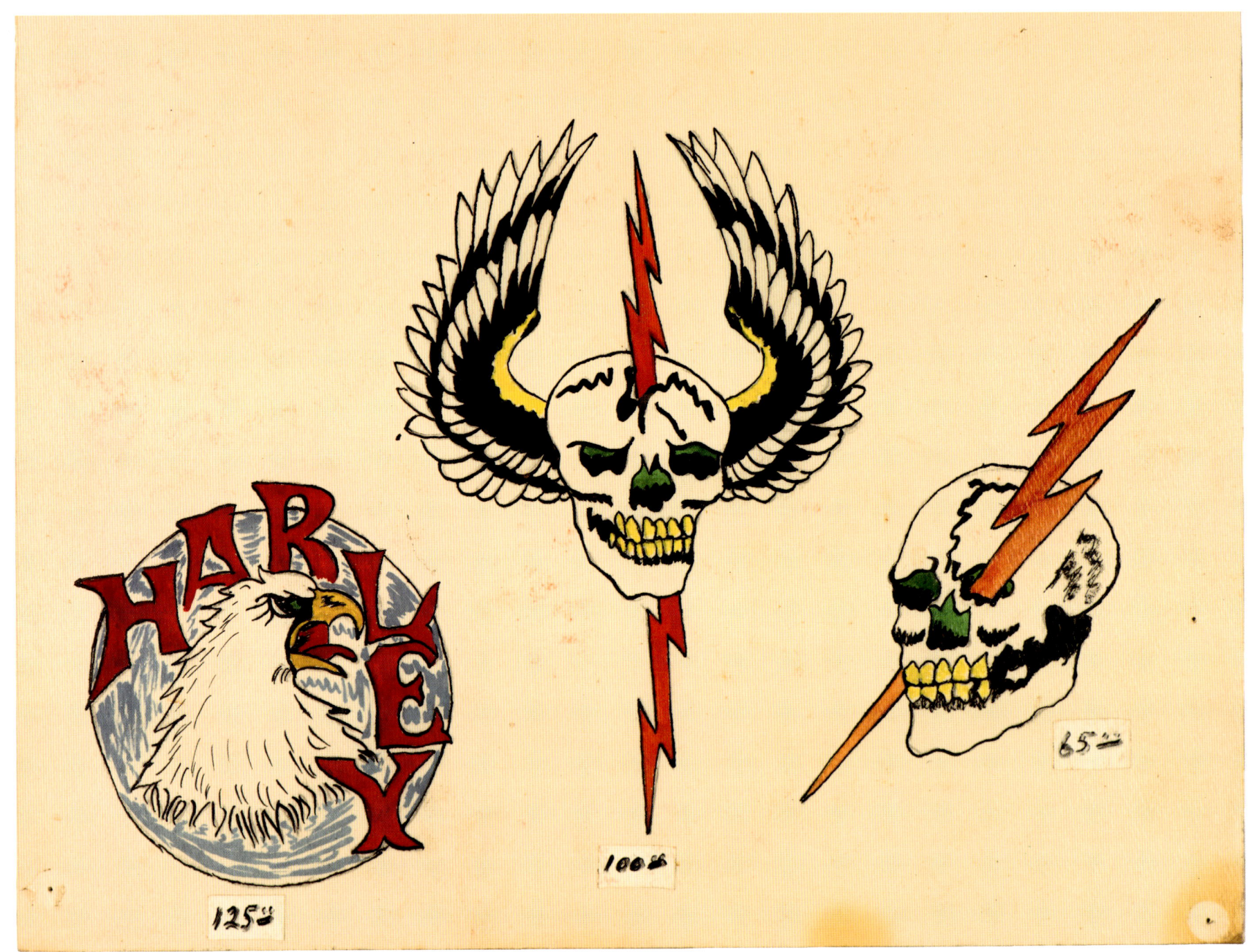

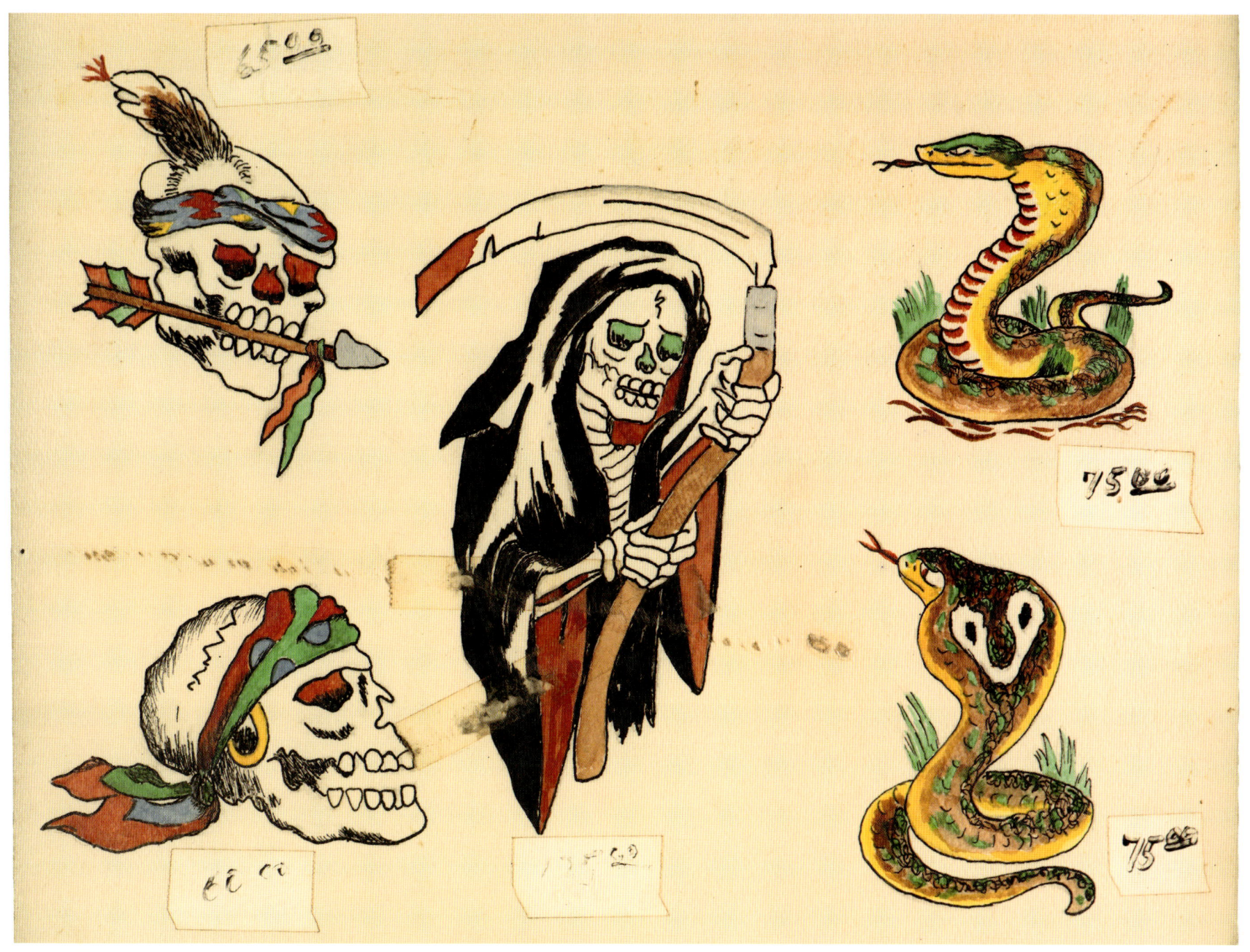

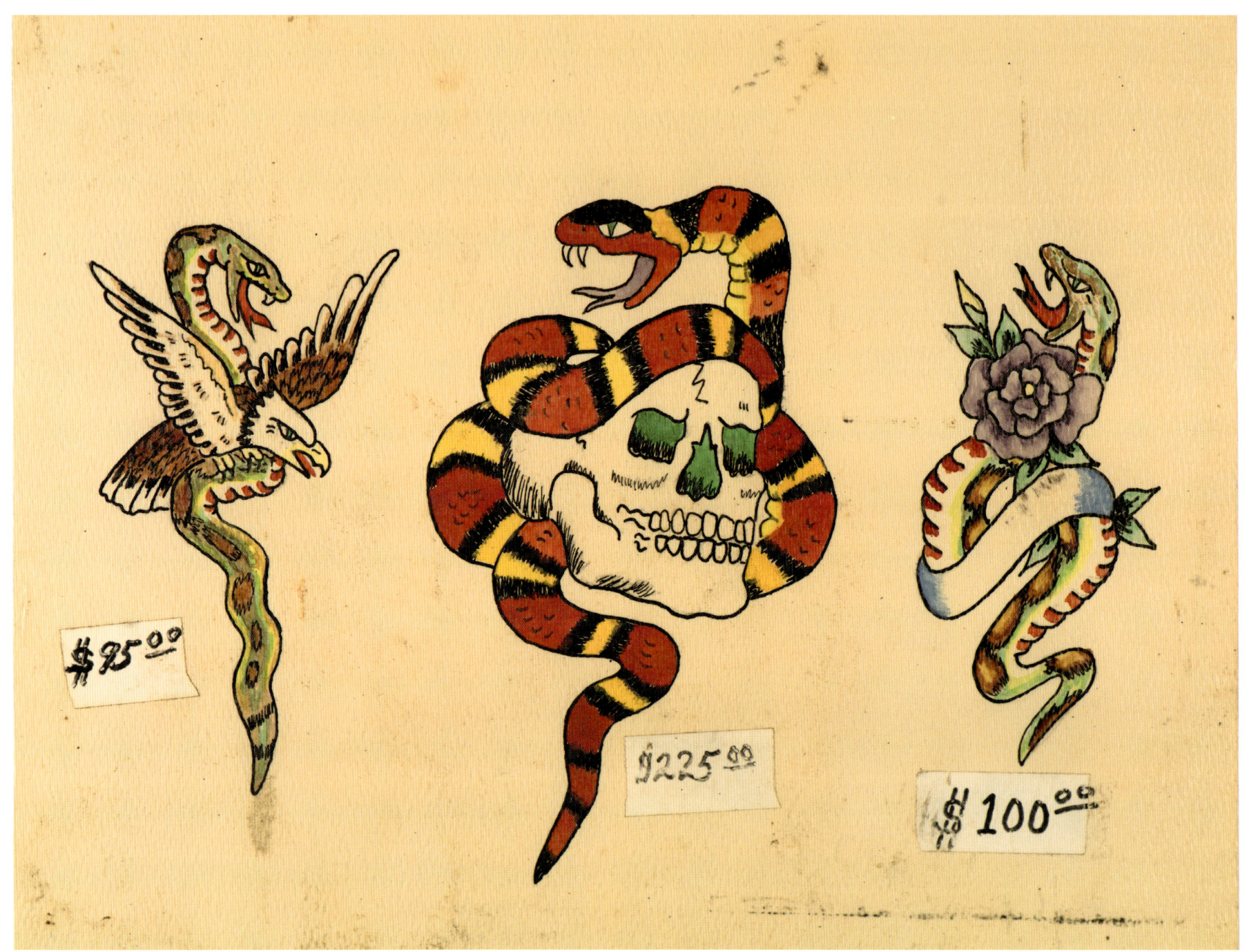

Lotteva Wagner Davis flash

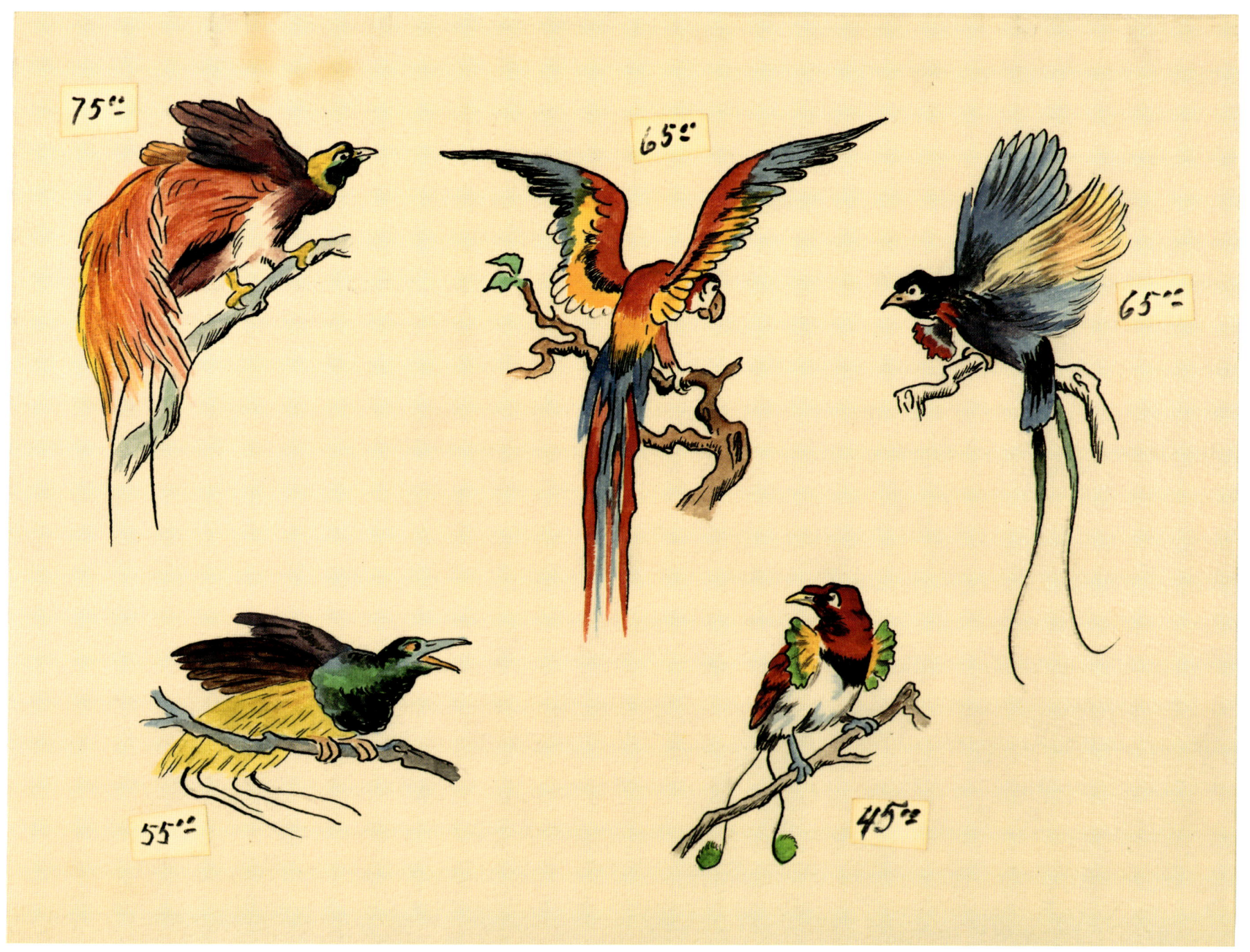

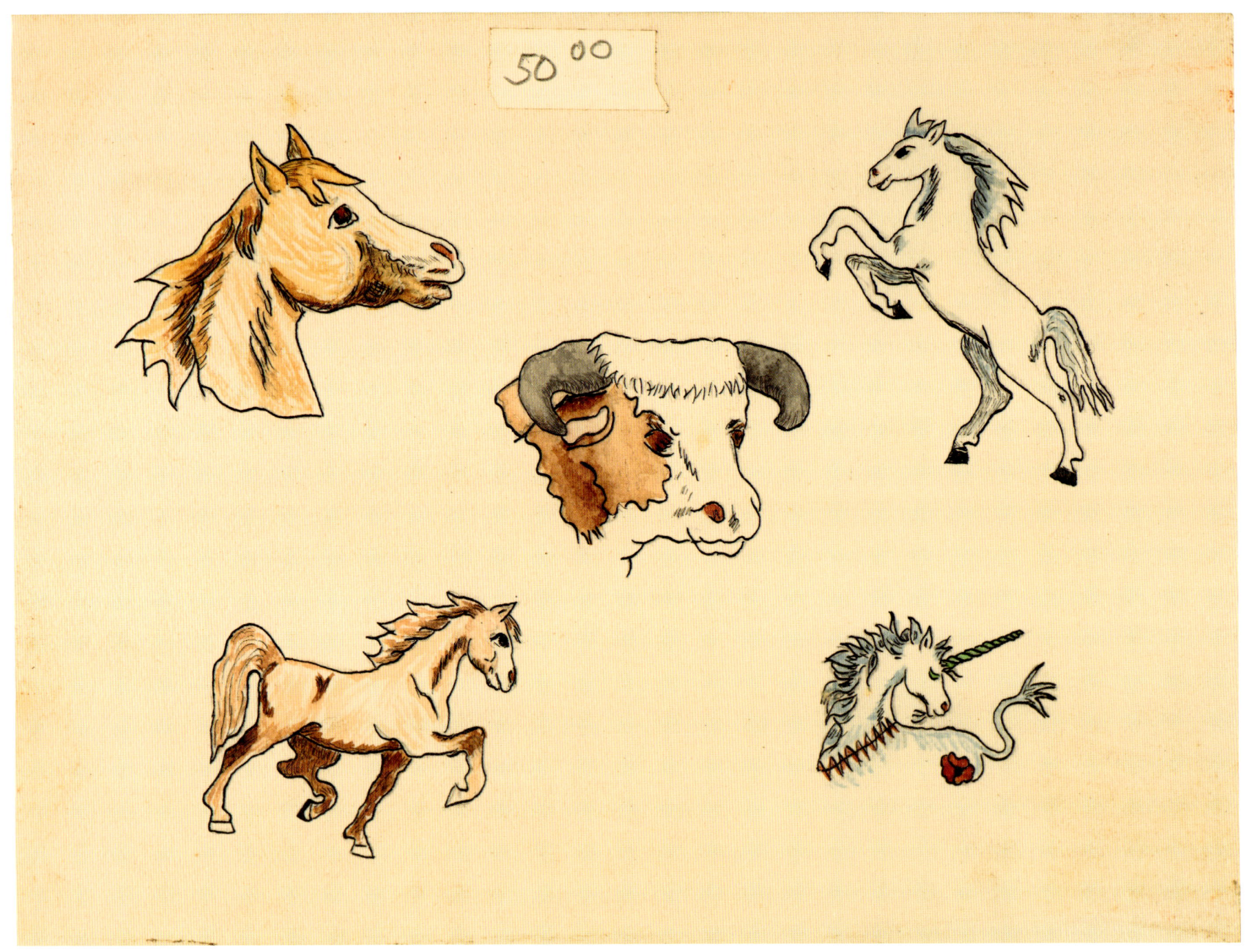

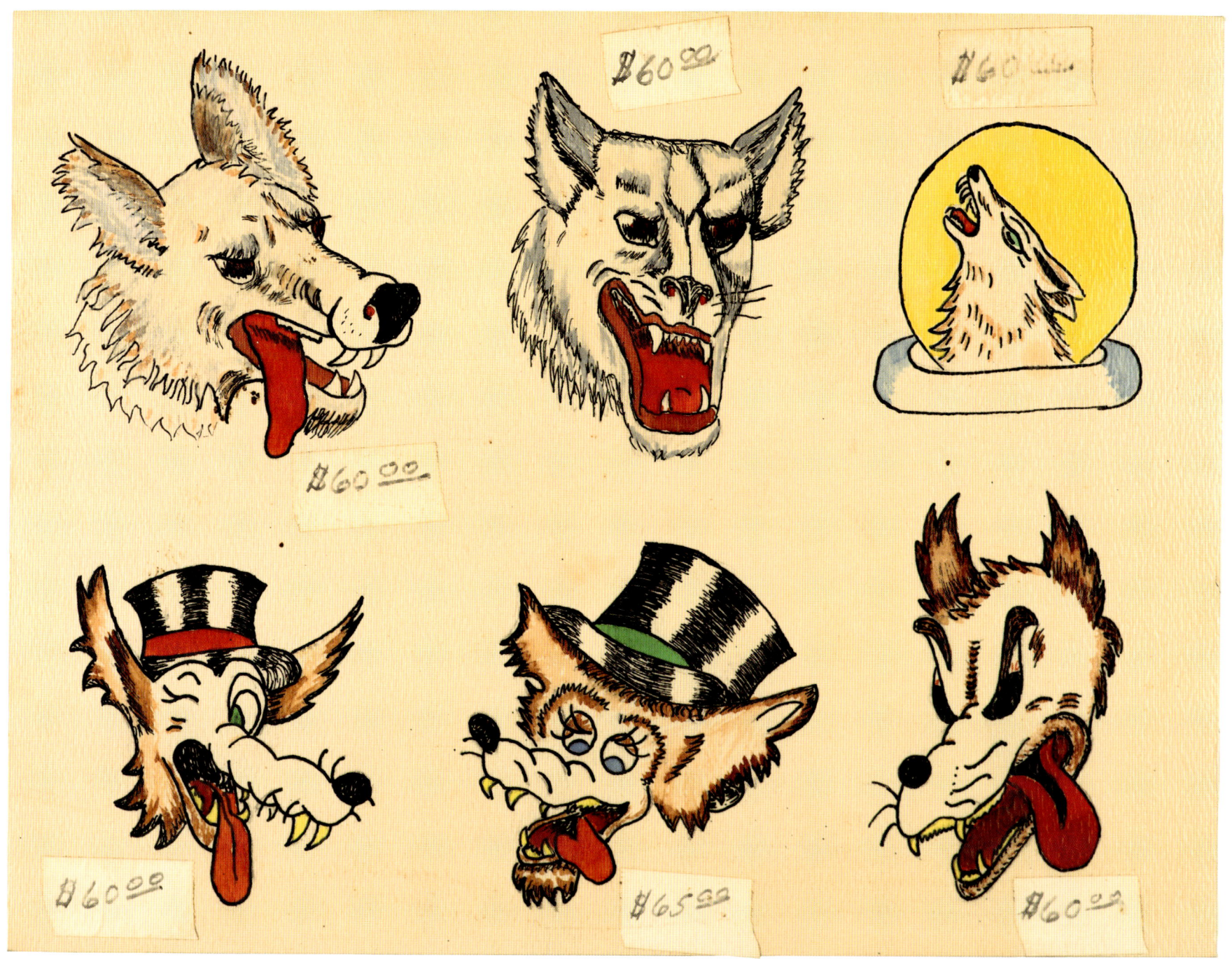

Lotteva Wagner Davis flash

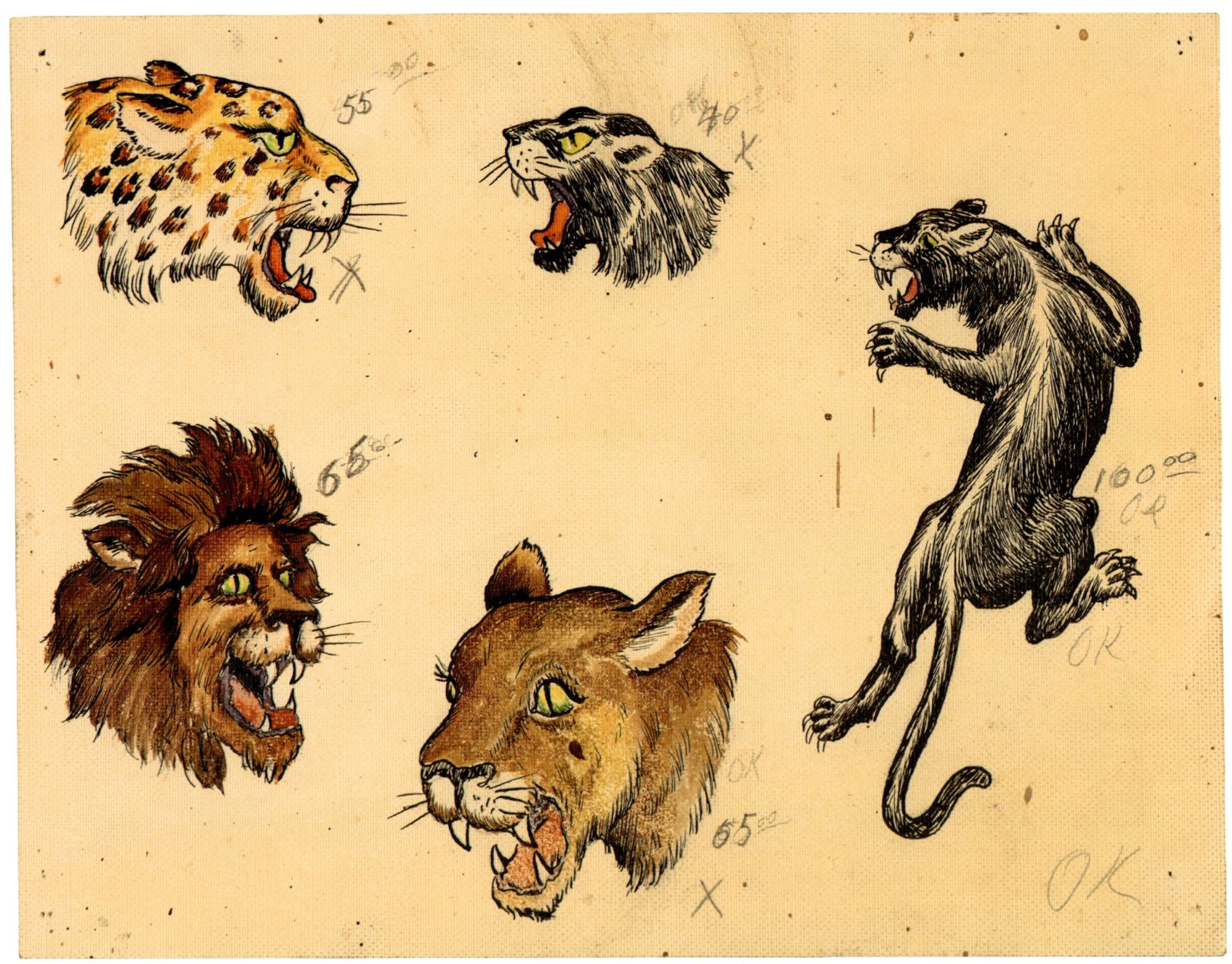

Lotteva Wagner Davis flash

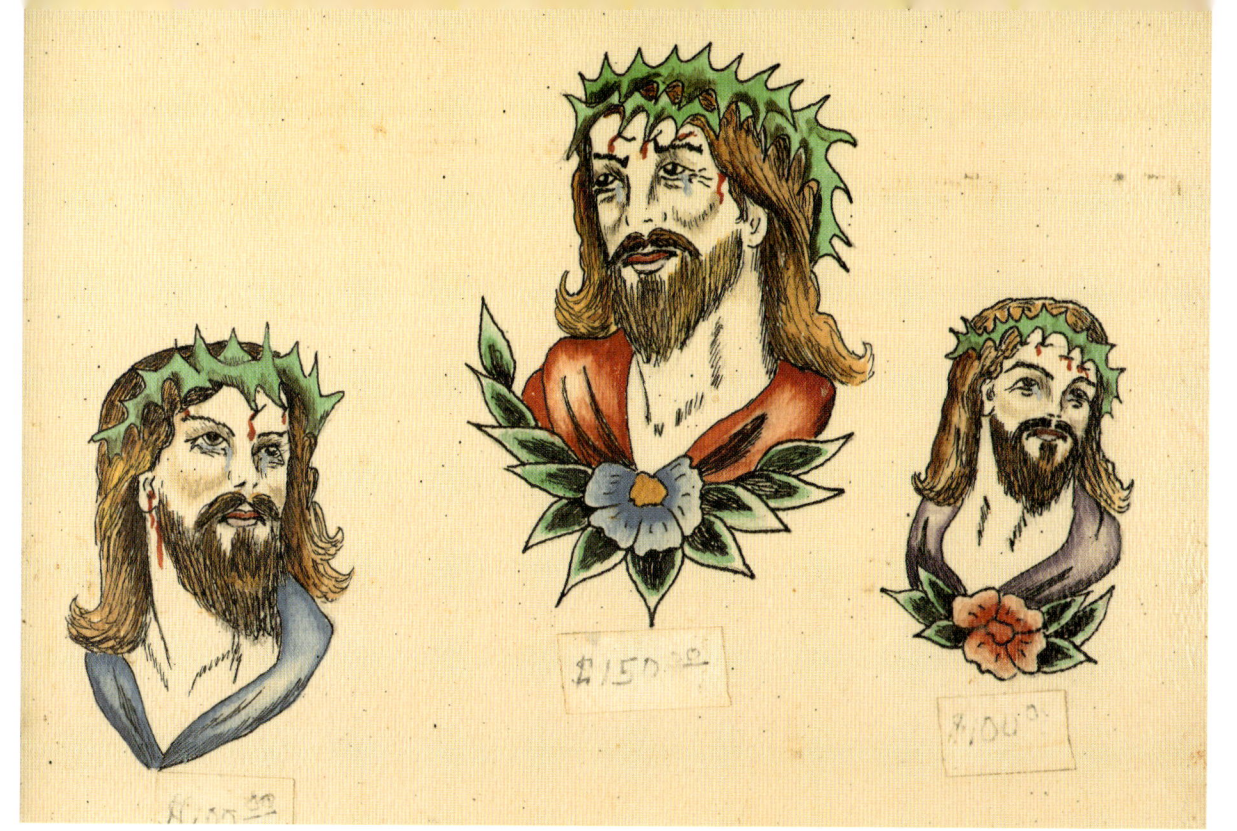

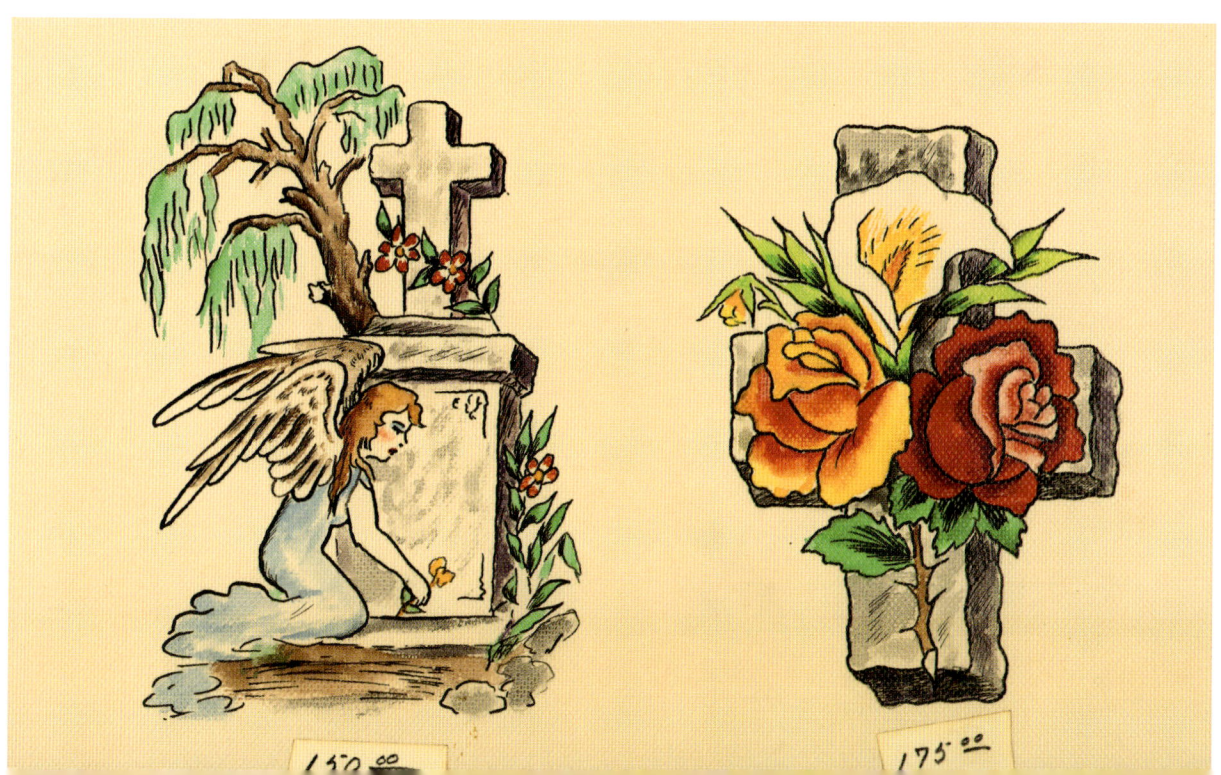

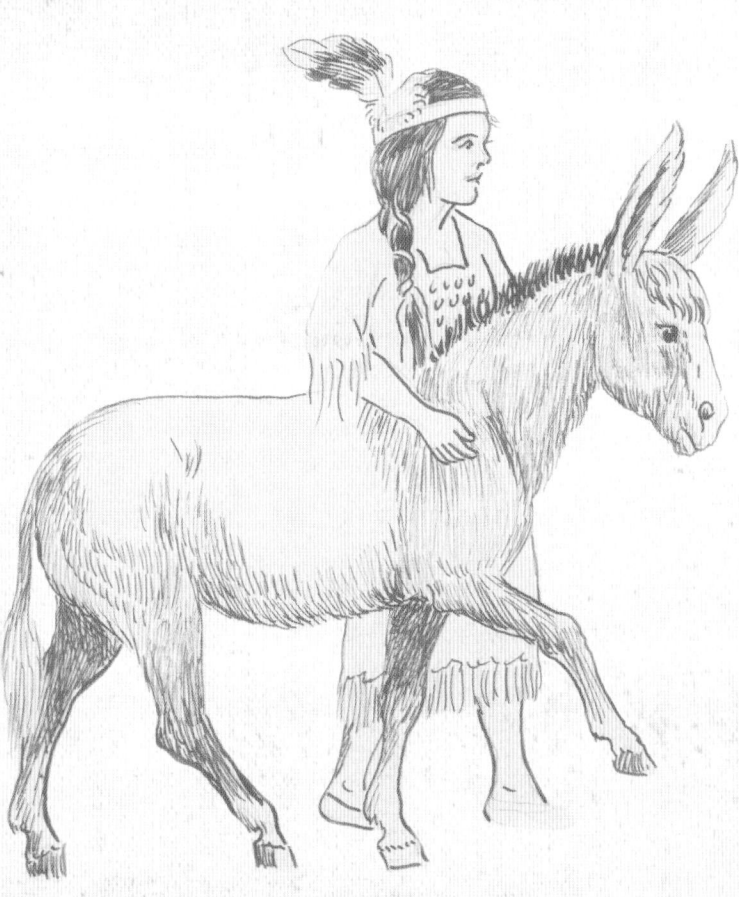

NOTES

1. Patricia Waynette Hook, handwritten notes of conversations with Lotteva Wagner Davis, June 1992.
2. Marie Harris, "Plainview Woman Uses Past in New Project: Color Book Series Reflects Artist's Life," *Plainview Daily Herald*, November 24, 1974, 6A–7A.
3. Ibid.
4. Ellen Sweets, "Tattoo Art a Family Tradition," *Dallas Morning News*, September 5, 1993.
5. Chuck Eldridge, interview with Lotteva Wagner Davis, 1989.
6. Ibid.
7. *Billy the Burro* and *Billy the Burro Joins the Circus,* with original artwork by L. Wagner Davis (Amarillo, TX: Tosh, n.d.), and *Bosco the Lazy Burro,* with drawings by L. Wagner Davis (Lawton, OK: Clover, n.d.). According to the *Plainview Daily Herald* (November 24, 1974), Lotteva was doing pen-and-ink drawings for a series of twenty-four books, and 28,800 copies of the first five books were finished and available, "printed and ready for distribution and sale through Ponca Wholesale."
8. Ibid.
9. Nicki B. Logan, "Round and Round They Go … Again," *Plainview Herald*, n.d.
10. Alan Govenar interview with Patricia Waynette Hook, February 11, 2024.
11. Alan Govenar interview with Ron Dolecek, February 8, 2024.
12. Alan Govenar interview with Patricia Waynette Hook, February 11, 2024.

INDEX

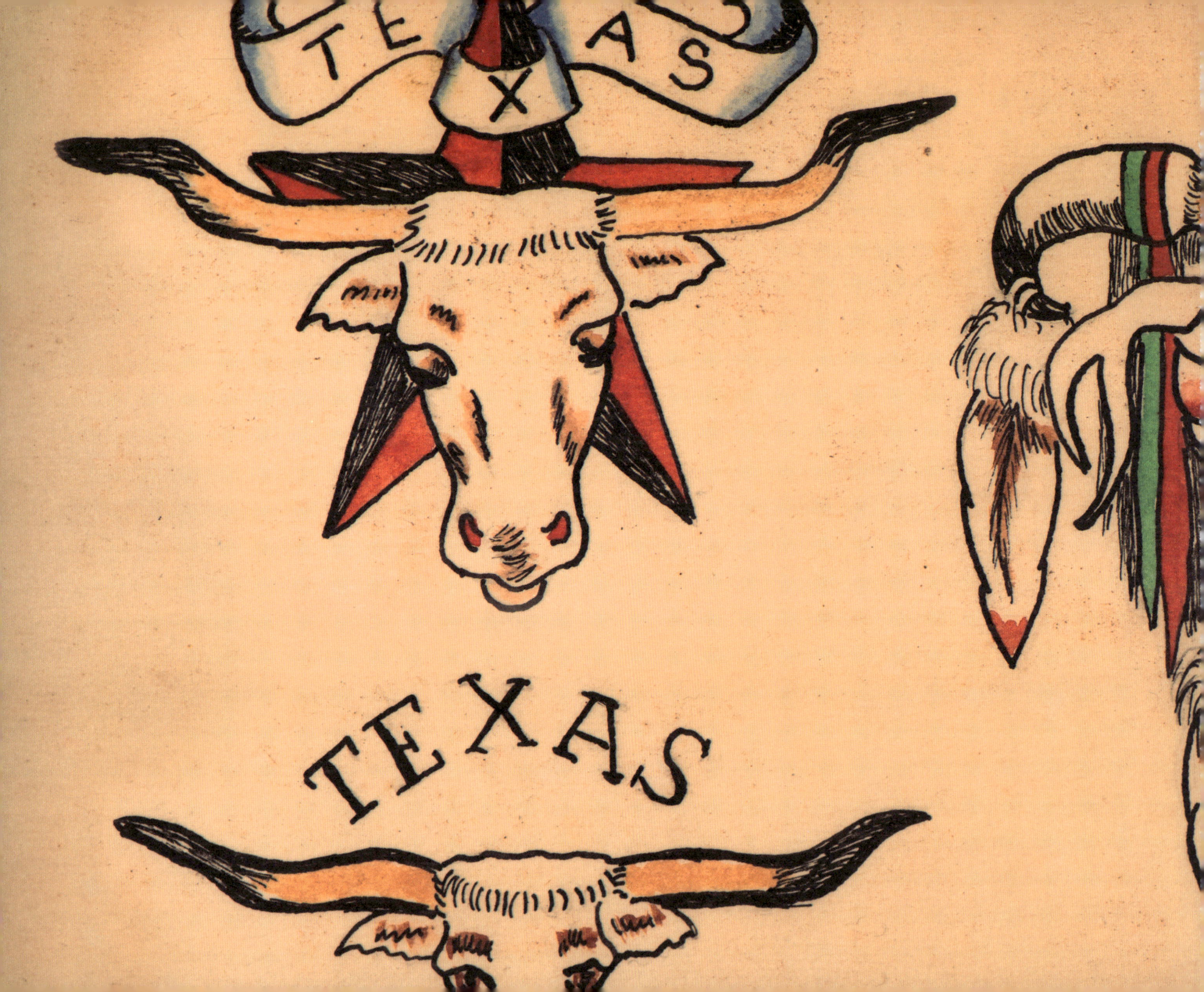